A PUN MY WORD

A PUN MY WORD

A Humorously Enlightened Path to English Usage

Robert Oliver Shipman

Littlefield Adams Quality Paperbacks

LITTLEFIELD ADAMS QUALITY PAPERBACKS

a division of Rowman & Littlefield Publishers, Inc.
8705 Bollman Place, Savage, Maryland 20763

British Cataloging in Publication Information Available

Library of Congress Cataloging-in-Publication Data

Shipman, Robert Oliver.
A pun my word : a humorously enlightened path to English usage / Robert Oliver Shipman.
p. cm.
Includes bibliographical references and index.
1. English language—Usage—Dictionaries. I. Title.
PE1460.S525 1991 428'.003—dc 20 91-13362 CIP

ISBN 0–8226–3011–7 (Littlefield, Adams, quality paperback : alk. paper)

Printed in the United States of America

The paper used in this publication meets the minimum requirements of American National Standard for Information Sciences—Permanence of Paper for Printed Library Materials, ANSI Z39.48–1984.

With love and gratitude
To
my wife,
Jeanille Hadden Shipman,
who has put up with my words
longer and better than anyone I know,
to
our daughter,
Anne Shipman Brennan,
whose editorial assistance with this book
has helped straighten out some of them,
and to
thousands of students
who made my day and way
in sharing a classroom with me.

To misuse the Word is to show contempt for Man. It undermines the bridges and poisons the wells. It causes Man to regress down the long path of his evolution.

DAG HAMMERSKJOLD
Secretary General
The United Nations
1953–1961

Contents

Acknowledgments

The seeds of this book were planted in my childhood by my parents, Bertram Francis and Elydia Foss Shipman, who instilled in me a regard and respect, and a reverence, for the English language. They insisted that words be pronounced and spelled correctly, that sentences adhere to proper syntax, and that spoken and written English reflect clear, logical thinking. They also considered language to be a source of pleasure and enjoyment. Now as I look back to my earliest years, I recall how as a family we participated in word games during meals, on drives in our Model T Ford, and on other occasions, and how I acquired a feeling for words, a capacity to work and play with them—to savor their sounds, their shades of meanings, their power—even to make puns with them!

In the years that followed others enriched me with their knowledge and love of language. All are gone, too. Yet I remember with fondness and gratitude Ruth Deakins, who taught English at Foxwood School in Flushing, New York; Grace Thompson, my sixth-grade teacher at Hindley School in Darien, Connecticut, and Elsa Petterson and Helen Shaub of its high school, my English and Latin teachers; David Thompson and William Henry, my English and Latin masters at Brunswick School in Greenwich, Connecticut; Paul Nixon, dean of Bowdoin College in Brunswick, Maine, and professor of Latin; Robert Peter Tristam Coffin and Herbert Ross Brown, professors of English at Bowdoin; Theodore N. Bernstein, assistant managing editor of the *New York Times* and adjunct associate professor at the Columbia University Graduate School of Journalism; and Harry Hazeldine, chief copy editor of the *Christian Science Monitor*. The lessons gleaned from these gifted, learned cultivators of language are an intrinsic part of *A Pun My Word*.

Nor should I overlook those friends and former colleagues at Mankato State University who have helped me with the manuscript. They are Jane F. Earley, dean of the College of Arts and Humanities; Charles K. Piehl, its associate dean; Marshel Rossow, director of the Mass Communications Institute; Kathleen Vetter Steiner, formerly its and my secretary; Terrance Flaherty, English Department chairperson; Ronald W. Gower and Nancy R. MacKenzie, professors of English; David W. Allan of Library Services; Marcia Baer, editor of *TODAY*, MSU's alumni magazine; Neil H. Nurre of University Operations; and Gregg Asher of Computer Services. Their encouragement, support, suggestions, and criticisms assisted me and the manuscript through its conceptual, research, writing, and computer-composition stages. To each I say thank you.

And to these people at Rowman & Littlefield, Publishers, Inc.—Jonathan Sisk, editor-in-chief; Lynn Gemmell, production editor; Lynda Hill, promotion director; and Kelli Gilbert, copy editor—go my thanks also. I am indebted to them for their professionalism and expertness, and for the kind and helpful ways they worked with me.

Thus I can say with much pleasure that this book is the fulfillment of a lifetime love affair with the English language. To all those, especially my thousands of students, who in some measure or means helped bring *A Pun My Word* to fruition I am indeed grateful.

Introduction

"Accuracy in the expresssion of ideas follows, not precedes, accurate use of language." These words, said to me more than forty years ago by Paul Deland, the then managing editor of the *Christian Science Monitor*, when I was a fledgling copy editor, have echoed in my mind ever since. His words not only inspired me then, they also have guided me in my personal and professional life ever since. They have served me well in my vocations as a communicator and as a teacher of writing and editing. And, most assuredly, they underlie the concept and content of *A Pun My Word: A Humorously Enlightened Path to English Usage*.

Language is a tool. It can be used precisely or clumsily depending upon the knowledge, competence, and caring of its user. Accuracy in the expression of ideas occurs when language is honed to the sharpness of a scalpel held in a steady, practiced hand. Yet honing of language makes demands on its user. It calls for knowing how words are spelled, what they mean, what their parts of speech are, and how they relate to one another. Accuracy in the use of language requires a disciplining of the mind. It calls for clarity of thought that precedes clarity of expression. It demands of one the ability to think in, through, and out on a straight line. And it insists that the speaker and/or writer use words, phrases, clauses, and sentences accordingly.

Ignorance, indifference, and illiteracy account in much measure for the inability of some people to express ideas accurately. As John Simon states in *Paradigms Lost*, "Language, for the most part, changes out of ignorance." Words can and do change in meaning because their users do not know their original meanings or because they believe that they have come up with new words. Yet ignorance, as any teacher will tell you, is curable. Knowledge is its best antidote.

Illiteracy is a scourge in the United States that permeates all levels of our society. It is not confined to those people who cannot read or write at all. It can be found among so-called educated people who ignorantly or unwittingly mix the number of subject and verb in a sentence such as, "**Anyone is** welcome to the party if **they** want to come." A knowing, caring speaker or writer, one who is thinking clearly, would state, "**All are** welcome to the party if **they** want to come." Illiteracy can be lessened, and will be, when each of us takes the time to think about what we really want to speak or write, and to know clearly how to state our words and sentences accurately.

The erosion of language starts at the top of society, not at its bottom, and trickles down. When public leaders, media people, clergy, teachers, parents, and other alleged standard-setters misspeak and miswrite English, the rest of us do likewise. Language at first is an imitative process that begins soon after birth and goes on and on. Literacy simply demonstrates one's ability to read and write, a minimal need in an age of instant and mass communication.

English is a beautiful language, rich and limitless in variety and opportunity for expressing ideas. Even so, English is not a simple language. It is filled with complexities and contradictions that confuse its would-be users as anyone who has adopted it as a second language well knows. To speak and write English accurately, one needs to be aware of and to understand its structure and composition, to recognize and respect its traditions, to be appreciative of its heritage as a means for conveying ideas from one generation to the next.

Edwin Newman, the renowned and extraordinary broadcast journalist and connoisseur of language, states it well in *A Civil Tongue*:

> American English, drawing on so many regional differences, so many immigrant groups, and such a range of business farming,

> industrial, and artistic experiences, can have an incomparable richness. Instead, high crimes and misdemeanors are visited upon it, and those who commit them do not understand that they are crimes against themselves. The language belongs to all of us. We have no more valuable possession.

A Pun My Word is not a cure-all for what may be ailing our society and its use of the English language. Nor does it contain all the answers to questions someone might have about using the language accurately. It is a simple guide in English usage that provides explanations, definitions, and examples of a variety of words and points of grammar and usage that are confusing, troublesome, misunderstood, ignored, misused, or abused. Numerous sources have been drawn upon for the items that appear in it. Books on usage and writing have been examined and studied. A number of dictionaries have been consulted. The media have been watched, heard, or read. Conversations, student papers, and classroom experiences have been recalled. I am indebted to all of them. They have helped to provide ideas and to reinforce my own.

Yet there are differences among some of these authorities. Dictionaries, for example, differ in their definitions and pronunciations of some words. Not all grammarians and scholars of language agree on how words should be used. Some are stricter in their concepts. Others are freer. What the user will find in this handbook is a compilation of items, as I have determined them, that represent a cross section, if not a consensus, of those points in verbal and grammatical usage that reflect modern standards of American English.

The distinguishing feature of *A Pun My Word* is its use of humor to inform, explain, and illustrate its many points in English usage. In this sense, it is a departure from most handbooks. Why not? Why should English, a language rich in nuances of meanings and in opportunities for play on words, be treated and used only seriously? A little enlightenment does ease the word and the way!

The book's organization, construction, and content have been designed with its users in mind. First, a word or words are explained in terms of their problem, difficulty, confusion, or misuse. Second, the word or words are defined, and their parts of speech are given. Third, an example or examples are offered to illustrate the word's or words' appropriate use. Some words or terms require longer explanations, definitions, and illustrations than do others. Discussion of them does involve some grammatical terms but is done at a minimum. *A Pun My Word* is a handbook on usage and not a grammar. I have sought to keep my exposition simple and clear, and to let the examples show or reinforce the points being made. Even so, as an aid to the book's use, I have compiled a glossary of grammatical terms, and for those who desire further knowledge, I have included the titles of numerous excellent grammars in the Bibliography.

Throughout the planning, compiling, and writing of *A Pun My Word*, I have been motivated by a love for the English language that stems from childhood when my mother taught me to read and write at the age of three. I marvel even now, almost seven decades later, at the fact that I can read and write, that I can put words on a piece of paper or on a blackboard or on a computer screen, and make them come out right. I find immense pleasure in speaking and writing well, and in having helped countless numbers of other people to do likewise. In remembrance of them and to those people who do care about accuracy in expressing ideas and the accurate use of language, I present this book, taking sole responsibility for its presumptiveness, content, errors, good and poor humor, and whatever.

ROBERT OLIVER SHIPMAN
Mankato, Minnesota
February 1991

A

a lot / alot

A lot consists of two words, **a**, an article, and **lot**, a noun. It means a considerable quantity or extent. It also means many. Other articles and nouns like **a lot** are a number, a heap, a bunch, a few.

Alot is not a word. It is a misspelling for **a lot**.

EXAMPLES:

Politicians are known to make a number, a heap, a bunch, **a lot** of promises. A few they keep.

a while See **awhile / a while**.

abdicate / abrogate / absolve

These three verbs are a dangerous trio. Judicious review of their meaning can lead to their civil use.

Abdicate means to abandon; formally to give up power, office, or throne.

Abrogate means to abolish, annul, or repeal by authority; to do away with.

Absolve means to set free from an obligation or the consequences of guilt.

EXAMPLES:

Kings ascend and **abdicate** thrones. Parliaments enact and **abrogate** laws. What do people do? They **absolve** themselves.

abjure / adjure

These look-alike verbs are not a compatible couple but quite the opposite. It might be said they are at odds with each other.

Abjure means to renounce upon oath; to swear off; to reject solemnly; to repudiate; to avoid or shun.

Adjure means to charge, bind, or command earnestly and solemnly, often under oath or the threat of a curse; to warn or admonish solemnly; to beg, entreat, or request earnestly.

EXAMPLES:

Have you ever noticed how some spouses are quick to **adjure** their mates about their bad habits yet are slow to **abjure** their own? One might call it the battle of the prefixes.

above See **over / above / more than**.

abrogate See **abdicate / abrogate / absolve**.

absolve See **abdicate / abrogate / absolve**.

accept / except

Accept, a verb, should not be confused with **except**, a conjunction, in pronunciation, spelling, and usage.

Accept means to receive willingly; to give admittance or approval to.

Except, as a conjunction, means on any other condition than that; only. As a verb, it means to take or leave out from a number or a whole.

EXAMPLES:

Accept what you are reading now. Otherwise, you will have no one **except** yourself to blame if you mispronounce, misspell, or misuse these words again, unless you choose, of course, to **except** them from your vocabulary.

accommodate

This popularly mispronounced and misspelled verb is a sticky one. It means to make fit or suitable. And, like a well-known candy, it has two **m**'s in it.

EXAMPLES:

When pronouncing or spelling **ac-co<u>m</u>-<u>m</u>o-date**, be sure to have more than one **m** on hand for making **acco<u>mm</u>odation** a noun suitable for gestation.

adapt / adopt

These look-alike verbs are different because of a single letter. It is the middle one, the second vowel. And the difference determines their spelling, pronunciation, and meaning. So if you are **a**pt, you will **o**pt for the right vowel for each word each time you use it.

Ad<u>a</u>pt means to make fit or suitable to requirements or conditions; to adjust; to make to correspond.

Ad<u>o</u>pt means to choose for or take to one's self; to take into one's family as a relation; to take as one's own child; to assume.

EXAMPLES:

Would-be parents **adopt** children sometimes. Children, however, seldom get a chance to choose would-be parents. Somehow they **adapt** to each other.

adduce / deduce / deduct

Reasoning and logic enter into the proper knowledge and use of these verbs.

Adduce (spelled with two **d**'s) means to offer an example, reason, or proof in discussion and analysis. **Adduce** suggests to lead to.

Deduce (no double **d**) is defined as to determine by deduction; to infer from a general principle; to trace the cause of. **Deduce** suggests to lead from.

Deduct, like **deduce**, comes from the Latin word *deducere*, to lead away from. It is defined as: to take away an amount from a total, such as subtract.

EXAMPLES:

The lecture system falters when professors fail to **adduce** their subjects clearly and when students are unable to **deduce** the lectures' meaning. The net result is to **deduct** a zero in the learning process.

adjectives

The comparing of adjectives has fallen into misuse and abuse thanks to the ignorance and indifference of some indiscriminate people and their desire to intensify their communication. Most single-syllable adjectives take **er** in forming the comparative and take **est** in forming the superlative. Most **adjectives** of more than one syllable require the word **more** in forming the comparative and require the words **the most** in forming the superlative. There are exceptions to these formations. So check a standard dictionary whenever you are in doubt about the comparison of a particular **adjective**.

EXAMPLES:

Cliff Hanger, the **most respected** guide on the mountain, was **surer** than the other climbers where the **safest** footholds were. Being **more familiar** with the terrain than they were, he made **severer** demands on himself than on them to be **sure** that no one slipped and fell head over heels into oblivion.

adjure See **abjure / adjure**.

adopt See **adapt / adopt**.

adverbs

Adverbs, which answer the question how, not what, have come into hard times. They have lost their tails—**ly**, the ending most commonly used in forming adverbs from adjectives. For some strange reason, ill-users of language are omitting the **ly** and are coming up with such illiteracies as: He ran swift. She slept bad. She sang beautiful. He threw natural.

EXAMPLES:

When communicators speak and write

- He ran **swiftly**
- She slept **badly**
- She sang **beautifully**
- He threw **naturally**

then respecters, preservers, and admirers of English will smile **broadly**, **knowingly**, and **gratefully**.

adverse / averse

These two adjectives, which seem to sound alike, are not synonyms even though both words express opposition. Each has its own distinct meaning.

Adverse means opposed, contrary, or unfavorable; opposite in position; and denotes a feeling of hostility.

Averse means reluctant or unwilling; having an active feeling of dislike, distaste, or repugnance.

EXAMPLES:

Gore Måy's **adverse** comment about Sue Perba's quiche accounts for why she is **averse** to having him taste any more of her cooking.

affect / effect

These totally different words—like drinking and driving—have a cause-and-effect relationship.

Affect is a verb. It means to influence; to impress; to act on; to produce an effect on; to produce a change. It also means to pretend; to feign; to make a show of, such as liking. **Affect**, actually, was used for a long time only as a verb until it began to be used in psychology as a noun to denote a feeling or emotion.

Effect, on the other hand, is a verb and a noun. As a verb, it means to bring about; to bring into existence; to make happen; to bring to an issue or to full success; to produce results; to achieve; to accomplish. As a noun, **effect** means something produced by an agent or a cause; something that follows as a consequence; a result. In distinguishing between **affect** and **effect** as verbs, think of **affect** as meaning to bring about partial results and **effect** as meaning to produce complete results.

EXAMPLES:

When Thurston Toper has been drinking, the **effect** of alcohol could **affect** how he drives a car. A drink too many could **effect** his involvement with the police, a point at which he might be likely to do his best to **affect** sobriety.

aid / aide

One way to give less comfort to the adversaries of good usage is to make a distinction in the meaning and in the spelling of these two tiny words.

Aid, the tinier of the pair, does not have an **e**. It is a noun and a verb. As a verb, it means to assist or help. As a noun, it means assistance, support, or help.

Aide, even though a letter longer (**e**) than **aid**, is a noun only. It means one who aids, helps, or assists; assistant.

EXAMPLES:

One time a general asked an **aide** to **aid** him. And the **aide** obeyed. He **aided** the general. In appreciation for the **aide's aid**, the general ordered a drink for himself and his assistant. Would you say their drink was lemon**aid** or lemon**aide**, or just plain lemon**ade**?

aide See **aid / aide**.

all / any / most / some

These four pronouns definitely need to be used definitively. Otherwise, their misuse can lead to problems in number in that each pronoun can be singular and plural.

All means the whole number, quantity, or amount.

Any means one or more persons, things, or portions out of a number.

Most means the greatest number or part.

Some means one indeterminate quantity, portion, or number as distinguished from the rest.

When the meaning of general amount or quantity can be read into a sentence, a singular verb should be used. When the meaning of individual and number can be read into a sentence, a plural verb should be used.

EXAMPLES:

All of the apples were picked. Not **any** of them was left. **Most** were packed. **Some** were made into applesauce, of which **all** was served at a political dinner. Were **any** of the apples served? No, but **most** of the applesauce was eaten. **Some** was tossed out, along with a dissident who said he hadn't paid $100 for baby food. He'd come to get the real applesauce from the candidate.

all ready / already

Words are like members of a family. They are fine as long as they say the right things. They even can speak for one another sometimes. These words may look alike, but they are not interchangeable.

All and **ready** are two words and are adjectives. **All** means wholly or altogether. **Ready** means prepared or immediately available.

Already is an adverb. It is one word. It means previously or before.

EXAMPLES:

Mom and the kids were **all ready** to go with Dad to a movie. The trouble began when he arrived home and said he had seen it **already**.

all right / alright

Look to the antonymns—or opposites—of this pair of words for the right and wrong way to use them.

All right are two words and are the spelling for the adjective phrase, Joe is **all right**, and for the adverb phrase, **All right**, let's go.

Alright appears to be a cousin to altogether and already. It is not. **Alright** is not a word. It is not an acceptable substitute for **all right**. In time, perhaps, **alright** will replace **all right** if illiteracy prevails. Meanwhile, try keeping **alright all right**. **All right**?

EXAMPLES:

If **all right** were to become **alright** and ''alwrong'' remain as ''all wrong,'' would it then be a case of having things ''halfright'' and ''half wrong''?

allot

This word is a verb. Sometimes it is confused with **alot**, a nonword and a misspelling of **a lot**, two words: an article and a noun. **Allot** means to assign a share or a portion; to distribute by lot or as if by lot. Teams, for example, **allot** blocks of tickets for their players. See **a lot / alot**.

alot See **a lot / alot**.

allusion See **delusion / illusion / allusion**.

already See **all ready / already**.

alright See **all right / alright**.

although See **though / although**.

among / between

Knowing when and how to use these two prepositions is not a matter of simple arithmetic as one may be led to believe. **Among** is used in referring to groups of three or more. **Between** is used in referring to two or more persons or things. But not always. When three or more entities are considered individually or are closely related, **between** may be preferable.

EXAMPLES:

It's simple to divide two apples **between** John and Jerry. And it's easy to divide three apples **among** John, Jerry, and Jimmy. But it's tough to divide four apples **between** John, Jerry, and Jimmy if one doesn't like applesauce.

anticipate See **expect / anticipate**.

anxious See **eager / anxious**.

any See **all / any / most / some**.

apostrophe

The **apostrophe** ('), a punctuation mark, because of its abuse, misuse, and nonuse, may soon join the bald eagle on the endangered species list. It, like America's national bird, requires tender loving care.

An **apostrophe** is needed for forming the plural of single letters, such as a's, b's, c's or A's, B's, C's, and for some words and figures to avoid confusion, such as Ph.D's, SOS's, two and's, three that's, four 4's.

An **apostrophe** is not needed for forming the plural of multiple letters, such as ABCs, VIPs. An **apostrophe** is not needed to form the plural of years, such as **1500s**, **1980s**, but one is needed when figures are omitted, such as the **'80s**.

An **apostrophe** is needed to indicate possessiveness of singular and plural proper and common nouns, such as Ludlum**'s** book, the book**'s** cover, Keats**'** poems, the people**'s** choice, the victors**'** prizes, boys**'** basketball, witches**'** brew, Los Angeles**'** smog, Ross**'s** flag, Sanchez**'s** mule.

An **apostrophe** is used to show possessiveness of indefinite pronouns, such as another**'s**, anyone**'s**, everybody**'s**, everyone**'s**, one**'s**, someone**'s**.

An **apostrophe** is not used to form the possessive of personal pronouns ending in **s**, such as **his**, **hers**, **ours**, **theirs**, and **yours**.

And an **apostrophe** is never used to form the possessive of the neuter pronoun **its**.

An **apostrophe** is needed to indicate the contractions of words such as **it's** (it is), **haven't** (have not), **let's** (let us), **you're** (you are).

And an **apostrophe** is needed to show the omitting of letters, such as in **'bout** (about), **runnin'** (running) wild, rock **'n'** (and) roll.

apt See **likable / likely / apt**.

as See **like / as**.

assure See **insure / ensure / assure**.

average See **mean / median / average**.

averse See **adverse / averse**.

avert / avoid

These two verbs, whose origins are in Latin and French, should not, like romance, be exercised too lightly.

Avert means to turn away or aside from; to ward off; to prevent.

Avoid means to stay or keep clear of; to keep away from; to shun; to evade.

EXAMPLES:

Olga Ogle has a problem in double vision. She knows she ought to **avert** her eyes even though, at long last, a man has made a pass at her. She knows she had better not **avoid** his eyes, or romance once again will have passed her by.

avoid See **avert / avoid**.

awhile / a while

Some words, depending on their function, fuse. Others remain fractured. This pair, which means in a short time, is a case in point.

Awhile, one word, is an adverb. It means for a short time or period.

A while, an article, **a**, and a noun, **while**, are two words and are used when they follow a preposition.

EXAMPLES:

Awhile ago Francesca Fidget fell down the stairs in a neighbor's house and broke her leg. Her neighbor did not mind putting her up for **a while**, but now, to that person's dismay, Francesca's decided to stay until the cast comes off.

B

bad / badly

Mixed feelings can occur when these two words get confused in their use and meaning.

Bad is an adjective and means not good, unfavorable, severe, offensive. It is used to modify nouns. It also is used as a predicate adjective with copulative or linking verbs to indicate a state of being.

Badly is an adverb and means in a bad, unfavorable, or offensive manner. It is used with verbs of action to indicate how someone or something acted.

EXAMPLES:

Angus Argyle doubled how **bad** he felt when he felt **badly** in the dark for some socks and came upon a **badly** mixed pair. Now wasn't that just too **bad** for him to end up with two **bad** socks that **badly** matched the **bad** mood he started with?

badly See **bad / badly.**

bail / bale

Baleful misuse of these look-alike and sound-alike words can be avoided when they are spelled and defined correctly.

As a noun, **bail** has several different meanings. It is the security given for the due appearance of a prisoner in order to obtain his or her release from jail. It is a container used to remove water from a boat. And it is a hinged bar for holding paper against the platen on a typewriter. As a verb, **bail** means to release under **bail** or to procure the release of by giving **bail**; to clear (water) from a boat by dipping and throwing over the side; and, when used with the preposition out, to parachute from a plane.

Bale, as a noun, has two different meanings: (1) a great evil, sorrow, or woe; (2) a large bundle of goods or a closely pressed package of merchandise bound and usually wrapped, such as paper or hay. As a verb, it has one meaning only: to make up into a **bale.**

EXAMPLES:

The **bail** Doreen Denim used to **bail** her husband out of jail was the money she received from the sale of some pigs and a **bale** or two of cotton she had gotten someone to **bale** for her.

balance / remainder

Proper use of these nouns requires weighing their definitions separately even though in informal use they have become interchangeable.

Balance, in bookkeeping terms, means equal weight to two sides: income and expenditure. More largely stated, **balance** means both sides are even.

Remainder means what is left after something has been removed.

EXAMPLES:

The team's offense and defense were in **balance**. So Coach Pigskin sat back and relaxed, ready to enjoy the **remainder** of the game when . . . !

barely / hardly / scarcely

These three common words have four things in common: All are adverbs. All imply a negative and should not be used with another negative word to form a double negative such as **hardly never**. All should be used with the word **when**, not **than**. And all suggest a happening of the narrowest of margins even though each word has its own shades of meaning.

Barely means only; just; no more than; openly; in a meager manner. It implies narrowness and thinness.

Hardly means barely also. And it means almost not at all; not quite; with little likelihood. It implies a degree of difficulty.

Scarcely means barely and hardly, too; not quite; definitely not; probably not. It implies an unbelievably small quantity.

EXAMPLES:

The sardine players **barely** squeezed into the closet. They had **hardly** found room for themselves and were **scarcely** breathing, when the door opened and someone from the other team shouted with delight: "Wow, I've caught me a bunch of stuffed fish! And wouldn't you know! They're smelling already!"

bazaar / bizarre

These words look like cousins, but they are not. Unrelated in derivation and definition as they are, the words obviously are spelled differently.

Bazaar is a noun and comes from the Persian word *bazar*. It means a fair, a place for the sale of goods.

Bizarre is an adjective and is derived from the Italian word *bizzarro*. It means odd, extravagant, or eccentric in style or mode. As a noun, it means a flower with atypical striped marking.

EXAMPLES:

''Come with me to the **bazaar**,'' Pepe said. ''But remember. Lay off all that **bizarre** stuff!''

beat / beaten

Two sure signs of illiteracy are not knowing the principle parts of this verb and not knowing how to use them correctly. They are **beat** (present), **beat** (past), **beaten** (past perfect and participle). The word means, among its numerous definitions, to strike, hit; to defeat, win, or overcome. A colloquial meaning is fatigued, worn-out.

EXAMPLES:

Vic Torious was elated he **beat** Smither Reens in tennis, but the latter was not. **Beaten** three sets to two in a match that took nearly four hours to play, Reens said he was really **beat**.

because of See **due to / because of.**

beside / besides

These look-alike words, through common usage—especially speech and the nonexistent or faint sounding of the final **s** in **besides**—have become virtually interchangeable. Yet each word has its own meaning and part of speech that merit clear recognition as well as precise spoken and written expression.

Beside is a preposition. It means by the side of or next to as well as apart or disjoined from. It also is used in comparisons.

Besides is a preposition, an adverb, and a conjunctive adverb. It means, as a preposition, in addition to, other than, except for; as an adverb, also; and, as a conjunctive adverb, moreover, furthermore, also, in addition to.

EXAMPLES:

"Come, my love, and sit **beside** me," Beau Regarde said. "**Besides** holding you in my arms, let me kiss your sweet lips. Say you'll marry me. No one's love **beside** yours means so much to my life and happiness. **Besides**, your father is standing behind me with a shotgun!"

besides See **beside / besides**.

between See **among / between**.

between you and I / between you and me

The first prepositional phrase is a perversion of English. Furthermore, it smacks of illiteracy nurtured by egotistical people who persist in its use. **I** should be **me**, for it, like **you**, is the object of the preposition **between**. The phrase should read **between you and me.** One way for testing when to use **I** or **me** is to substitute another personal pronoun for **you**, since its subjective and objective forms are both **you**. The same substitution can be used for testing for subjective or objective case when a noun and a pronoun are part of a prepositional phrase.

EXAMPLES:

"Do I split the pie **between you** (him) and **me**, Flakey, or **between** Krisko (him) and **me**?" Krusto asked, eyeing the half he had "carved out" for himself.

between you and me See **between you and I / between you and me.**

bi / semi

Ambiguity, the foe of the careful speaker and writer, would lessen in the use of these two prefexes if **bi** meant two only and **semi** meant half only. But they don't. The trouble arises with **bi**. Sometimes **bi** can mean two, and other times **bi** can mean twice. **Semi** behaves itself and always means half. **Bi**monthly means every two months, and nothing else. **Bi**weekly means every two weeks, but it also can mean twice a week. **Bi**annual means twice a year, whereas **bi**ennial means every two years. **Semi**monthly means twice a month, **semi**weekly means twice a week, and **semi**annually means twice a year. No problem.

EXAMPLES:

Tab Lloyd couldn't decide whether to publish a **bi**weekly or **semi**weekly, or a **bi**monthly or **semi**monthly, or a **bi**annual or **semi**annual magazine. He looked at his horoscope—and his bank balance—and settled for a **bi**ennial.

bizarre See **bazaar / bizarre.**

board See **collective nouns.**

boat / ship

One should continue to exercise care with these nouns and not move them about too freely even though, for most practical purposes, they have drifted together and have become interchangeable. As any seasoned sailor knows, a **boat** is a small water craft and a **ship** is a big one. He or she will tell you that there are row**boats**, life**boats,** sail**boats**, steam**boats**, steam**ships**, battle**ships**—even air**ships**—but no air**boats**.

EXAMPLES:

When it comes to using the words **boat** and **ship**, Steve Adore has no trouble. He interchanges them except when he is around ancient mariners and language preservers. Otherwise, he is known to have loaded a **boat** or two on a **ship**, but he is yet to have been seen lifting a **ship** on a **boat**.

born / borne

These words bear watching, for they are not alike in meaning and use, and can lead to confused communication when one is misused for the other.

Born is an adjective and means brought forth by or as if by birth.

Borne is the past participle of the verb **bear**. It means to carry, hold up, endure, sustain, accept, allow, stand.

EXAMPLES:

Born with a nettlesome nature, Ann Tagonistic was **borne** by her parents from analyst to analyst, until no one could **bear** her any longer.

borne See **born / borne.**

both

Both means being of two. It functions as a conjunction, as a pronoun, and as an adjective. Its overuse as a pronoun creates redundancy. One can avoid such repetition by replacing **both** with a noun or another pronoun.

EXAMPLES:

"**Both** Larry and Harry like to date, and **both** said they (both) were coming to our party. Should one conclude that **both** men will show up with dates?" Hy Pertension asked anxiously. "One conclusion is as good as two or four," his wife replied.

bring / take

When your point of view is correct, you are bound to fetch the admiration of language lovers. That is why knowing whether you are coming or going is essential for using these verbs when dealing with physical movement.

Bring means to convey, lead, carry, or cause something to come to a place or a person.

Take means to convey, lead, carry, or cause something to go away from a place or a person.

EXAMPLES:

"**Bring** all the good potatoes from the shed," Spud Grower said to his wife. "We'll **take** them to the store. They should **bring** a good price. We'll split what we get. I'll **take** two thirds."

burglary / larceny / robbery / thievery

Indiscriminate use of these nouns steals upon their individual meanings and disallows their honest use.

Burglary is the entering (not necessarily breaking into) a premise with the intent of theft.

Larceny is the unlawful taking of property with the intent to deprive the rightful owner of it permanently. **Larceny** can be grand or petty depending on its magnitude.

Robbery is the committing of larceny with force or the threat of force and can occur when a person is present or not.

Thievery is the act or practice or instance of stealing. Except in baseball, it is unlawful.

EXAMPLES:

What a burglar does is called **burglary** and what a larcenist does is called **larceny** and what a robber does is called **robbery** and what a thief does is called **thievery.** You have guessed it. What a crook does is called crookery.

burst / bust

These two words can be a drain and a strain on the emotions if one is not knowledgeable of their meanings and use.

Burst is a verb. It means to break open, apart, or into pieces, usually from impact or pressure from within; to give way with an excess of emotion; to give vent suddenly to repressed emotion; to be filled to the breaking point. Its principal parts are **burst**, **burst** or **bursted**, **bursting**.

Bust is a noun or a verb depending on its use. As a noun, **bust** means the upper part of the human torso between the neck and waist, especially of women; a sculptured representation of the human figure including the neck and head. It also is slang for failure or washout. As a verb, **bust** means to hit, slug; to break or smash, especially with force; to breakup; to demote; to tame; to ruin financially; to raid. It also means to go broke; to lose at cards by exceeding a limit. Its principal parts are **bust**, **busted** or **bust**, **busting**.

EXAMPLES:

Harvey Haddit knocked his father-in-law's **bust** off the mantle, and his wife **burst** into tears and threatened to break every bone in his body. Later she caught him staring at a woman whose **bust** was about to **burst** her dress. And when he neglected to turn off the hot water heater and the pipes **burst** or **bursted**, she **busted** or **bust** him one on the lip. No wonder Haddit **burst** out of the house, yelling, "Today has been one big **bust** after another!"

bus / buss / buzz

These words have to do with riding or kissing—or both. Sensitive and sensible people are careful to observe the distinctiveness of each word's spelling and definition.

Bus is the present tense of the verb **bus**, **bused**. It means to travel by bus, a large motor-driven passenger vehicle, or to be transported in one.

Buss is the present tense of the verb **buss**, **bussed**. It means to kiss or be kissed.

Buzz is a verb but is spelled differently. It means to utter covertly by or as if by whispering.

EXAMPLES:

The teenagers didn't mind having to **bus** to and from school as long as they had someone in the back seat to **buzz**—and **buss**—with.

buss See **bus / buss / buzz**.

bust See **burst / bust.**

but also See **not only . . . but also**.

buy / by / bye

Like so many other words in the English language, these three tiny ones are pronounced alike. Similarities such as theirs account in part for why English is fascinating and, at times, terribly frustrating to speak and write clearly.

Buy is both a verb and a noun. When used as a verb, it means to acquire possession, ownership, or the rights to the use or services of by payment, especially of money. When used as a noun, it means something of value at a favorable price; an act of buying; anything bought or about to be bought.

By can function as an adjective, as an adverb, or, most commonly, as a preposition. As an adjective, it is defined as being off the main route; incidental. As an adverb, it means close at hand; near; past; aside; away. As a preposition, it is defined as in proximity to, near; through or through the medium of; in the direction of; in accordance with; in the name, presence, or view of.

Bye is a variant of **by.** As an adjective, it means principal or main; not secondary or private. As a noun, it is the position of a participant in a tournament who has no opponent after pairs are drawn and who advances to the next round without playing. **Bye** also is the diminutive of good**bye**, a noun meaning farewell.

EXAMPLES:

Dee Fault tried to **buy** a **bye by** offering money to the tennis officials. "**By** no means," they told her, "are you going to **buy** anything from us, certainly not the **bye** you want. All you're getting from us is one great big '**bye, bye**'!"

by See **buy / by / bye.**

buzz See **bus / buss / buzz.**

bye See **buy / by / bye.**

C

can / may / might

Permissiveness has so enthralled the way people speak and write these days that little care is given to the nuances in language. These verbs are good examples of how shades of meaning control precise and clear communication.

Can means to be able; to make, do, or accomplish. Ability to act is implied.

May means to have permission, to indicate possibility.

Might, originally the past tense of **may**, also means to have permission, to indicate possibility. It suggests doubt or reservation as well.

Strictly speaking, **can** and **may** are not interchangeable words even though such usage has fallen into popular practice. Caring communicators should and do make the nicety of distinction between ability to do and permission to do when using these verbs.

EXAMPLES:

King Pinn **can** bowl as well as any of his buddies. Yet he bowls with them only when his wife says he **may**. Do you suppose Pinn someday **might** make a strike at home and roll out on his own—with something to spare?

cannon See **canon / cannon**.

canon / cannon

There is no need to sound off about these same-sounding words. One deals with law and order and the other with straight shooting.

Canon means a criterion of standard of judgment; an accepted principle or rule; a body of principles, rules, or standards, particularly of a church.

A **cannon** is an artillery piece, a large gun. Its plural is **cannon**, not **cannons**.

EXAMPLES:

After the guardsmen had fired many **cannon**, they went into the chapel to hear the **canon** read.

canvas / canvass

These words are close enough in their spelling to lend confusion to those would-be users who do not know their definitions.

Canvas with one **s**, is a noun. It means a firm, closely woven cloth.

Canvass, spelled with two **s**'s, is a verb. It means to examine in detail; to solicit political support; to determine opinions or sentiments. As a noun, it means the act of doing the foregoing.

EXAMPLES:

"As we **canvass** the precinct," the candidate said, "we will have to write the results on this old **canvas** since no one brought any paper."

canvass See **canvas / canvass**.

capital / capitol

These nouns are not at all difficult to use if one keeps each word's vowels straight and knows the difference between a place and a building.

Capital, spelled **al**, means, among its numerous definitions, a city or town serving as the seat of government.

Capitol, spelled **ol**, is the building housing the seat of government.

EXAMPLES:

After the seniors had visited the state **capital**, their teacher suggested that they have their picture taken on the steps of the **capitol**. "What a **capital** idea!" a would-be punster among them quipped.

capitol See **capital / capitol**.

carat See **caret / carat / carrot / karat.**

caret / carat / carrot / karat

All that glitters is not gold, as these four nouns indicate. Each has its own nugget of meaning despite similarities in appearance and pronunciation.

A **caret** is a writer's or proofreader's mark that is used to indicate where something is to be inserted. Like the other nouns, it is pronounced ′kar-ət.

A **carat** is a unit of weight for precious stones, such as diamonds.

A **carrot** is a vegetable, an orange spindle-shaped edible root.

A **karat** is a unit for measuring the purity of pure gold, pure gold being 24 **karats**. Some dictionaries show it as a variant of **carat**.

EXAMPLES:

Peter Rarebit, the jeweler, weighed the ruby's **carats** and the **karats** in the gold ring. Next he inserted a **caret** in the advertising copy to show a change. Then he rubbed his hands and, leaning back, munched contentedly on a **carrot**.

carrot See **caret / carat / carrot / karat**.

catchup See **catsup / catchup / ketchup.**

catsup / catchup / ketchup

As defined, these words call for tomatoes in their recipes regardless of how each is spelled. **Catsup** and **catchup** are variants of **ketchup**, a noun, which came into the English language from the Malayan word *kechap*, meaning a spiced fish sauce. Tomato sauce is the main ingredient. In England **ketchup** can be made from mushrooms and nuts, and from other edibles. The words, for all practical purposes, have become interchangeable in the United States.

EXAMPLES:

"Honey," Beau Nanza called to the waitress, "how 'bout bringin' som'thin' to go on these french fries?" "How about some **catsup** or **catchup** or **ketchup**?" she asked. "Naw, none of that fancy stuff," he said. "Jus' bring me some tamata sauce."

censer / censor / censure

These words need not be confused and become a burning issue once their definitions and parts of speech are understood correctly.

Censer is a noun. It is a container in which incense, a pleasing fragrance, perfume, or scent is burned. Its verb form is **cense**.

Censor is a verb and a noun. As a verb, it means to examine something in order to suppress, delete, or remove whatever is considered to be offensive. As a noun, it means one who examines to suppress, delete, or remove.

Censure is a verb and a noun. As a verb, it means to find fault with; to criticize as blameworthy; to condemn. As a noun, it means a judgment involving condemnation; the act of blaming or condemning sternly.

EXAMPLES:

Who would **censure** someone, what's more, seek to **censor** that person's actions, because he or she ignited the incense in the **censer**, unless the would-be **censor** lacked a sense of smell?

censor See **censer / censor / censure**.

censure See **censer / censor / censure**.

character / reputation

These two nouns appear to be synonyms. They are not. Like human beings, each word has its own individuality that requires recognition and respect.

Character refers to the moral qualities or attributes that mark a person.

Reputation refers to the qualities and traits of a person as regarded by other people.

EXAMPLES:

Reputation, which some people consider to be good, bad, or a mixture of the two, can precede or follow a person. **Character**, regardless of what others may try to say about it, doesn't go anywhere. We all are stuck with our own.

children's / childrens'

One of these words is for real. The other is not. To know the difference, one needs to recognize what is singular and what is plural, and how to use an apostrophe to form the possessive case. **Children's** is the plural possessive of the singular noun child. As a plural noun, it is spelled **children** without an s. There is no such construction as **childrens'**. It is a corruption of **children's** and smacks of illiteracy.

childrens' See **children's / childrens'**.

chord / cord

There's no need to get tied up in knots over these two nouns just because they are pronounced alike and have quite different meanings, and, therefore, strictly speaking, are not interchangeable. Once the words have been clearly defined, a speaker or writer can be in accord with their accurate use.

Chord means three or more musical tones struck simultaneously; a straight line joining two points on a curve; an individual emotion or disposition; either of the two outside members of a truss connected and braced by web members; the straight line joining the leading and trailing edge of an airfoil.

Cord means a long slender flexible material usually consisting of several strands woven or twisted together; a moral, spiritual, or emotional bond; an anatomical structure (as a nerve or umbilical cord) resembling a cord; a small flexible insulated cable; a unit of wood cut for fuel.

EXAMPLES:

Someone struck a **chord** on the accordian. The lumberjacks cleared their vocal **cords** and raised their voices in song. Soon their sound was joined by that of axes felling the nearby oaks. In no time the crew had a **chord** of fellowship and a **cord** of wood with which to keep themselves warm.

cinch See **clench / clinch / cinch**.

cite See **sight / site / cite**.

clean / cleanse

These two verbs have a sense of purity about them so that defining them flawlessly is the perfect thing to do.

Clean means to rid of dirt, impurities, or extraneous matter.

Cleanse also means to rid of dirt. In its figurative sense it means to make oneself or to be made spiritually and morally pure.

EXAMPLES:

Even Luke Warm knows that one uses soap to **clean** the body and prayer to **cleanse** the soul.

cleanse See **clean / cleanse**.

clench / clinch / cinch

A definitive outlook and a firm grasp of the meaning of each of these three words can make a difference in how each is used correctly.

Clench, as a verb, means to hold fast to something or to clutch, such as a tool; to set or close tight, such as one's teeth or fists. As a noun, it means the end of a nail that is turned back in the clinching process.

Clinch, as a verb, means to turn over or flatten the protruding point of a driven nail, rivet, or bolt, or to treat a screw in like manner; to make final or irrefutable; to settle; to win; to hold an opponent, as in boxing, at close quarters with one or both arms; to hold fast or firmly. As a noun, it means a fastening by means of a clinched nail, rivet, bolt, or screw; an instance or act of clinching in boxing; embrace.

Cinch, as a verb, means to put a cinch on; to make certain or assure; to perform the act of cinching or of tightening the cinch. As a noun, it means a girth for a pack or saddle; a thing done with ease; a certainty to happen.

EXAMPLES:

Buck Aroo was a **cinch** to **clinch** the main event at the rodeo until the **cinch** on his saddle broke and he had to **clench** the bronco's mane to keep himself and his championship from being thrown for a loss.

clinch See **clench / clinch / cinch**.

closure / cloture

These two nouns mean the same thing. Keeping an open mind on their derivation helps to pronounce and spell each word correctly even though for all practical purposes the prevailing preference for **closure** has made its use an open-and-shut case.

Closure is derived from the Latin word *clausus*. It means an act of closing; the condition of being closed; something that closes, such as a pocketbook with a zipper.

Cloture comes from the French word *cloture*. It means the closing of debate in a legislative body, especially by calling for a vote.

EXAMPLES:

Closure of the filibuster came after a call for **cloture** that closed the mouths of some long-winded senators.

cloture See **closure / cloture**.

collective nouns

Staying calm, cool, and all together adds up to how to handle singular nouns that many unknowledgeable and witless people around us are using as plurals. After all, it is a simple matter of having or making those nouns, verbs, and pronouns that relate to one another agree in number. Such nouns as board, club, council, committee, company, congress, crowd, faculty, family, group, herd, house, jury, orchestra, public, senate, and team are singular. Each calls for a singular verb and the singular pronoun **it** or **its**. Such nouns as boards, clubs, councils, committees, companies, congresses, crowds, faculties, groups, herds, juries, orchestras, publics, senates, and teams are plural. Each calls for a plural verb and the plural pronoun **they**, **their**, or **them**.

EXAMPLES:

The finance **board faces its** own problems when **it meets** next week to take up the city budget. **Its** bored **members have** gone **their** separate ways, but **they were** heard grumbling as **they were** leaving last night's meeting that other city **boards are** known to keep **their** meetings boredom free.

collision / crash

There's no need to get upset over the use of these two nouns. Hit their definitions head-on and then steer straight ahead so that they no longer rub or bump you or each other the wrong way.

A **collision**, by definition and logic, requires that two or more objects be in motion when they strike, hit, bump, crash, or skid into one another.

A **crash**, by definition, means that two or more objects strike, hit, or bump. One or two or more objects can be in motion, and the other or others can be stationary, at a standstill, or motionless.

EXAMPLES:

The **collision** occurred when the drivers of the two slow-moving cars failed to agree who had the right of way. The **crash** occurred when the ground did not yield the right of way to the plunging airplane.

compared to / compared with

Knowing how to use these prepositions with the verb **compare** depends on understanding right relationships and classes of things. When liking one thing to another, the use of **compared to** is called for. When items are placed side by side and examined for their similarities and differences, **compared with** is called for.

EXAMPLES:

Libby Lobb's serve has been **compared to** the flight of a feather. **Compared with** a tennis champion's, it just about clears the net.

compared with See **compared to / compared with**.

complacent / complaisant

Simply stated, these adjectives, whose nicety of difference in meaning and use often is overlooked, have to do with pleasing one's self and others. As for who is pleasing to whom, that requires discrimination on the user's part.

Complacent means self-satisfied; pleased, especially with oneself or with one's abilities, accomplishments, or advantages.

Complaisant means obliging; agreeable, or gracious; eager to please others; inclined or disposed to please.

EXAMPLES:

Complacent people seldom make **complaisant** lovers, especially so when their love affairs are one-sided and are directed at pleasing only themselves.

complaisant See **complacent / complaisant**.

complement / compliment

These words are both verbs and nouns. Their proper use depends on how they are appraised and completed in thought before being spoken or written.

Complement has to do with completeness. As a verb, it means to fill up; to make entire or complete. As a noun, it means something that fills up, makes perfect, or completes.

Compliment has to do with praise. As a verb, it means to congratulate; to praise, to express admiration or approval. As a noun, it is an expression of esteem, respect, affection, admiration, congratulation; a flattering remark.

EXAMPLES:

When Dudley Dudds **complemented** his outfit with an expensive tie, it drew a **compliment** from his wife, but when he bought a cheap-looking scarf for her wardrobe's **complement**, she did not **compliment** him again for a long, long time.

complex / complicated

These adjectives are not all that involved once you sort out the difference in their meaning. It is a matter of parts and intricacy.

Complex means consisting of interwoven or interconnected parts; composed of two or more parts; hard to separate, analyze, or solve. It often implies many varying parts.

Complicated means composed of intricately combined or involved parts, and emphasizes elaborate relationship of parts rather than number.

EXAMPLES:

Slim Plistic faced a **complex** question. He looked at the parts of his broken watch spread out before him. Should he try to put them together or should he take them to a jeweler? He decided it was too **complicated**—even for him. So he stuffed everything in a pocket and reached for his hat.

complicated See **complex / complicated**.

compliment See **complement**.

compose / comprise / consist / include

All these verbs appear on the surface to be interchangeable. A closer look shows they are not when one considers that a whole is made up of its parts and that the parts make up a whole. When you think about it, the four words have to do with large and small matters.

Compose is transitive and means to make; to form; to combine things.

Comprise is also transitive. It means to contain, encompass, or comprehend.

Consist is intransitive and means to stand together; to be made up of; to be capable of existing.

Include, which is transitive, means to take in as a part of a whole. It has achieved popularity as a synonym for **comprise** when actually it has to do with part and not the whole of something.

EXAMPLES:

One can **compose** one's thoughts, and one's thoughts can **comprise** one's intellect, but what one **includes** in one's thoughts does not always **consist** of what one should think.

comprise See **compose / comprise / consist / include**.

connote See **denote / connote**.

consist See **compose / comprise / consist / include**.

consul / counsel / council

Tact and diplomacy, as well as deliberativeness and a legal bent, are needed in taking under advisement how to use these nouns.

Consul means an official appointed by a government who resides in a foreign country and who represents the commercial interests of the citizens of the appointing country.

Counsel means advice given especially as the result of consultation; guarded thoughts, or intentions; a lawyer engaged in the trial or management of a case in court.

Council means a group elected or appointed as an advisory or legislative body; an assembly or meeting for consultation, advice, or discussion.

EXAMPLES:

The **consul** was uncertain of the **counsel** he should give to the ambassador's **council**. So he **consul**ted with his **counsel**ors in the **consul**ate before he went to the embassy with words of **consul**tation in hand for the **council**ors.

continual / continuous

To use these look-alike adjectives properly, one needs to understand which means now and then and which means ceaseless.

Continual means recurring regularly and frequently; stopping and resuming.

Continuous means extending or prolonged without interruption; ceaseless.

EXAMPLES:

Politicians gladly welcome **continuous** praise but will settle for any that is **continual**, particularly when it enables them to get into or remain in office.

continuous See **continual / continuous**.

convince / persuade

These verbs have to do with influencing and being influenced. Contrary to their persistent misuse, the words are not identical in meaning nor are they interchangeable in expression. To use them properly, one needs to distinguish between to and of, that and into.

Convince means to bring by argument and evidence to belief; to cause to believe something. It is used with **of**, and **that**. It is not used with **to**. One can be **convinced of** something or be **convinced that** something is. One cannot be **convinced to** do something.

Persuade means to cause (someone) to do something by means of argument, reasoning, or entreaty; to win over to a course of action by reasoning or inducement. It is used with **to**, **of**, **that**, and **into**. One can be **persuaded to** do something. One can be **persuaded of** something. One can be **persuaded that** something is. And one can be **persuaded into** doing something.

EXAMPLES:

People who advertise on television are **convinced that** they can **persuade** viewers **to** buy anything. They could be right.

cord See **chord / cord**.

council See **consul / counsel / council**.

counsel See **consul / counsel / council**.

crash See **collision / crash**.

credible / creditable

These look-alike adjectives often are misused. They have to do with honor and believability, so that giving credit where credit is due becomes a means for determining their correct use.

Credible means capable of being believed; believable; plausible; worthy of confidence; reliable.

Creditable means worthy of belief; sufficiently good to bring honor or esteem; deserving of commendation; worthy of commercial credit.

EXAMPLES:

Should Bea Reft come up with a **credible** payment plan, her bank might find her **creditable**. Even so, it may be stretching credit in her case a bit too far.

creditable See **credible / creditable**.

cynic / skeptic

One need remain no longer in doubt about the use of these nouns once doubt is established as part of the meaning of one of them.

Cynic means a faultfinding captious critic; especially one who believes that human conduct is motivated wholly by self-interest.

Skeptic means a person who holds an attitude of doubt or uncertainty, or a disposition to incredulity either in general or toward a particular subject.

EXAMPLES:

Some politicians have only to open their mouths to change an undecided voter from a **skeptic** to a **cynic**.

D

data and other Latin plurals

Some words add up and some do not, and others can be counted both ways. It all has to do with number, one way or another. The matter of number pertains particularly to Latin plural nouns that have been absorbed in the English language, such as **agenda**, **alumni**, **data**, **media**, and **trivia**, to name a few, whose singulars are **agendum**, **alumnus**, **datum**, **medium**, and **trivium**.

Popular usage has divided the ways in which these Latin plural nouns are used in spoken and written English. **Trivia** is used only with singular verbs, and so is **agenda**. **Agendas** has become the Americanized plural of **agendum**, but **alumni** and **media** have retained their plural forms.

Data, on the other hand, is a double-duty word. It is the plural of **datum**, a Latin noun that means factual information used as a basis for reasoning, discussion, or calculation. The plural form has become Americanized to the point that it is used in both singular and plural constructions. When its meaning is collective and stress is placed on a group of facts as a unit, a singular verb is used. When **data** refers to the individual facts, a plural verb is used.

EXAMPLES:

Alumni sometimes find that **data** about them get into the hands of the **media**, which place the facts on their **agendas** despite the fact that some readers, listeners, and viewers say such **data** is boring and is sheer **trivia**.

decimate / demolish / destroy

Some words, such as these three verbs, are whole in their meaning. There is nothing halfway or partial about them. They are called absolutes and cannot be qualified.

Decimate, which comes from the Latin, means to select by lot and kill every tenth man of; to take a tenth from; to destroy a large part of. The word describes the method of punishment given to rebellious or cowardly soldiers in the Roman legions. Their leaders would choose one in every ten soldiers by lot to be put to death. Think of the word decimal and you have the partial concept: one in ten.

Decimate is not used with fractions or percentages, such as in "Half or 50 percent of the people were decimated." Nor is it used with abstractions, as in "Almost all of the deer were decimated." One does not say that something has been totally or completely decimated because the killing off that the word implies is partial, less than total or complete.

Demolish means to break to pieces; to do away with completely; to destroy.

Destroy means to ruin the structure, organic existence, or condition of something; to put out of existence; to put an end to; to annihilate; to kill.

To say something has been totally or completely **demolished** or has been totally or completely **destroyed** would be redundant.

EXAMPLES:

Roger Roulette says farming is too risky. Diseases can **decimate** cattle, storms can **demolish** buildings, and frosts can **destroy** crops. He says he prefers to make his living by playing the sweepstakes that come in the mail.

deduce See **adduce / deduce / deduct.**

deduct See **adduce / deduce / deduct.**

delusion / illusion / allusion

Some things seem to be so when they are not, such as believing that these nouns are synonyms because they look and sound somewhat alike.

A **delusion** is a false belief often entailing some peril. It is believing (self-deception) or causing others to believe that false is true. It is something that is falsely or delusively believed.

An **illusion** is a false belief or impression; a deceptive appearance; that which appears to the mind or eye to be natural but is not; a misperception.

An **allusion** is an indirect, passing, or casual reference to something.

EXAMPLES:

Delusion is when a husband brags that he is the boss in his own home. **Illusion** is what magicians create by sleight of hand. **Allusion** is what scantily knowledgeable students seek to slip past teachers on examinations.

demolish See **decimate / destroy / demolish.**

denote / connote

The plain and simple fact about these verbs is that one means what it says, while the other hints or implies beyond what it means.

Denote means to make known; to be explicit; to name; to specify; to mark plainly; to indicate; to signify.

Connote means to convey in addition to exact explicit meaning; to suggest or imply beyond the explicit meaning; to hint beyond the obvious or explicit.

EXAMPLES:

To many people marriage **denotes** bliss. To others it sometimes **connotes** experiencing something less than that.

desert / dessert

A grain or two of dry wit and a sweet sense of things help keep these words in proper perspective and definition.

Desert, as a noun, means an arid barren land and is pronounced ′dez-ərt. As a verb, it means to abandon and is pronounced di-′zərt.

Dessert means a sweet course or dish served at the end of a meal.

EXAMPLES:

Norman Nomad was not about to **desert** his **dessert** in the **desert.** Despite the heat and the blowing sand, he managed to get down the rest of his camel curds. Then, reaching in his rucksack, he pulled out the last of his sweetened dates and enjoyed what might be called his "just **deserts**."

dessert See **desert / dessert.**

destroy See **decimate / demolish / destroy.**

differ from / differ with

These two verbs can be troublesome until you "preposition" them properly.

Differ from means to be unlike or distinct in nature from something else.

Differ with means to disagree; to express dissent; to dispute.

EXAMPLES:

What would politics be like if the participants were not **different from** one another and they did not **differ with** each other whenever they got together?

differ with See **differ from / differ with.**

disc / disk

These nouns, which have to do with flat round objects, are not identical twins. Each spins its own meaning and revolution.

A **disc** is a phonograph record. It also is any of various rounded and flattened animal anatomical structures.

A **disk** is any thin, flat, circular object.

EXAMPLES:

What do you get when a radio announcer slips a **disc** on a turntable, stands up and reaches to get another **disc**, and slips on a **disk** that had slipped from a chain around his or her neck? A slipped **disc** jockey.

discreet / discrete

A bit of tact is needed in distinguishing between these adjectives. Although they are pronounced the same way, they have different meanings.

Discreet means having or showing discernment or good judgment in conduct, especially in speech; keeping confidences; being prudent.

Discrete means constituting a separate entity; consisting of distinct or unconnected elements.

EXAMPLES:

A **discreet** maid is one who guards her tongue when the husband and wife she works for engage in **discrete** romances.

discrete See **discreet / discrete.**

disinterested / uninterested

These adjectives, despite their similarity of appearance, are not synonyms. The meaning of each has a slant of its own.

Disinterested means to be neutral; to be free of prejudice or selfish motive or interest.

Uninterested means lacking interest; aloofness and indifference; taking no part in something.

EXAMPLES:

If given a choice, politicians most likely would opt for **disinterested** journalists rather than for **uninterested** ones. Sometimes they get both.

disk See **disc / disk.**

drunk / drunken

These words, despite popular imbibing, are not interchangeable even though both are the same part of speech.

Drunk is an adjective and is the spelling used after a form of the verb **to be**. It also is a participle, a verbal adjective that is formed from the past tense of the verb **drink**.

Drunken also is an adjective and is the spelling used before a noun.

EXAMPLES:

Stanley Stag had **drunk** his fill at the bachelor's party. In fact, he was **drunk.** He reeled his car homeward, but police bagged him for **drunken** driving and wheeled him to jail, where he was left to unwind overnight.

drunken See **drunk / drunken.**

due to / because of

These two sets of words are examples of how popular usage and proper English take separate paths. It might be called the syntax split. Therefore, one needs to know the individual parts of speech to use the phrases correctly.

Due to, contrary to popular misbelief and misuse, is not a prepositional construction but an adjectival one. It is used with linking verbs and modifies nouns and pronouns. It has to do with answering the question **what**. The words **owing to** are a proper substitution for **due to**. Some people use the phrase, but most do not because they consider it to be old-fashioned, stilted, or too literary.

Because of is adverbial in construction and modifies verbs, adjectives, and other adverbs. It has to do with answering the question **why**.

Both **due to** and **because of** have to do with cause and effect. That is where the confusion in their use appears to arise.

EXAMPLES:

Someone told Farnsworth Freestyle that the swimming pool's closing was **due to** lack of water. Someone else said the pool was closed **because of** lack of water. Regardless of the cause given and how it was worded, the effect on Freestyle was the same. He didn't take a plunge yesterday. But his hopes did!

E

each / either / neither

The singular thing to do with these pronouns is to keep them singular.

Each means being one of two or more distinct individuals having a similar relation and often constituting an aggregate.

Either means being the one or the other.

Neither means not the one or the other.

EXAMPLES:

Each of the women wants to lose weight. Even though **either** is likely to try anything she can to do so, **neither** is likely to drop an ounce.

each other / one another

For a long time **each other** was limited to mean two persons or things and **one another** meant two or more persons or things. It is not so any longer. Modern usage has made them interchangeable.

EXAMPLES:

How often it is that honeymooners gaze fondly at **each other.** Yet, when the glow has faded, they face **one another** with individual demands for divorce.

eager / anxious

The distinction in the meaning of these adjectives does not worry most people. Careful speakers and writers, however, should be and are desirous of using them correctly, for one of the words, in its own way, is worrisome.

Eager means marked by keen, enthusiastic, or impatient desire or interest.

Anxious also has a sense of desire, but it means characterized by extreme uneasiness of mind or brooding fear about some contingency.

EXAMPLES:

When a child is **eager** to bake a cake, his or her mother, you can be sure, will be **anxious** about what it looks and tastes like when it comes out of the oven.

easy / easily

The distinction between these words is that **easy** is an adjective and **easily** is an adverb. To use **easy** as an adverb, except in colloquial expressions, such as "easy come, easy go," is to mark one as an illiterate.

EXAMPLES:

Ann O'Tate read the exam all the way through, marking those questions she considered to be **easy**. She answered them first and then did the hard ones. Even so, she passed **easily**, much to the annoyance of those who did poorly.

easily See **easy / easily**.

effect See **affect / effect**.

either See **each / either / neither**.

either . . . or / neither . . . nor

These correlative conjunctions require synchronization of syntax as well as parallelism of thought in connecting their grammatical elements and in forming agreement of nouns, pronouns, and verbs. Keep in mind that these words work together in pairs and that the same kind of phrasing follows each correlative conjunction. Keep in mind, too, that the noun or pronoun closest to the verb determines the latter's number.

EXAMPLES:

Artie Choke will **either** scale the cliff **or** fall into the river. **Neither** his wife **nor** his friends are betting money he'll rise to the occasion. Instead, they have a wad of towels and a change of clothing handy.

elude See **escape / elude / evade**.

emigrate / immigrate

These verbs call for a sense of direction. It is a matter of knowing out from in. Better still, it is knowing who is going and who is coming, for these actions are not simultaneous or exactly coincidental events.

Emigrate is to **leave** one's place or residence or country to live elsewhere.

Immigrate is to **come** into a country of which one is not a native for the purpose of residing permanently.

EXAMPLES:

Some things are impossible for one person to do at the same time. Even the redoubtable Superman could not **emigrate** from Krypton and **immigrate** to Earth in a single leap—much less do so in the single panel of a comic strip!

empty / vacant

Although these adjectives, generally speaking, are synonyms having to do with lack of content, they are used in differing connotations and contexts.

Empty means containing nothing; not occupied or inhabited; lacking reality, substance, or value; devoid of sense.

Vacant means not occupied by an incumbent, possessor, or officer; being without content or occupant; free from activity or work; devoid of thought, reflection, or expression. It has with it a sense of a temporary condition.

EXAMPLES:

Some heads are **vacant** during tests, while others remain **empty** afterward.

enigma / puzzle / riddle

These nouns have a way of baffling the mind. Mysterious as they appear to be, each has a definition that provides a solution to its individual use.

An **enigma** is an obscure speech or writing; something hard to understand or explain; an inscrutable or mysterious person.

A **puzzle** is a question, problem, or contrivance, such as a toy or a jigsaw or a crossword puzzle, that amuses, perplexes, or challenges the mind. It is difficult to solve and is designed to test one's ingenuity or cleverness.

A **riddle** is a mystifying verbal question or problem that is posed for solving, whose parts seem to be paradoxical or contradictory and often obscure, and that is answered only by guessing or by a flash of insight.

EXAMPLES:

Igno Ramus was an **enigma** to others but not to his wife when he was read a **riddle** while doing a jigsaw **puzzle**. She knew it was all show and no know.

enormity / enormousness

Many people interchange these nouns, thinking they are synonyms, when in fact to so do could be seen as immoderation or the baring of one's ignorance.

Enormity is a grave offense against order, right, and decency; the state or quality of being immoderate, monstrous, or outrageous; great wickedness.

Enormousness is extraordinarily great size, number, or degree exceeding usual bounds or accepted notions.

EXAMPLES:

The **enormousness** of Chester Chortle's off-color jokes can be measured by their **enormity** whenever he seeks to unload them on unreceptive audiences.

enormousness See **enormity / enormousness**.

ensure See **insure / ensure / assure**.

envy / jealousy

These nouns denoting ill will are not synonyms really. Their difference in use depends on the intensity of the feeling that is being expressed.

Envy is painful or resentful awareness of, a discontented longing for an advantage enjoyed by another person joined with a desire to possess the same advantage.

Jealousy is unpleasant suspicion, intolerance of rivalry, or unfaithfulness; a disposition, attitude, or feeling to suspect rivalry or unfaithfulness; hostility toward a rival or one believed to enjoy an advantage.

EXAMPLES:

Charlie Coveter's **jealousy** of his wife's love affair with their next-door neighbor was overshadowed by his **envy** of the man's overwhelming wealth.

escape / elude / evade

These verbs are a bit tricky. Unwary communicators have a tendency to flee from their correct use by not making a distinction in their definitions.

Escape, as an intransitive verb, means to break free; to regain liberty; to get free from confinement. It is followed by the prepositions **from** or **out of**. As a transitive verb, **escape** is not followed by a preposition. It means to avoid danger, pursuit, observation, or the like.

Elude is to escape by means of dexterity, artifice, or cunning; to escape the perception, understanding, or grasp of; to avoid adroitly.

Evade is to slip away; to dodge something or someone who intends to stop us; to escape by trickery or cleverness; to duck doing something; to avoid answering directly.

EXAMPLES:

For Cy Cellblock to **escape** from jail, he either has to **elude** the guards and **evade** their bloodhounds or have all go to lunch and leave the doors unlocked.

essential / indispensible / vital

The use of these adjectives is one of degree and comparision, or the lack thereof. Yet all deal with what is necessary.

Essential means of, relating to, or constituting existence or life; of the utmost importance. It is an absolute term and therefore is not expressed in degrees. Something cannot be more essential or most essential. The fact that something is essential states its necessity, its unqualified being.

Indispensible means not subject to being set aside or neglected;

that which cannot be passed off, let go, or left out without harming the basic purpose or usefulness of a thing; that which is required or is necessary, often as an integral component.

Vital means existing as a manifestation of life; necessary to or concerned with the maintenance of life. **Vital** is the equivalent of **essential**. It is an absolute term and cannot be qualified. Something cannot be more or most **vital**. It is **vital**. Period.

EXAMPLES:

Choosing one's words adroitly is **essential** when going steady. Right ones are **indispensible.** In fact, they're **vital** or the relationship won't last long.

evade See **escape / elude / evade**.

every one / everyone

These indefinite pronouns can be like busybodies, for one insists on being singular, the other plural, and on occupying space according to its number.

Everyone is one word. It is singular in number and means every person. A singular verb and a singular pronoun are used to form agreement of all three parts of speech. Some speakers and writers hesitate to use his, or his or her, as singular pronouns in referring to **everyone**. Perhaps they find these pronouns sexist, awkward, or annoying. The way to get around what appears to be offensive is to use the plural pronoun **all**.

Every one becomes two words when their meaning involves each individual item and they are followed by a preposition. Then a plural verb and a plural pronoun are used to form agreement of all three parts of speech.

EXAMPLES:

Everyone is standing on his or her feet except Stanley Sittingstill. **All** are standing on their feet except. . . . **Every one** of the fans are standing on their feet except. . . . **All** of the fans are standing on their feet except. . . .

everyone See **every one / everyone**.

evoke / invoke

A difference in vowels in the prefixes of these verbs makes them discrete.

E̲voke, whose prefix **e** means **out**, is defined as to call forth or up; to elicit; to summon; to cite especially with approval or for support.

I̲nvoke, whose prefix **i** means **in** or **into**, is defined as to petition for help or support; to appeal to or cite as an authority; to make an earnest request for.

EXAMPLES:

The U.S. Congress has its muted moments when its committees **evoke** people to appear before them and witnesses **invoke** their right to button their lips.

except See **accept / except**.

expect / anticipate

Caring communicators look forward to using and are prepared to use these and other words precisely and correctly.

Expect means to look foward to, to await some occurrence or outcome. It implies a high degree of certainty and involves the idea of envisioning.

Anticipate means to give advance thought, discussion, or treatment to; to look forward to as certain. It embraces the concept of doing something before or in concurrence with a coming event; of preparing.

EXAMPLES:

Students can **expect** to fail exams if they do not **anticipate** the questions.

F

farther / further

Conscientious communicators, those who truly care, make a distinction between these two words even though **further** is outdistancing **farther** in indiscriminate popularity. Still, one would not ask, "How fur is it?"

Farther is both an adjective and an adverb, and is the comparative for the word **far**. It has to do with ideas of physical distance.

Further, as an adjective and an adverb, has to do with everything else. As a verb, the word means to advance; to promote; to give progress to.

EXAMPLES:

There is no need to **further** the cause of using these adjectives, adverbs, and verbs correctly by discussing **further further**. Therefore, to assure an end to its **further** discussion, read no **farther** than this period.

faze / phase

These odd-looking but alike-sounding words may seem disconcerting to a would-be user until their parts of speech are understood and each word is defined precisely and spelled correctly.

Faze is a verb. It means to disturb the composure of; to disconcert; to throw into confusiuon; to daunt; to unnerve.

Phase is a noun. It means a stage in development; an aspect of a moon or a planet; an aspect of a subject or a question.

EXAMPLES:

Mrs. Wuzzy says Fuzzy's wearing of a fez is a **phase** her son is going through that doesn't **faze** her—or him—one bit.

felony / misdemeanor

The right and wrong use of these nouns having to do with criminality is a matter of corrigibility since each is capable of being set right in one's mind and in type.

A **felony** is a serious crime. Definition of what constitutes one depends on the governmental jurisdiction involved. At the federal level, a **felony** is a crime that carries a potential penalty of more than a year in jail or prison.

A **misdemeanor** is a minor offense against the law. At the federal level, it carries a potential penalty of less than a year in jail. Judges can impose a fine or probation in addition to or instead of a jail sentence when a statute gives them the option to do so.

EXAMPLES:

Hugh Hack is likely to spend more time with his bride in the years ahead if he is convicted of a **misdemeanor**, such as shoplifting, than if he is sent to a state prison on a **felony** conviction, such as grand theft. Should she try slipping him a cake with a saw in it, they could end up really severed apart.

fewer / less

These too-often abused adjectives have to do with number and quantity. Their precise and correct use calls for exercising a matter of degree and keeping individual items and those in bulk distinctly separate.

Fewer is the comparative of **few.** It means a smaller number of persons or things. It applies to matters of number and modifies plural nouns.

Less means constituting a more limited number; of reduced size, extent, or degree. It applies to matters of degree and modifies collective nouns, mass nouns, or nouns denoting an abstract whole.

EXAMPLES:

''How come I get **less** wine than you do?'' Saul Sultana asked, eyeing his tiny half-filled glass with a crushed look. ''You picked **fewer** grapes than I did,'' Mickey Muscatel answered, slurping steadily from his tall, full one.

figuratively / literally

People who like to interchange these adverbs do so not realizing that they are confusing what is meant to be said with what actually is said. Thus it is a matter of keeping one's senses—or meaning—distinctively clear.

Figuratively means in an analogous sense; similar to something else but not in the exact sense.

Literally means in an exact sense; in an actual manner.

EXAMPLES:

A drunkard can be said to be **figuratively** stewed to the gills, while a fish submerged in a chowder **literally** is in that sodden condition.

flack / flak

One can avoid a barrage of criticism by using these nouns with discretion.

A **flack** is one who provides publicity; a press agent; a publicist.

Flak means antiaircraft fire; the bursting of shells fired from such guns. It also is slang for criticism.

EXAMPLES:

A **flack** who tries to captalize on an air battle he has witnessed could draw as much **flak** as the **flak** he has seen.

flair / flare

Even though these words look alike and are pronounced the same, they should give no difficulty to anyone with a bent for defining words properly.

Flair is a noun. It means a skill or instinctive ability to appreciate or make good use of something; inborn talent.

Flare is both a noun and a verb. As a noun, it means an unsteady glaring light; a fire or a blaze of light used to signal, illuminate, or attract attention; a sudden outburst as of sound, excitement, or anger. As a verb, **flare** means to burn with an unsteady flame; to shine with sudden light; to break out or intensify—often used with up; to express strong emotion, such as sudden zeal, temper, or anger.

EXAMPLES:

El Torcho the Terribly Tempered One has a **flair** for sword swallowing. As long as he has a **flare** to work by, he downs the blade well. It is when the flame goes out that things really **flare** up.

flak See **flack / flak**.

flare See **flair / flare**.

flaunt / flout

These often misused and confused verbs call for a show of respect to avoid a show of contempt from those people who know how to use them correctly.

Flaunt means to display or obtrude oneself to public notice; to wave showily; to display ostentatiously or imprudently.

Flout means to treat with contemptuous disregard; to indulge in scornful behavior; to show contempt in derision or mockery.

EXAMPLES:

Isn't it interesting how some politicians who **flaunt** themselves and **flout** their opponents drop from sight and hearing when they no longer are elected?

flounder / founder

There are two keys to using these words correctly. One is to recognize that they are both nouns and verbs. The other is to thrash out their definitions and let them sink in.

Flounder, as a noun, means a flat fish. As a verb, it means to struggle to move or obtain footing; to thrash about.

Founder, as a noun, means one who founds or establishes. As a verb, it means to become disabled; to give way; to sink below the surface of the water; to come to grief.

EXAMPLES:

A fishing fleet **founder** saw that a **flounder** no longer could **flounder**. Thinking it was dead, he tossed it overboard to let it **founder** in the sea, only to see it not **founder** but swim away, perhaps to **flounder** another day.

flout See **flaunt / flout**.

forbear / forebear / forego / forgo

Knowing when and when not to use an **e** enables one to spell these four words correctly and not to interchange the paired ones.

Forbear, spelled with a single **e**, is a verb. It means to leave alone; to hold oneself back from, especially with an effort of self-restraint.

Forebear, spelled with two **e**'s, is a noun. It means ancestor, one from whom a person is descended; a forefather or a foremother.

Forego, spelled with one **e**, means to go before; to precede in time or place.

Forgo, spelled without an **e**, means to abstain from; to forsake; to renounce.

EXAMPLES:

"Please **forbear** from any further comment about my **forebear** and help me shoot the four bears that are scratching at the door," Glenn Grizzle said to Percy Prattle, "or I'll **forego** you out the window and you'll have to **forgo** the further pleasure of my company!"

forebear See **forbear / forebear / forego / forgo**.

forego See **forbear / forebear / forego / forgo**.

forgo See **forbear / forebear / forego / forgo**.

forthwith See **present / presently / now / forthwith**.

fortuitous / fortunate

These adjectives are not synonyms, for one has to do with chance and the other with luck.

Fortuitous means occurring by chance; accidental; unplanned; unexpected.

Fortunate means bringing something not foreseen as certain; receiving some unexpected good; lucky.

EXAMPLES:

A **fortuitous** meeting can be **fortunate** or otherwise, depending on who sees whom, and where and when. If each side were to seek the other, such a meeting would not be **fortuitous** but could be a **fortunate** one nonetheless.

fortunate See **fortuitous / fortunate**.

foul / fowl

These words are not of the same weather or feather even though they are pronounced the same way.

Foul is an adjective, a noun, and a verb. As an adjective, it means offensive to the senses; constituting an infringement of rules in a game or sports. As a noun, it means an entanglement or collision especially in angling and sailing; an infringement of the rules in a game or sport. And, as a verb, it means to become or be **foul**; to become encrusted, clogged, or choked with a foreign substance; to become entangled or come into collision; to commit a violation in the rules of a game or sport.

Fowl is a noun and a verb. As a noun, it means a bird of any kind, such as a hen, duck, turkey, goose, or pheasant. As a verb, it means to seek, catch, or kill wild**fowl**.

EXAMPLES:

Thaddeus Teedoff drove a golf ball down the fairway that glanced off a **fowl** passing overhead. The ball continued on its way and rolled into the cup for a stroke under par. No one yelled: "**Foul**, Teedoff! You have **foul**ed!" Nor did anyone shout, "Thaddeus, you **fowl**ed the **fowl**!" And so Teedoff wrote down the score on his card, giving himself, one would have to suppose, a "double birdie" for the hole.

founder See **flounder / founder**.

fowl See **foul / fowl**.

further See **farther / further**.

futile See **hopeless / futile**.

G

gage / gauge

A conscientious communicator will pledge to measure the meaning of these nouns carefully before using them.

Gage means something, as a glove, thrown down in token of a challenge to combat; a challenge; a pledge or pawn; security.

Gauge means a standard of measure or measurement; a standard dimension, size, or quantity; any device or instrument for measuring, testing something, or registering measurements.

EXAMPLES:

When it comes to throwing down a **gage**, A. Tad Timid wouldn't know his left hand from his right, but give him a **gauge** and he knows how to take the measure of almost anything.

gamut / gantlet / gauntlet

These nouns, which often are, but need not be, confused, range or run in meaning from a series of musical notes, to a form of punishment, to a protective glove, respectively.

Gamut means the whole series of recognized musical notes; an entire range or series of something, such as colors, letters, or figures.

Gantlet means a double file of men facing each other and armed with clubs or other weapons with which to strike at an individual who is made to run between them; an ordeal from two or all sides; trying conditions; an ordeal. It also is a term used in railroading dealing with the merging of two tracks.

Gauntlet means a glove worn with medieval armor to protect the hand; any of various protective gloves used especially in industry; a glove with an extended cuff for the wrist; a challenge to combat.

EXAMPLES:

Oso Gamie felt a **gamut** of emotions as he ran the **gantlet**, trying to ward off blows from both sides with an old **gauntlet** he had thrown down earlier.

gantlet See **gamut / gantlet / gauntlet.**

gauge See **gage / gauge.**

gauntlet See **gamut / gantlet / gauntlet**.

genius / talent

Even though both these nouns have to do with extraordinary ability and often are contrasted with each other, they should not be confused or be considered synonyms, for one has a higher sense of things than does the other. One can be a **genius** and have **talent**. Yet one can be a **genius** and not have a particular **talent**. Or one can have **talent** and not be a **genius**.

Genius means an exceptional natural capacity of intellect, especially as shown in creative and original thought, expression, discovery, or invention; impressive inborn creative ability; a person having such capacity; a person with a very high intelligence quotient; a guardian or attendant spirit; a person who influences another for good or bad.

Talent means a special natural ability or aptitude; a capacity for success or achievement; a marked natural ability endowed within a person for use, development, or improvement; a unit of money used in ancient countries.

EXAMPLES:

"With that potato's aptitude for laziness," muttered Lucinda Lounger as she looked at her husband's outstretched body on the couch, "it would take at least the **genius** of an Einstein and the **talent** of a Baryshnikov to get him off his back and up on his toes!"

gerund

Thanks to the increased emphasis of informal language, particularly in advertising copy, in commercials, and in broadcasting, the **gerund** has become misunderstood, ignored, or misused. It is a part of speech called a verbal noun. Its form is the same as that of another part of speech, the participle, a verbal adjective, which ends in **ing**. There similarity ends, for each part of speech has its own function to perform in a phrase or sentence. That is why speakers and writers who want their meaning to be clear adhere to proper grammar and syntax when using both parts of speech.

The **gerund** is distinctive in that it often deals with possessiveness. It requires making a distinction between an agent and what an agent does. For example, there is a difference in meaning between these sentences: "Lapso didn't remember a woman entering (participle) the room," and "Lapso didn't remember a woman**'s** entering (**gerund**) the room." The differentiation is between Lapso**'s** not recalling who entered the room and his being unaware a woman had entered the room, let alone identifying her. The use of the **gerund** in the second sentence dealing with Lapso's memory accounts for why there is a considerable difference in meaning between the two sentences.

The **gerund** can function: as a subject (Remembering is not one of Lapso's claims to fame.); as an object (Paulette Pirouette teaches dancing. Lardo tried running for exercise.); or as a modifier (a swimming pool—not a pool that swims). But to say "Bo is a growing boy" means a boy named Bo grows, for growing, so used, is a participle and functions as an adjective.

get / got / gotten

Get (present), **got** (past), and **gotten** (past perfect) form the principle parts of what may be the most versatile and overused verb in the English language. Of the three forms, **gotten** is least used and is not used when it should be. **Get** and **got** have become catch-all verbs that lack discrimination in their use and precise expression in their meaning.

The original meaning of **get** was to seize or take hold of. Today dictionaries list numerous meanings for both **get** and **got**. Careful communicators can—and do—display the depth of their vocabularies and their adroitness in the handling of language by using verbs other than **get** and **got** to express ideas precisely and accurately.

EXAMPLES:

"I **get** (understand, know, recognize) your meaning," Artie Ficial said, "but I've **got** to (I need to, ought to, should, must, have to) think it over before it's **got** away from (it's **gotten** away from, slipped from, disappeared from, gone from) my mind."

gibe / jibe

Competent communicators will not drift with the tides of popular misuse and abuse of language by interchanging these same-sounding nouns and verbs. Instead, they will mark the distinction between them and thus avoid the jeers of those people who know how to use them properly.

Gibe, as a noun, means a taunting or sarcastic remark. As a verb, it means to utter mocking words; to taunt; to deride; to jeer.

Jibe, as a noun, means the act of jibing. As a verb, it means to shift from one side to the other when running before the wind as a fore-and-aft sail or its boom; to change a ship's course so that a fore-and-aft sail acts in this manner. **Jibe** also means to be in harmony or accord with; to agree.

EXAMPLES:

Tom Foolery can **jibe** before the wind as well as any sailor, but when he casts a **gibe** or two at his crew mates about their performance, somehow the wind goes out of their sails and they no longer **jibe** with him.

glamour / glamorous

The connotation of magic that originally was found in this pair of words is rapidly disappearing. The mass media can be thanked for this waning, for with their customary exuberance and pervasiveness they have overworked and vulgarized these words to the point where each is used indiscriminately. The result is that both words have lost almost whatever effectiveness they once had for expressing ideas of charm, excitement, enchantment, and magic.

Glamour is both a noun and an adjective. It is derived from *grammar*, a Scottish word dealing with occult learning. The word **glamor**, no **u**, is the corruption of *grammar* brought into common English use by Sir Walter Scott. The Americanization of **glamor** into **glamour** by adding the letter **u**, perhaps because of the magic associated with the word, runs counter to the insistence and persistence of Noah Webster, America's first lexicographer, in dropping the **u** in such English words as **favour**, **honour**, and

labour, and making them **favor**, **honor**, and **labor**. Like amour, **glamour** has its **u**, although most modern dictionaries list **glamor**, no **u**, as a variant spelling. So much for the romanticization—or nonromanticization—of language! As a noun, **glamour** is the word for alluring charm, witchery, fascination, excitement, enchantment, and magic. As an adjective, it is the word for a person or thing that expresses one or more of these qualities.

Glamorous is an adjective. (Note that it is **glamor**, no **u**, plus **ous**.) It means full of **glamour**, that is full of alluring charm, witchery, fascination, excitement, enchantment, or magic.

EXAMPLES:

"The night is young, and I'm so amorous. How about it, **glamorous** lady?" Eddie Eagerly proposed, snuggling up against his wife's side. "Sorry, old boy," she said, "but the magic is gone." "Are you saying our marriage has lost its **glamour**?" he asked. "That's right," she replied as she adjusted the curlers in her hair, turned her back to him, and drifted off to sleep.

glamorous See **glamour / glamorous.**

glance / glimpse

At first sight, these words appear to be synonyms. A closer look reveals they are not, for their difference has to do with how briefly or how quickly objects are perceived.

Glance, as a noun, means a quick look. As a verb, it means to look quickly. It also has a quite different meaning: to strike a surface so as to bounce off at an angle.

Glimpse, as a noun, means a brief fleeting view or look. As a verb, it means to take, catch, or get a brief view of.

EXAMPLES:

In a **glance** Vel Veteen caught a **glimpse** of Polly Ester. To **glimpse** her friend in a suit like her own did more than **glance** off her ego. It crushed it.

glimpse See **glance / glimpse.**

glutton / gourmand / gourmet

These three nouns have to do with the quantity and quality of ingestion and the taste of things. Their definitions, it could be said, provide food—and drink—for thought.

Glutton, the least savory of the three words, is defined as a person who eats excessively, one who is given habitually to greedy and voracious eating and drinking. A **glutton** also can be a person with a remarkably great desire or capacity for something.

Gourmand is a bit tastier. It comes from the French and means a person who is excessively fond of food and drink, one who is heartily interested in good food and drink.

Gourmet has its own refinement. It also comes from the French and means a connoisseur of food and drink; a person who is especially competent to pass judgments in an art or in matters of taste; a discerning judge of the best in any field.

EXAMPLES:

Gerry Gobbler devoured all that was brought to him, Gilda Glossie savored all she consumed, and Grayson Gratified sat back, satisfied, wiping his mouth daintily and saying all he had consumed had been just right. So who, do you suppose, picked up the tab: the **glutton**, the **gourmand**, or the **gourmet**?

good / well

Ordinarily what is **well** and **good** should be left alone but not so in the case of these two words. They have been subjected to such abuse and misuse that it would be **good** to look at them and to determine how to use them properly and **well**.

Good primarily is an adjective. It occurs as an adverb chiefly in speech and is considered by educated people to be less than standard English. **Good** has many meanings, the most common of which are: morally excellent; pious; virtuous; righteous; satisfactory in quantity, quality, or degree; proper, fit, right, suitable.

Well is both an adjective and an adverb. As either part of speech, it has many meanings. As an adjective, it means in good health; satisfactory; comfortable; fortunate. As an adverb, it means skillfully; satisfactorily; agreeably; favorably; intimately; soundly.

Good and **well** also function as nouns, a discussion of which is not needed.

EXAMPLES:

Coach Pigskin is **well**-pleased to have many **good** players. When they all are **well** and are in **good** health, and they play **well**, he says: "**Well** and **good.** It's about time things went both ways for me!"

gorilla / guerrilla

These nouns, despite their look-alike appearance, cannot ape each other or be interchanged. Clearly, they are the names of separate species that are—or often are—jungles apart.

A **gorilla** is an animal, the largest of anthropoid apes of western equitorial Africa. It is related to the chimpanzee but is less erect and much larger. The word **gorilla** also means an ugly or brutal man.

A **guerrilla** is a person who engages in irregular warfare especially as a member of an independent unit that harasses the enemy by surprise raids and attacks on, and sabotage of, communication and supply lines.

EXAMPLES:

Grego, the **gorilla**, scratched his huge, hairy chest in awe as he watched the **guerrilla** gingerly place dynamite under the bridge. "Wow!" he said. "I'd better blow this scene before it becomes an explosive situation!"

got See **get / got / gotten**.

gotten See **get / got / gotten.**

gourmand See **glutton / gourmand / gourmet.**

gourmet See **glutton / gourmand / gourmet.**

graduate / graduated

These verbs, which come from the Latin word *gradus*, meaning step or degree, can be spoken and written correctly or incorrectly depending upon the degree to which communicators watch their step in using them by noting the distinction between an act and an agent.

Graduate is a transitive verb. It means to grant an academic degree or diploma on someone or to admit a person to a particular standing or grade. Such an act is done by an agent, such as the faculty of a school, college, or some other institution. A person receiving such action is called a **graduate**. It is correct to say a person plans or hopes to **graduate from** an institution. In such usage, the preposition **from** is required.

Graduated is both a transitive and an intransitive verb. In its transitive form as the past tense of **graduate**, the word means that an agent has granted an academic degree or diploma on a person or that an individual is the recipient of such action. In its intransitive form, **graduated** can mean that either the agent acted or a person is or was the recipient of the action.

Thus schools **graduate** students, and students are **graduated from** or they **graduate from** schools. To omit the preposition **from** and say someone **graduated** college is not acceptable English (either in or out of school). It is illiteracy as any **graduate** or would-be **graduate** should know.

EXAMPLES :

For years Nanette Needles had looked to the day when she would **graduate** from The School for Designing Women. Now that the school had **graduated** her, she wondered what to fashion first—a husband or a new line of clothes.

graduated See **graduate / graduated.**

grateful / gratified

Being appreciative of or thankful for what is pleasing is not always a concurrent state of thought or emotion. This distinction is what marks the difference in these two words and in their individual meaning even though they often are interchanged. Such a practice may be so because both words stem from the Latin root *gratus*, meaning pleasing.

Grateful is an adjective. It means appreciative of kindness or benefits received; thankful; expressing gratitude; pleasing to the mind or senses; agreeable or welcome; refreshing.

Gratified is the past tense of the verb to gratify, to give pleasure by satisfying desires or humoring inclinations or feelings. Unlike

grateful, **gratified** does not have the connotation of gratitude or thankful. But like **grateful**, it can function as a participle, a verbal adjective.

EXAMPLES:

Grateful for little things in life, Uriah Underling was **gratified** when his boss, Petrovich Parsimonious, gave him a one-dollar raise.

gratified See **grateful / gratified.**

grisly / gristly / grizzly / grizzled

Once one gets one's bearings on these adjectives, one should not find it altogether hairy to use them correctly.

Grisly means inspiring or causing fear or horror or disgust.

Gristly means resembling or containing gristle, tough flexible tissue of animal bodies, especially in meat.

Grizzly means gray, gray haired. A large gray-haired bear of North America is called a **grizzly** bear. The word is used also as a noun to name this kind of bear.

Grizzled means gray, gray haired and is a synonym for **grizzly** but not for **grizzly** bear.

EXAMPLES:

Under a **grizzled** sky, a **grisly grizzly** bear sniffed about an abandoned camp site for food. Looking up at the **grizzly** sky, the **grizzly** growled under its breath: "Typical tourists. Not a thing here but **gristly** leftovers!"

gristly See **grisly / gristly / grizzly / grizzled.**

grizzled See **grisly / gristly / grizzly / grizzled.**

grizzly See **grisly / gristly / grizzly / grizzled.**

group See **collective nouns.**

guarantee / guaranty / warranty

There are ways to make things certain or to assure that matters will be done as pledged. It is what these three words do if their users are sure of each word's precise meaning.

Guarantee is both a noun and a verb, and is commonly used either way. As a noun, it means a formal promise or assurance, usually in writing, for the fulfillment of what has been agreed, such as an assurance of the quality of or length of use to be expected from a product offered for sale with a promise of reimbursement. As a verb, **guarantee** means to give or make such promise or assurance.

Guaranty is also a noun and a verb. Its meaning, for the most part, is the same as that of **guarantee**. The two words, therefore, are interchangeable. Even so, **guaranty** has the added meaning of a pledge or formal assurance given as security that another's debt or obligation will be fulfilled. It means also that which is given or presented as security; the act of giving security.

Warranty is a noun only. It has a variety of legal meanings, but basically it means a written assurance, especially one given to a buyer of an article and involving a pledge to repair defects that become apparent in it within a specified period. It also means that which authorizes, sanctions, supports, or justifies doing something.

EXAMPLES:

"Does the **warranty** on this car mean that you **guarantee**, without cost to me, the replacement of parts?" Ben Byer asked the salesperson. "Yes, it does," Sammy Slick answered eagerly, rubbing his hands. "If I want to finance the car's purchase and can't provide collateral, will I have to have someone sign the note with me to **guaranty** the payments?" Byer asked. "That's right," Slick replied dejectedly, seeing the sale about to slip from his hands.

guaranty See **guarantee / guaranty / warranty.**

guerrilla See **gorilla / guerrilla.**

guess / suppose / surmise

One need not conjecture whether these verbs are synonyms or not. Despite popular opinion, they do not mean exactly the same thing. Each has its own shade of meaning that careful communicators who believe language should be handled like a honed tool use flawlessly and with precision and accuracy.

Guess means to arrive at or to form an opinion without having sufficient evidence to support the opinion fully; to think something is likely without calculating or measuring and without definite knowledge.

Suppose means to be inclined to think; to accept as true or probable; to believe, to assume, or to take for granted as true, in the absence of positive knowledge or of evidence to the contrary; to assume as true for the purpose of argument.

Surmise means to imagine, to infer, or to make a conjecture that may or may not be correct; to suspect on slight grounds or without proof that something in question is so.

EXAMPLES:

"I **suppose** because of last night's parties not all of you studied for this morning's exam," Professor Stickler said with a twinkle in his eye as he handed out the questions. "All of which leads me to **surmise**," he added with a self-appreciating smile, "that some of you will **guess** at the answers."

H

habitual / usual

These adjectives have a commonness to them in that both refer to a settled, constant, accustomed practice. Yet each has a distinctiveness in meaning that calls for its precise use.

Habitual means doing, practicing, or acting in some manner that has become regular, settled, and constant as the result of unconscious and compulsive behavior, as from habit. It suggests a practice settled or established by much repetition.

Usual means in accord with usage, custom, or habit; commonly met with or observed in experience; common place, everyday; found in ordinary practice or in the ordinary course of events. It stresses an absence of strangeness or unexpectedness and indicates what is to be expected by reason of previous experience, which shows it to occur more often than not.

EXAMPLES:

Teddy Tardy's **habitual** lateness for work led to the **usual**, and inevitable, consequence: his dismissal.

hail / hale

These words sometimes get confused and should not, for there is a healthy difference in their meanings.

Hail is a verb, a noun, and an adjective. As a verb, it means to greet or salute; welcome; to call out in order to stop, to attract attention, to ask aid, and the like. It means also to pour down pellets of frozen rain in a shower. As a noun, **hail** means pellets of frozen rain falling in a shower; something coming in great numbers; an exclamation of greeting or acclamation; a calling to attention. And, as an adjective, **hail** means sociable; heartily genial, as in **hail** fellow.

Hale is a verb and an adjective only. As a verb, it means to haul, pull, drag, draw, or compel to go by force. As an adjective, **hale** means strong and healthy; robust; vigorous; free from defect, disease, or infirmity.

EXAMPLES:

Despite the **hail** that came down in torrents, Officer Phineas Pinchem was able to **hail** a taxi. After that it was easy for him, thanks to his **hale** condition, to **hale** his prisoner to the police station, where jail, not a **hail**, awaited the somewhat drained, drenched, and dejected desperado.

hair / heir

There is room for air, depending on the spelling, but not for error, in using these look-alike nouns correctly.

Hair means a slender threadlike strand that grows from the skin of people and animals or on certain plants; a mass of these strands on the human head.

Heir means a person who inherits or who is entitled to inherit property; a person who inherits or who is entitled to inherit a rank, title, or office.

EXAMPLES:

"You cut one more **hair** from the head of the **heir**," King Tonsorial said to the royal barber as he sought to console his sobbing infant son, "and it is your head ere the sun sets!"

hairbrained / harebrained

Fuzzy thinking could account for the confusion some people encounter when they try to use these two words. No wonder. One is for real; the other is not.

Hairbrained has nothing to do with hair and brains. It is a nonword.

Harebrained is an adjective and derives its meaning from the antics of a hare, a swift rodentlike mammal that leaps about in various directions for no apparent reason. The word means flighty; foolish; giddy; reckless; not clearly reasoned; brainless.

EXAMPLES:

It is not possible for people, especially bald men, to have **hair-brained** schemes, but it is possible for them and others to have **harebrained** ones.

hale See **hail / hale**.

hang / hanged / hung

To execute the principle parts of this verb, one should keep capital punishment in mind. Otherwise, there is no restraint on their use.

Hang means to fasten to some elevated point without support from below; to place in position by means of pivots, hooks, nails, or other fastenings; to depend, swing, wave, or flutter from any support; to suspend by the neck until dead. **Hang** (present) and **hanged** (past), rather than **hung**, are used in referring to a legal sentence of death by hanging and its execution.

EXAMPLES:

The sheriff's deputies, who **hanged** the horse thief at night, are expected to **hang** around until they are sober, after which they could well end up with **hanged** or **hung** looks on their faces—and **hang**overs for sure.

hangar / hanger

A slip of the tongue or sloppy enunciation can lead to the misuse of these nouns, for the correct spelling and/or pronunciation of **ar** or **er** makes a real difference in the words' meaning and use. It could be said to be a case of knowing where to park one thing and to hang something else.

A **hangar** is a shed or a shelter; any enclosed building for parking, housing, storing, or repairing aircraft.

A hanger is a shoulder-shaped frame with a hook at the top, usually of wire, wood, or plastic, for draping or hanging an article of clothing when not in use; one who suspends or hangs something.

EXAMPLES:

The pilot searched the **hangar** for a **hanger** on which to hang his flight jacket and couldn't find one. So he barked, "The hang with it!" and kept it on.

hanged See **hang / hanged / hunged**.

hanger See **hangar / hanger**.

happen See **take place / happen /occur / transpire**.

hardly See **barely / hardly / scarcely**.

hardy / hearty

There is a strength in the meaning of these adjectives that should not be confused and that accounts for each word's individuality.

Hardy means capable of enduring fatigue, hardship, exposure, and so forth; sturdy; strong; robust; vigorous; unduly bold; resolute; brave.

Hearty means warm-hearted; affectionate; cordial; jovial; sincere; genuine; heartfelt; enthusiastic; zealous; exhuberent; unrestrained; strong; large; abundant; substantial; nourishing.

EXAMPLES:

With a **hearty** greeting to the cook, the **hardy** lumberjack sat down and ate a **hearty** breakfast before heading for the forest to cut some **hardy** timber.

harebrained See **hairbrained / harebrained**.

healthful / healthy

These adjectives call for putting first things first in that one can lead to the other. Even though some uneducated people interchange them needlessly, the words can be kept separate in thought and, therefore, be used accurately.

Healthful means producing good health; wholesome; salutary; beneficial.

Healthy means having or showing good health; functioning well; enjoying health and vigor of mind, body, or spirit; freedom from signs of illness, sickness, or disease.

EXAMPLES:

"You know," Miguel Medico said to Nick O'Tine, taking a cigarette from his patient's fingers, "**healthful** habits could help you to enjoy a **healthy** life."

healthy See **healthful / healthy**.

hearty See **hardy / hearty.**

heinous

This adjective often is mispronounced. With a bit of horse sense or food for thought, it can be made to sound correct: ′hā-nəs. It means hateful; odious; offensive; outrageous; very wicked; totally reprehensible; hatefully or shockingly evil; abominable.

EXAMPLE:

What could be more **heinous** (′hā-nəs) to the ear than when an ignorant person pronounces this descriptive word hē-′nas?

heir See **hair / heir**.

hesitate See **vacillate / hesitate**.

historic / historical

An understanding of the past and its events and their significance makes a distinguishable difference in how these two adjectives are used.

Historic means famous or well known in history; having considerable importance in the past.

Historical means of, pertaining, or relating to, or characteristic of history; dealing with or treating of history or past events.

EXAMPLES:

"This could become a **historic** moment," Artie Fact said, fumbling on his dresser for his wallet. "Hysterical maybe but **historical** never," his wife said with a gleam in her eyes as she took a bunch of ten-dollar bills from it.

historical See **historic / historical**.

home / house

Contrary to how indolent users of language or how sentimentalists may interchange these nouns when they write or speak them, or how real estate people do likewise when they are trying to make a sale, there is a difference between a **home** and a **house**. Accurate defining of each word so indicates.

A **home** is one's place of residence; an abode, dwelling, shelter, structure, or place where one's domestic affections are centered.

It also is an institution for the sick, infirm, poor, retired, and the like.

A **house** is a building that serves as living quarters for one or a few families; a shelter or refuge of a wild animal; a gambling casino. It also is a building in which a legislative or official deliberative body meets.

EXAMPLES:

It may have been the best little gambling **house** in Nevada, but it was never called a **home** of chance.

hopefully

There is little hope that this tiresome, overworked word will be restored to correct diction until its misusers give it a proper point of view. **Hopefully** is an adverb. It means in a hopeful manner. It does not mean "it is hoped," "let us hope," or "we hope." When used, it modifies a verb with an animate subject that is capable of feeling hope and that is doing the action.

EXAMPLES:

Let us hope, even be hopeful, that we **hopefully** can look forward to when **hopefully** is seldom or hardly ever or never used even by well-intentioned speakers and writers. Or is **hopefully** a hopeless case, thanks to illiteracy?

hopeless / futile

When something is not working out, these two adjectives might come to mind to describe the situation. A concept of nonaccomplishment underlies their meaning. Yet each adjective deals with nonsuccess in its own way. Their use, therefore, is not interchangeable. It is individual.

Hopeless means providing or giving no ground for hope; incapable of being accomplished, solved, or resolved; having no expectation of good or success.

Futile means incapable of producing results; ineffective; serving no useful purpose; useless.

EXAMPLES:

"Would you go to the dance with me?" Stuart Stumbler asked Nancy Nimble, shifting from one foot to the other. "No," she replied. "I guess my chances are **hopeless**, aren't they?" he asked. "Yes, they are," she said, shuddering at the thought of what his feet would do. "It is **futile** for you to ask again."

house See **home / house**.

however See **so / however / therefore**.

hung See **hang / hanged / hung**.

hurdle See **hurl / hurdle / hurtle**.

hurl / hurdle / hurtle

Like an elopement, one should not throw oneself or leap or rush too quickly into something without considering the implications of one's actions. The definitions of these words need to be noted carefully and their parts of speech understood if one is to make clear and precise use of them.

Hurl is both a verb and a noun. As a verb, it means to throw or fling with great force or vigor such objects as a stone or a javelin or a baseball. It also means to utter or speak with vehemence. As a noun, **hurl** means a forcible or violent throw or fling.

Hurdle also is a verb and a noun. As a verb, it means to leap over or to clear a barrier, such as a hurdle, fence, or wall. It also means to master a difficulty or problem; to overcome. As a noun, **hurdle** means a portable fence, usually wooden, over which people and animals must jump or leap in a race; barrier.

Hurtle is a verb and noun, too. As a verb, it means to rush violently; to move with great speed; to go noisily or resoundingly, as with violent or rapid motion; to strike together noisily; to resound noisily, as in a collision. As a noun, **hurtle** means clash; collision; shock; clatter.

EXAMPLES:

''You can **hurl** whatever insults about him you want to, Mother, but I'm going to marry Warren Worthless. I can **hurdle** anything you and Father put up against me,'' Dee Termined shouted in the car's phone as she felt the Jaguar **hurtle** its way to her rendezvous with her lover.

hurtle See **hurl / hurdle / hurtle**.

I

idle / indolent / lazy / slothful

When some people don't get things done, any one or all of these adjectives can provide the reason why.

Idle means doing no work; not employed; not active or in use. It also means avoiding work; worthless; shiftless; having no special purpose. The word is derogatory at times, but not always, for one may be relaxing or be without work involuntarily or through necessity.

Indolent is a derogatory word. It means having or showing an inclination to avoid exertion, activity, or movement, and suggests a love of ease and a settled dislike for activity or movement.

Lazy means disinclined to work; being inactive; having an aversion to work or effort; not energetic or vigorous; moving slowly; sluggish. It usually is a derogative word in that it suggests a disinclination to work or take trouble.

Slothful is the most derogative of the four adjectives. It means totally unwilling to work, to be active, to be energetic, to be employed; spiritually apathetic and inactive; sluggardly; torpid; slack. It suggests a reprehensible unwillingness to do such work as is demanded of a person, a tempermental inability to act promptly or speedily when action or speed is called for.

EXAMPLES:

Is it any wonder that Lee Thargic and his farm are run-down all the time even though he has four sons? The first is **idle** because his broken leg has failed to mend. The second is **indolent**, a couch potato who breathes, eats, and sleeps in front of the television set. The third is **lazy** and doesn't get up before noon and then piddles the afternoon away. And the fourth is **slothful** and does nothing by being sure to stay clear of work as if it were poison ivy.

illegal / illegitimate / illicit / unlawful

When people get into trouble or do wrong things, within or outside the law, one of more of these adjectives could be involved, for it is often a matter of degree, definition, or statute, depending upon the circumstances and the nature of the offense.

Illegal means not legal; against the law; not according to or authorized by law; contrary to existing statutes, regulations, and the like; unauthorized. It relates to matters forbidden by law.

Illegitimate also means not legal, not authorized by law. Its scope is wider than **illegal**, for it includes not only what is not authorized by law but also what is against propriety or reason, such as a child born of parents who are not married or an argument formulated from invalid premises.

Illicit means not allowed or permitted; unlicensed; unauthorized; contrary to moral standards; impermissible but not necessarily **illegal**.

Unlawful, a word that is falling into disuse, means not lawful; contrary or against the law; not sanctioned by or according to law; not morally right or conventional. **Illegal** often is used for **unlawful** when meaning contrary to law, while **illicit** is substituted when meaning contrary to moral standards.

EXAMPLES:

Rodney Rogue's **illegal** taking of bank funds and his having an **illegitimate** child born out of an **illicit** romance with a teller would suggest that he is more than your ordinary **unlawful** fellow when it comes to acquiring things.

illegitimate See **illegal / illegitimate / illicit / unlawful.**

illicit See **illegal / illegitimate / illicit / unlawful.**

illusion See **delusion / illusion / allusion.**

immigrate See **emigrate / immigrate.**

immunity / impunity

These nouns, despite popular confusion over them, do not mean the same thing and, therefore, should not be interchanged. Each has its own sense of freedom that should, and can, be exercised with caution and care.

Immunity means exemption from or insusceptibilty to disease; exemption from usual obligation, service, duty, or liability to taxation or jurisdiction; freedom from anything evil or harmful or disagreeable or threatening.

Impunity is a less extensive word. Its meaning is restricted to exemption or freedom from punishment, penalty, harm, or loss.

EXAMPLES:

"If you want **immunity** from the flu," Red Wyne, the bartender, said to the sniffling patron, "get a shot from your doctor, but if you want to drive home with **impunity** from arrest, put down that shot glass and drink this pot of black coffee!"

impact / influence

Even though both these words are nouns and verbs, they are not, contrary to popular misconception, interchangeable. Each word, regardless of its part of speech, is able to function within its own definition and thus avoid needless collision or confusion with the other.

Impact, as a noun, means an impinging or striking of one body against another; a forceful contact, collision, or onset; the force of an impression of one thing on another. As a verb, it means to fix firmly by or as if by packing or wedging; to press together; to have an impact on; to strike forcefully; to impinge or make contact forcefully.

Influence, as a noun, means the act or power of producing an effect without apparent exertion of force or direct exercise of command. As a verb, it means to affect or alter by indirect or tangible means; to sway.

EXAMPLES:

When dentists work on **impact**ed molars, the size of their bills can well **influence** whether patients visit them again. It might be called **impact** on the teeth and **influence** on the wallet or a double bite all in one treatment.

impassable / impassible / impassive

These look-alike adjectives, when confused, can be troublesome and thus can block communication. But when each word is defined correctly and its derivation is understood, a clear way for its proper use becomes evident.

Impassable comes from the Latin *pando*, stretch. It means incapable of being passed, traveled, traversed, crossed, or surmounted.

Impassible is derived from a very different Latin word, *patior*, feel. It means incapable of suffering or feeling pain, harm, or emotion, or of experiencing injury; incapable of feeling.

Impassive comes from the same root word as **impassible**. They have or had several meanings in common. Even so, **impassive** has the connotation of serenity: calm, without emotion, unmoved, apathetic; not feeling or showing emotion; expressionless.

EXAMPLES:

"The road is **impassable**," Big Mack said as he pulled his truck over on the shoulder and stopped, his knuckles white from gripping the wheel. He glared at his wife's **impassive** face and barked: "How can you be **impassible** at a time like this? Can't you see how much I'm suffering?"

impassible See **impassable / impassible / impassive.**

impassive See **impassable / impassible / impassive.**

impetus See **momentum / impetus.**

imply / infer

These verbs often are confused in their use and meaning when all that is required is an understanding of their give-and-take relationship.

Imply is the **giving out** or stating of ideas, facts, or opinions. It means to hint, suggest, or insinuate a meaning not expressed; to involve or intimate as a necessary circumstance.

Infer is the **taking in** or deducing of ideas, facts, or opinions. It means to derive as a conclusion from facts or premises; to surmise; to speculate; to guess; to deduce; to conclude.

EXAMPLES:

"Do you mean to **imply** that I am dishonest?" the shopkeeper asked, his hand resting in the cash register. "You can **infer** whatever you like," the customer replied, slamming the drawer shut.

impunity See **immunity / impunity.**

in / into / in to

The way to keep these four words separate in thought and in usage is to know their parts of speech and their functions as well as their meaning.

In is a preposition. Used as a function word, it indicates inclusion within space, location, position, place, time, or limits.

Into is a preposition. It is used as a function word to indicate motion, entry, introduction, insertion, superposition, inclusion, or immersion in.

In to are two words and are two different parts of speech: an adverb and a preposition. They should not be confused with **into** even though the words often are used to express motion following a verb.

EXAMPLES:

For Putoff to ask for a pay raise, he has to meet with his boss **in** her office. To get there, Putoff can run, hop, leap, jump, walk, creep, or crawl **into** it. But if he really wants a raise, he'll start getting his work **in to** her on time.

include See **compose / comprise / consist / include.**

incredible / incredulous

Misuse of these adjectives arises when one assumes incorrectly that they are synonyms. Each has a meaning that is uniquely its own. Believe it or not!

Incredible means too extraordinary and improbable to be believed; hard to believe; so extraordinary as to seem impossible; unbelievable.

Incredulous means unwilling to accept or admit what is offered as true; disinclined or indisposed to believe; refusing belief; skeptical.

EXAMPLES:

"I find your excuse for keeping me waiting **incredible**," Abby Normal said to Al Legorical. "Does it mean you are **incredulous**?" he asked. "Yes," she replied, "but you still are late!"

incredulous See **incredible / incredulous.**

indict / indite

This pair of transitive verbs are pronounced alike, in-'dīt. Otherwise, they have nothing in common. They should not be confused, therefore, and should be used with care, especially when they are committed to writing.

Indict, primarily a legal term, means to charge with an offense or crime; to accuse of wrongdoing; to charge with crime by the finding or presentment of a jury, such as a grand jury.

Indite, a dated word, means to put down in writing; to put into words; to compose, make up, or write, such as a speech, a poem, and the like.

EXAMPLES:

"Have the grand jurors voted to **indict** the trio?" Judge Dee Murrer asked. "Yes, we have, your honor," Mal Feasance, the foreman, replied. "Then **indite** 'true bill' on the prepared form," she said, "and hand it to the clerk."

indispensible See **essential / indispensible / vital.**

indite See **indict / indite.**

indolent See **idle / indolent / lazy / slothful.**

infantile See **juvenile / puerile / infantile.**

infer See **imply / infer**.

influence See **impact / influence.**

ingenious / ingenuous

When words look alike they have a way of being confused with each other and with being used as if they were synonyms. Yet one need not be a genius to recognize that the difference in the spelling—and, consequently, in the meaning—of these adjectives is a single letter. It is the vowel **i** or **u** right after the consonant **n**, the difference between being clever and candid.

Ingenious means skilled in inventing and thinking out new ideas; marked by particular aptitude at discovering, inventing, or contriving; marked by originality, resourcefulness, and cleverness in conception and execution; artful; clever; resourceful.

Ingenuous means showing innocent or childlike simplicity and candidness; lacking craft or subtley; free from reserve, restraint, or dissimulation; artless; frank; candid; innocent; high minded; sincere.

EXAMPLES:

If it is said an **ingenious** boy chases an **ingenuous** girl until she catches him, could it be a case that he is smart and she is innocent? Or could it be the other way around?

ingenuous See **ingenious / ingenuous.**

inherent / innate / intrinsic

Some things are the way they are because something within them makes them so. Such it is with these adjectives. Their meanings may be similar, but they are not identical words. Each has a definition of its very own.

Inherent means existing in something or someone as a permanent element, quality, characteristic, or attribute; existing in or belonging by nature or by settled habit so as to be inseparable.

Innate means possessed from birth; inborn; native; natural; originating in or arising from the constitution of the mind or intellect rather than learned from experience.

Intrinsic means having internal value; of or pertaining to the essential constitution or nature of something or someone; belonging to something by its very nature; from within.

EXAMPLES:

Inherent in Ava Rice, the pawnbroker, and her **innate** greed is her resolve to pay Destie Toot less for his watch than its **instrinsic** value.

innate See **inherent / innate / intrinsic**.

insipid See **vapid / insipid.**

insure / ensure / assure

One can set one's mind at ease over these similar-looking verbs by making certain of their individual meaning and thus resist using them as synonyms.

Insure means to provide or obtain insurance on or for; to secure indemnity to or on, in the event of loss, accident, damage, or death; to make certain by taking necessary measures and precautions.

Ensure means to guarantee; to make certain, safe, or sure; to bring about.

Assure means to give confidence to; to state with confidence; to make certain the coming or attainment to; to declare earnestly to; to affirm; to convince; to inform or tell positively.

EXAMPLES:

"I know you can **insure** this package's contents, said Saul Skeptical to the postal clerk, "but can you **ensure** that it will get there and **assure** me so?" Parsell Post didn't respond. Instead, he tossed the package on top of the huge pile of Christmas mail, muttering to himself, "It beats me the way some people expect me to be Santa Claus!"

intellectual See **intelligent / intellectual / intelligible.**

intelligible See **intelligent / intellectual / intelligible.**

intelligent / intellectual / intelligible

"The mind," as the saying goes, "is a terrible thing to waste." This is true for these adjectives, each of which has to do with thinking. Yet nothing need be wasted in their use so long as their individual meanings are clear in the communicator's mind.

Intelligent means mentally keen; having great mental ability; quick to comprehend or understand; ability to adapt to new situations and to solve problems; showing sound thought and good judgment.

Intellectual means possessing or showing the power or faculty of the mind by which one knows and understands as distinguished from what one feels or what one wills; keen mental capacity for thinking and acquiring knowledge, especially of a high order; given to study, reflection, and speculation.

Intelligible has a meaning apart from **intelligent** and **intellectual**. It means capable of being understood or comprehended; that which is clear and can be understood or apprehended readily by the intellect or the mind alone.

EXAMPLES:

''You may think you're pretty **intelligent**, Brunhilda Brain, with all those **intellectual** pursuits of yours, but what comes out of your mouth isn't **intelligible** to me,'' Dossie Dullard said as she resumed reading the tabloid she had picked up at the supermarket checkout.

into See **in / into / in to.**

intractable / intransigent / recalcitrant

Stubbornness can be manifested in various ways as these three adjectives unopposedly indicate. The key to their proper use is to keep an open mind about them and to define them correctly.

Intractable means stubborn, obstinate, hardheaded, headstrong, unbending, inflexible; hard to shape or to work with; not easily managed, governed, or directed; hard or difficult to deal with or control, or to alleviate or cure.

Intransigent means uncompromising; refusing to agree, to compromise or to make a settlement, or to abandon or moderate an extreme position in any way; unyielding; adamant; inflexible; stubborn.

Recalcitrant, which is derived from the Latin *recalcitro*, kick backwards, means refusing to submit to authority, domination, guidance, or control; stubbornly or obstinately defiant of authority or restraint; not obedient or compliant; not responsive to treatment.

EXAMPLES:

Poor ole frustrated Cal Cutter really knows what stubbornness is. He has an **intractable** son who refuses to get up and go to school in the morning. He has an **intransigent** wife who refuses to agree that their wedding vows included the word "obey." And he has a **recalcitrant** mule that kicks back at him whenever he prods it to get going.

intransigent See **intractable / intransigent / recalcitrant.**

intrinsic See **inherent / innate / intrinsic.**

invoke See **evoke / invoke.**

irregardless See **regardless / irregardless.**

it / it's / its

Who would think that a tiny word, such as this two-letter singular pronoun, would be subject to abuse, misuse, and disuse. But **it** is. Confusion arises over how to form the possessive of **it**, how to form the contraction of **it** with the verb **to be**, and how to make **it** agree in number with other parts of speech. **It's** not all that difficult to use **it** correctly once one understands that this pronoun has these three forms of expression, each of which is peculiarly **its** own.

It means that one. The word is always singular and refers to something expressed by a singular noun: the name of a person, a place, or a thing.

It's is the combining of two words, **it** and **is**, two different parts of speech, a pronoun and a verb. An apostrophe is used to indicate their contraction into one word.

Its, without an apostrophe, is the possessive of **it**.

EXAMPLES:

It's about time that **its** users treat **it** with respect.

it's See **it / it's / its.**

its See **it / it's / its.**

J

jail / prison

It is largely a matter of time and a sentence or two to understand why and how these two nouns are not interchangeable in their use.

Jail is a place used for confining people serving misdemeanors or awaiting trial or sentencing on either felony or misdeameanor charges. It also is used for confining people convicted of civil matters related to contempt of court and the like, whose stay in jail, in any event, is usually no more than a year.

Prison is a place used for confining people serving felony sentences of one year or longer. Confinement can be in a maximum security facility, such as a penitentiary, or in a medium security facility, such as a correctional institution or reformatory.

EXAMPLES:

Nerdo must like having time on his hands or maybe he likes turkey and all the trimmings. Anyway, he beat a deputy sheriff on the head and broke out of county **jail**, where he was serving twenty days for disturbing the peace. Now Nerdo resides in state **prison**, where the warden says he has planned full-course Christmas dinners for his guest to enjoy in the next three years.

jangle See **jingle / jangle**.

jaunt / junket

These nouns, which primarily have to do with going places and having a good time, should not be confused. Although both may relate to pleasure, the distinction rests with who is paying for it.

Jaunt means a short or brief trip or journey, especially for pleasure.

Junket, apart from being a sweet, custardlike food of flavored milk curded with rennet, means a pleasure excursion, such as a picnic or an outing. It also means a trip taken by an official at public expense.

EXAMPLES:

When Phil A. Buster goes on a trip overseas, his detractors say he is on a **jaunt**. The news media describe it as a **junket**. And his staff swears he is on a fact-finding mission for a Senate committee.

jealousy See **envy / jealousy**.

jetsam / jettison

Sometimes what these words are about is left to be seen, for they have to do with something that is done deliberately and with the doing of it.

Jetsam is a noun only. It means the goods, which either sink or are washed ashore, that are cast overboard deliberately to lighten or stabilize a vessel in distress. It has taken on the meaning of discarded odds and ends.

Jettison is both a verb and a noun. As a verb, it means to cast goods overboard in order to lighten a vessel or an aircraft. As a noun, it means the act of doing the foregoing.

EXAMPLES:

The **jetsam** was sinking steadily into the sea. If the balloon were to rise only a little, it could reach shore and not end up in the water. Pilot Horace Helium looked about the gondola for something more to **jettison.** Shrugging his shoulders, he turned to his passenger and said, "Sorry, old boy, but I guess it is your turn to go over the side and make matters lighter. Goodbye!"

jettison See **jetsam / jettison**.

jibe See **gibe / jibe**.

jingle / jangle

These words, even though they look almost alike, have opposite meanings. In fact, they are discordant when you consider the effect they have on the ears.

Jingle, as a verb, means to make a light clinking, ringing, or tinkling sound, such as keys, coins, and other metals striking together; to rhyme or sound in a catchy manner. As a noun, it means the clinking, ringing, or tinkling sound of light metal being struck together; the repetition of sounds in music and of rhymes in verse, so as to catch the ear. A **jingle** also is a two-wheeled, horse-drawn roofed carriage found in Ireland and Australia.

Jangle, as a verb, means to cause or make a harsh, discordant sound such as when metal pieces hit, strike, or come together; to ring with a discordant sound; to annoy; to irritate; to grate (as on the nerves). As a noun, it means a harsh or discordant sound; an argument, dispute, or noisy quarrel; idle talk.

EXAMPLES :

When Sam Squareshooter calls on his girl, his spurs **jingle**, **jangle**, **jingle**, much to her father's irritation, who says he doesn't care to hear another **jingle** and can do without another **jangle** from that "blankety-blank" cowboy.

journey / voyage / trip

These nouns have one thing in common: They have to do with traveling. Yet their meanings are dissimilar when it comes to where the traveling is being done and to its duration and distance.

A **journey** is travel or passage from one place to another that usually takes a long time and covers many miles.

A **voyage** is travel on water, in the air, or in space that is of long duration and considerable distance.

A **trip** is travel either for business or for pleasure on land or water or in the air that is of short duration and limited distance. It also is an intense visionary experience undergone by anyone who has taken a psychedelic drug.

EXAMPLES:

A **journey** to the moon is a long, long **voyage**, but a **trip** to a supermarket and a slow-moving checkout lane can seem like light years longer.

judge / jurist

Contrary to popular misuse, especially by the news media, these nouns, which are titles of people who deal with the law and with legal knowledge, are not interchangeable. A **judge** should be and usually is a **jurist**, whereas a **jurist** does not have to be and not always is a **judge**.

A **judge** is a public officer who is authorized by election or by appointment to hear and decide cases and causes in a court of law; also a magistrate who is charged with the administering of justice.

A **jurist** is a person versed or skilled in the knowledge and practice of law, such as a judge, a legal scholar, or a law professor.

EXAMPLES:

"Here comes the **judge**," the baliff said. "Now where is that **jurist** who says he knows a thing a two about the law? He's supposed—ugh—to testify next."

judicial / judicious

Communicators would do well to take these adjectives under advisement before using them. They are not synonyms. One has to do with judgment in courts of justice and the administration of justice. The other has to do with the kind of judgment made elsewhere. Even so, a **judicial** decision can be a **judicious** one depending on the intellect of the person making the decision.

Judicial means of or relating to a judgment, the function of judging, the administration of justice, or the judiciary; of a judge or judgment; inclined to make or give judgments; giving or making judgments as in a dispute or contest; critical; discriminating.

Judicious means having, using, or showing sound judgment or good sense; rational; sober; enlightened; wise; prudent; reasonable.

EXAMPLES:

A person who reads a **judicial** frown accurately will be **judicious** in what he or she has to say in or out of court.

judicious See **judicial / judicious**.

junction / juncture

Although these nouns are similar in meaning in the sense that they denote the act of joining or the condition of being joined, there comes a point in time when it is evident that the words are not interchangeable.

Junction is used in the sense of crossroads, a place where two or more things meet or converge; an intersection of highways and roads; a place where railroad lines meet, cross, and diverge. It also means a place where two or more things are joined together, such as a seam or a joint. And it means something that joins other things together.

Juncture is used in the sense of a point of time, especially one made critical or important by a concurrence of circumstances; a very serious state of affairs; crisis. It also means the line or point at which two bodies are joined; the act of joining; the state of being joined.

EXAMPLES:

When Glenn Miller and his orchestra in 1940 recorded "Tuxedo **Junction**," a tune named for a railroad crossing point in Alabama, the event marked the **juncture** in the tune and the band's rise to immense popularity during the Big Band Era and ever since.

juncture See **junction / juncture**.

junket See **jaunt / junket**.

jurist See **judge / jurist**.

jury See **collective nouns**.

just / only

For **just** $59.99 one can have this, or for **only** $99.99 one can have that. What would advertising copy and radio and television commercials be like if they never contained these adverbs? Would their disappearance be a blessing or a loss to consumers? It is difficult to say what the effect would be. What is not difficult to say about **just** and **only**, apart from how they are used in advertising, is that they should be handled with care, especially by placing each adverb next or close to the word or words it modifies and thus assuring that the meaning of its modification is clear.

Just appears to be contradictory. It means very recently, as in "Prompto **just** arrived." It means by a very small margin, as in "Victor **just** won the match." And it means exactly, precisely, none other, as in "Fancier **just** wanted the gold watch."

Only also appears to be contradictory. It means without others or anything; exclusively; solely; alone, as in "**Only** Prompto arrived." It means at the very least, as in "Victor won the match by one game **only**." It means no more than or merely, as in "Fancier wanted **only** the gold watch."

EXAMPLES:

Only time will tell **just** how these adverbs will be used in the future. So check a large dictionary for their shades of meaning and select **only** that one which means **just** what you really want to speak or write and then place it **just** before or after the word it modifies and there **only**.

juvenile / puerile / infantile

Caution and care should be exercised with these adjectives. They describe young people in various ways, and, depending on how the words are used, they can be spoken or written in either a proper or a derogatory manner.

Juvenile means young, youthful, not fully developed, not an adult. It takes on a pejorative meaning in the term **juvenile** delinquent, words used for describing a young person considered unworthy of approval from adults or who is in trouble either with the law or with authorities, or with both.

Puerile is an adjective of another taint. It means of or pertaining to a child; boyish (Latin *puerilis*, boy); belonging to childhood. Through usage, however, it has acquired the derogatory connotations of childish, childishly foolish, silly, immature, trivial.

Infantile means of or pertaining to infants, babies, or infancy. **Infantile** paralysis, the term that identifies a disease largely afflicting children before Jonas Salk found a vaccine for it, has a positive connotation. Like the other adjectives, **infantile** has taken on such pejorative meanings as extremely childish, very immature, babyish, and the like.

EXAMPLES:

"Let's take a break," Adelaide Aside, director of the summer theater, called to the cast rehearsing a new play. She turned to Silas Stagestruck and said: "You're supposed to be the **juvenile** lead, not a two-year-old baby. Thus far your performance has been **puerile**. In fact it's been **infantile**. You'd better grow up in the next ten minutes or find yourself a cradle. You show any more childishness and you can be sure you've had your final curtain with me!"

K

karat See **caret / carat / carrot / karat**.

ketchup See **catsup / catchup / ketchup**.

kilt / kith / kin

These look-alike nouns are not cousins, not even distant ones, even though they have to do with what one wears, with whom one associates, and from whom one is descended.

Kilt is any short, pleated skirt, especially a tartan wrap-around, as that worn by men in the Scottish Highlands. A man wears a kilt. Two or more men wear kilts. A man wears a pair of pants. Other men wear pairs of pants, not to mention what women wear, which is material cut from another cloth.

Kith means acquaintances, friends, neighbors, or the like; persons living in the same general locality and forming a more or less cohesive group; a group of people living in the same area and forming a culture with common language, customs, and economy.

Kin means one's relatives collectively; a group of people descended from a common ancestor or constituting a family, clan, tribe, or race; kinsfolk.

EXAMPLES:

MacAdam Rhodes made sure his **kilt** was tightly wrapped about him before he opened the door and faced the **kith** gathered at his front steps. "I'm sorry I'm leaving you, my friends, but not your arctic temperatures," he told them through chattering teeth. "I'm taking the highway to my homeland and to my **kin** in the south where a man can bare his knees anytime he pleases and not have frigid air find its way up the rest of him!"

kin See **kilt / kith / kin**.

kind of / sort of

This pair of words, when used as adverbial phrases, can be rather or somewhat troublesome, for each suggests vagueness of thought and betrays a writer or speaker's inadequacy of expression. Rather and somewhat, as the previous sentence indicates, are appropriate substitutions, better still, replacements, for these phrases that **kind of** or **sort of**, that somewhat, have become colloquial English. Careful communicators who respect precise written and spoken expression are rather likely to shun substandard usage of these phrases, confining their use to mean "a species or subcategory of" and making sure that the phrases agree more than somewhat in number with the nouns they modify.

EXAMPLES:

"What **kind of** apple is this one?" Wilma Winesap asked, holding up a ripe, red one. "What **sort of** question is that to ask while I'm still sorting them?" Clarence Courtland answered rudely with a question. "Wait until I've sorted all of them and then I'll tell you what **kinds of** and **sorts of** apples I have."

kingly / queenly / regal / royal

Kings and queens reign and rule. They come and they go. There are words to describe their demeanor, the manner of their ways, and what pertains to their person. These adjectives do so but not in an interchangeable manner.

Kingly means that which belongs to or is fitting or worthy of or suitable for or like a king.

Queenly means that which belongs to or is fitting or worthy of or suitable for or like a queen.

Regal has to do with the office of kingship or queenship and to the outward manifestations of grandeur and majesty, stateliness, and splendidness.

Royal is applied especially to what pertains to or is associated with the person of a monarch, such as family, residence, household, robes, crown, and so on.

EXAMPLES:

The House of Richtenrovenwald has had many **kingly** and **queenly** monarchs who conducted their duties in a **regal** manner and had a **royal** time doing so.

kith See **kilt / kin / kith**.

kneel / knell

These look-alike words get confused, perhaps even bent in their meaning and use. They should not, for one has to do with the knees, the other with a bell.

Kneel, as a verb, means to fall or rest on the knees or a knee. As a noun, it means the position of kneeling or being on one's knees.

Knell, as a verb, means to sound, as a bell, especially a funeral bell; to give forth a mournful, ominous, or warning sound; to proclaim or summon by, or as by, a bell. As a noun, it means the sound made by a bell rung slowly for a death or a funeral; any sound made to announce the death, end, extinction, failure, and the like of something; any mournful sound.

EXAMPLES:

Nell knew the **knell** of the new bell in the chapel meant she should go down on her knees and **kneel** in prayer, maintaining her **kneel** until she heard the new bell in the chapel **knell** its final toll.

knell See **kneel / knell**.

knight / night

Although these nouns are pronounced alike, they do not mean the same thing. They should not be confused any more than should chivalry and darkness, but somehow they are, thanks to those people who have difficulty with spelling.

A **knight** is a mounted soldier serving a feudal superior; a man honored by a sovereign for merit, such as in Great Britain, who is addressed as "sir"; a man devoted to the service of a lady as her attendant or champion; a piece in the game of chess in the form of a horse's head.

Night is the period of time between sunset and sunrise; the time from dusk to dawn when there is no sunlight; the end of daylight; the dark or darkness.

EXAMPLES:

It is a good **knight** who knows when to say good **night** to a lady.

knot / not

Meanings can get tangled when these sound-alike words are misspelled. It need not be so. A positive approach to getting their letters right and to understanding their parts of speech can straighten things out and lead to their correct use.

Knot is a verb and a noun. As a verb, it means to tie in or with a **knot**; to unite or join closely or intricately; to hold together; to entangle. As a noun, **knot** has a variety of meanings: a complication of threads, cords, or ropes, formed by tying or entangling; a method of fastening a rope to another object or to another rope; a bond of union; a small group (of people or things); a hard lump, especially of wood; a division on a log line for measuring the speed of a ship; a unit of speed, one nautical mile per hour, about 1.5 statute miles per hour; a distance of one nautical mile.

Not is an adverb. It means in no way; in no degree. It is used to express negation, denial, refusal, or prohibition.

EXAMPLES:

"**Not** another **knot**!" cried Andy Angler, spotting a big one in his fishing line. "I was going to catch a record number of bass and hang them on a string, and **knot** the line, so the judges could check them out. But **not** now, **not** with the **knot** I did **not** want!" When Andy got home and told his wife, she quietly said, "Oh, my dear, it seems to have been all for naught or **knot**, doesn't it?"

knowable / know-how / knowledgeable

A little knowledge can go a long way, according to the saying, and these three words with their various meanings seem to support such a statement. Knowing how to use each word correctly is the test, of course, of one's real ability as a communicator.

Knowable is an adjective. It has one meaning: capable of being known.

Know-how is an Americanized word, a noun, that dictionaries differ as to whether it is a standard word or an informal one. Regardless of its status, the word is popularly used. It means possessing practical knowledge needed for doing something smoothly, efficiently, or correctly; having the faculty or skill for a particular activity.

Knowledgeable is an adjective. It means having or showing knowledge, insight, understanding, or intelligence; well-informed.

EXAMPLES:

Iris Intellectus, a **knowledgeable** woman, dated a **knowable** man named Will Wellmet. They shared **know-how** on many things. But when she realized he was a know-it-all, she vowed she wouldn't go out with him again, no how.

know-how See **knowable / know-how / knowledgeable**.

knowledgeable See **knowable / know-how / knowledgeable**.

L

lack / need / want

These words, whether used as nouns or adverbs, have one thing in common. They convey the sense that something is missing or is absent. Yet they are not interchangeable, for they, with their own individual meanings, indicate precisely how something is missed.

Lack, as a noun, means, the fact or state of being deficient; not having or possessing; the absence of something needed, desirable, or customary; something missed; shortage. As a verb, **lack** means to be destitute; to be without or deficient in; not to have possession of.

Need, as a noun, has numerous meanings: a requirement; a lack of something wanted or deemed necessary; necessity, duty, or obligation; urgent want of something requisite; necessity arising from the circumstances arising from a case; a situation or time of difficulty; exigency; destitution; extreme poverty. As a verb, it means to require; to be under a necessity; to be in want. **Need** conveys a connotation that makes it strong in emotional appeal.

Want, as a noun, means deficiency; grave and extreme poverty that denies one of the necessities of life; something desired, demanded, or required; the state of being without something desired or needed. As a verb, **want** means to be without or deficient in; to fall short by; to crave; to feel a desire for. It also has a connotation of lack of necessary things and an awareness of it.

EXAMPLES:

"Life's unfair," Benedict Buckless said, looking into his flattened, paper-thin wallet. "I **lack** transportation, I **need** a car, and I **want** a Cadillac. O.K., so I'll have to forget about my **need** and my **want**. But what about my **lack**? Why, I don't even have a dollar for making a down payment on a used bicycle!"

larceny See **burglary / larceny / robbery / thievery**.

last / latest

Careful communicators know, despite the interchanging less-educated and knowledgeable people give these adjectives, the superlative of **late**, that there is a distinction of finality and most recentness between the pair. That is why careful communicators allow each word its own time and place in the scheme of things.

Last means following all the rest; occurring or coming after all others, as in time, order, or place; being at the end; hindmost; belonging to the final stage; being the only remaining; in conclusion; finality.

Latest means the most recent in time of a series that may or may not be continued; happening just previous to the present time; current; that which follows all others in time only.

EXAMPLES:

The **last** thing Dora Drowsie had on her mind as she drifted off to sleep was the memory of her **last** date with her **latest** boyfriend. She hoped that **last** really meant **latest**, but of both she wasn't certain. So she headed straight for dreamland to find out.

later / latter

These words, which look alike, often are confused in their spelling. One has to do with time, the other with the second of two people or things. It could be a matter of putting first things first and the second of two things last.

Later, the comparative of the adjective **late**, is both an adjective and an adverb. It has the limited meaning of after in time.

Latter also is the comparative of the adjective **late**. It is an adjective, never an adverb, and means of or being related or closer or nearer to the end; being the second mentioned of two, as distinguished from former.

EXAMPLES:

''It is **later** than you think,'' Moe Beal said to Rich Mond. ''Don't ask why. I'll tell you **later**. Meanwhile, let me look at the study you made of the city's reservoir.'' ''Which one do you want to see: the first or the second?'' Mond asked. ''The **latter**, dummy,'' Beal replied. ''The first one was so full of holes it wouldn't, hah, hah, hold water!''

latest See **last / latest**.

Latin plurals See **data and other Latin plurals**.

latter See **later / latter**.

laudable / laudatory

Something of praise can be said about these two adjectives as long as a distinction is made between what is worthy and what is giving about them. To do so, one needs to look at their roots and their suffixes. Both words stem from *laud*, the Latin word for praise. The similarity ends there, for the adjectives go their separate ways. **Laudable** comes from the Latin noun *laudabilis*, praiseworthy, while **laudatory** is derived from the Latin noun *laudatorius*, praise-giving. Thus the suffixes **able** and **atory**, when added to **laud**, account for the individuality of each word.

Laudable means worthy or deserving of praise; praiseworthy; commendable.

Laudatory means of, relating to, containing, giving, or expressing praise.

EXAMPLES:

Willie Wayward behaved in a **laudable** manner once, and his mother nearly fainted in disbelief before offering a **laudatory** word for what he had done.

laudatory See **laudable / laudatory**.

lavish / prodigal / profuse

One should not be hesitant about being extravagant with these words, for all three have to do with unstinted extravagance. To use them accurately, one should be aware of the degrees of difference in their meanings even though, through popular usage, each word is being interchanged now with the others.

Lavish is both a verb and an adjective. As a verb, it means to squander; to expend, give, or bestow profusely, generously, or liberally, and to do so in great amounts, quantities, or abundance unstintingly and without limit. As an adjective, it means expending, using, giving, bestowing, or producing in great amount, quantities, or profusion.; unlimited; generous; extravagant.

Prodigal is a noun and an adjective. As a noun, it means a person who spends, or has spent, his or her money or substance wastefully, foolishly, or with wasteful extravagance; one who spends recklessly; a spendthrift; a wasteful person; a wastrel. As an adjective, **prodigal** means wastefully or recklessly extravagant; giving or yielding profusely; lavishly, exceedingly, or foolishly abundant, profuse, or generous.

Profuse is an adjective. It is the least in intensity of these three words. It means spending, giving, or given freely or generously in large amount, often to excess; pouring forth liberally; exhibiting or showing great abundance; plentiful; copious; extravagant.

EXAMPLES:

"How much longer do you think I can **lavish** my riches on you?" a father asked his **prodigal** son. "**Lavish** amounts do not seem to impress you." "I suppose what you want from me," the **prodigal** replied, "is a promise that I will stop my wasteful ways." "Yes," his father said. "If you were to cease your **prodigal** ways, you would have my **profuse** thanks. And they may be all that is left when you consider the rate at which my fortune is shrinking!"

lawful / legal

To the extent that these two words pertain to the law, they are synonyms. Even so, each adjective has a distinctive meaning that its users will note and will apply in seeking to make their expression legitimate.

Lawful means allowed, appointed, authorized, established, constituted, permitted, recognized, or sanctioned by law; not contrary to law; legally qualified; legitimate; acting or living by law.

Legal means of, according or pertaining to, or connected with or defined by the law, especially as written and administered by the courts; recognized by law rather than by equity; binding; statutory; constitutional; of, pertaining, or relating to or characteristic of the profession of law or its practitioners.

EXAMPLES:

When it comes to anticlimaxes, few can top a **lawful** marriage that ends in a **legal** divorce almost before the ink has dried on the marriage license.

lay / lie

Sometimes even the best of speakers and writers confuse these two verbs. No one need do so, for there is a decided distinction between them that once it is understood leads to their proper, precise, and perfect use. The key is to recognize transitive verbs, those that convey action and take objects, and intransitive ones, those that do not convey action and do not take objects. When in doubt about whether a verb is transitive or intransitive, consult a standard dictionary for such indication.

Lay is a transitive verb. It takes an object to which it conveys influence or action. **Lay** has several definitions. Essentially it means to put or set down; to put or place in a horizontal position or position of rest. Its principal parts are **lay**, **laid**, **laid**, **laying.** As a transitive verb, it conveys action from its subject to an object. The way to test for the uses of **lay** is to see whether or not the noun following it is essential to the meaning of the sentence.

Lie, an intransitive verb, does not take an object. Why not? Because it does not convey any action. It means to be or stay at rest in a horizontal position; to be prostrate; to assume a horizontal position. Its principal parts are **lie**, **lay**, **lain**, **lying**. As an intransitive verb, it conveys no action to an object. **Lie** also means to speak falsely or utter untruth knowingly, as with intent to deceive; to state what is false or to convey a false impression. It, like the other form of **lie,** is an intransitive verb and does not take an object. Its principal parts are, however, **lie**, **lied**, **lying**.

EXAMPLES:

"**Lay** the book on the table and let it **lie** there," Lydia Librarius said. "And don't **lie** to me that you don't have it. It's about to fall out of your backpack!"

lazy See **idle / indolent / lazy / slothful**.

leave / let

To substitute "**Leave** him do it" for "**Let** him do it" smacks of illiteracy. Its use should be avoided as if it were a hound dog that has met up with a skunk. A close look at the meanings of these two verbs indicates why they are not interchangeable as some ignorant people would like to make them.

Leave means to go away from; to depart from; withdraw; to quit; to forsake. It does not mean to permit or allow. As a noun, however, it means absence from work or military duty; permission to do something.

Let means to permit, allow, award; to offer or grant for rent, lease, or hire.

EXAMPLES:

Nick Nimrod handles his dogs without a scratch. He knows it is smart to **leave** them alone when they are eating, to **let** them sleep after they have been on a hunt, and to keep plenty of flea powder around.

lectern / podium / pulpit / rostrum

Taking a proper stand with the proper preposition that goes with each of these nouns places them in their right place and positions them apart from one another.

A **lectern** is a desk or stand with a slanted top that is placed on a table or some other flat surface and **behind** which a speaker stands.

A **podium** is a small platform **on** which a conductor of an orchestra or a public leader stands.

A **pulpit** is a platform or raised structure **in** which a member of the clergy delivers a sermon or conducts a service.

A **rostrum** is a platform or stage, or the like, for public speaking **on** which, like a **podium**, a speaker or performer stands.

EXAMPLES:

The statewide celebrations, linked by closed-circuit television, were about to begin. Burton Bellows, the keynote speaker, was **behind** the **lectern** going over his notes; Louis Ledbetter was **on** the **podium**, baton in hand; and numerous dignitaries were grouped **on** the **rostrum**, when Pastor Pompous Preachem, standing **in** the **pulpit**, said, "Ladies and gentlemen, let all of us rise to the occasion—and pray!"

legal See **lawful / legal.**

lend / loan

There is an ocean of difference between how the English and Americans use these words. The British restrict them, using **lend** as a verb only and **loan** as a noun only. They frown on the use of **loan** as a verb. They consider such a departure to be an Americanism. Even so, **loan** is widespread in its use by their cousins across the Atlantic as a noun and as a verb. **Lend** functions as a verb only in American-English, playing a lesser role to **loan**, which no longer is confined as a verb for use in financial transactions only.

Lend means to allow, give, or grant the temporary use of something, such as money, on the condition that it or its equivalent will be returned; to furnish or impart; to give out in general; to give the assistance or support of; to adapt or apply oneself or itself. Its principal parts are **lend, lent, lent.**

Loan, as a noun, means the act of lending; something lent usually for the borrower's temporary use; money lent at interest; the temporary duty or service of a person transferred to another job or assignment. As a verb, **loan** means to make a loan of; to lend; to lend money at interest.

EXAMPLES:

Sally Studious likes to **lend** a hand to a classmate with an occasional **loan** of a book. What she objects to is when that person tries to **loan** her book to someone else and charge interest for it.

less See **fewer / less.**

let See **leave / let.**

liable / likely / apt

These adjectives have become so interchangeable in speech that they have almost lost their original meanings. Even so, when each word is defined separately, an able user of language will note its distinctiveness and use it when and where it is appropriate to do so.

Liable means obligated according to law or equity; responsible;

answerable; being in a position to occur; exposed, open, or subject to anything possible, especially something undesirable, disadvantageous, or unpleasant.

Likely means in all likelihood; of a nature or circumstance as to make something probable; having a high probability of occurring or being true; to be expected; apparently destined.

Apt means unusually fitted or qualified; ordinarily disposed; having a tendency; inclined; unusually intelligent; able to learn quickly and easily; to the point; pertinent.

EXAMPLES:

Some teenagers are **apt** to exceed their parents' curfew. When they do, they are **liable** to be grounded. What is more, they are **likely** to spend many nights at home counting the moments that might have been.

libel / slander

These words, which are worth noting carefully if one wishes to stay on the good side of the law and not be liable for action by the authorities, have to do with defamation, the slurring of a person's good name or reputation.

Libel, as a noun, means defamation, other than oral, that is made in print, in writing, in recorded speech, or by pictures, signs, or effigies and which subjects a person to ridicule, scorn, or contempt. As a verb, it means to do the foregoing.

Slander, as a noun, means oral defamation. As a verb, it means to defame.

EXAMPLES:

"If you put those words you've just uttered about me in writing and publish them," Thorton Thinskinned said to Lawton Loquacious, I'll sue you for both **slander** and **libel** faster than you can say 'defamation'!"

lie See **lay / lie.**

like See **like / as.**

like / as

Thanks to the informality of today's spoken word and its employment by broadcasters and advertising copy writers, these two words have fallen into casual and grammatical misuse. In view of this trend toward informal use of language, indifferent communicators will not concern themselves with the parts of speech or how these two words function in a given sentence or construction. For those speakers and writers who do care about holding to a high standard of usage, the distinction between **like** and **as** is clear. It has to do with the difference between a preposition and a conjunction. And it has to do with nouns and pronouns and with clauses and verbs.

A preposition is a linking or connecting word that is used to relate a noun or a pronoun to another word or to show what relation exists between two words. A preposition's function is not involved with clauses, a group of words that includes one or more verbs. That is the job of a conjunction.

A conjunction is a linking or connecting word. It joins two words of equal rank, such as nouns, adjectives, and adverbs, and also joins phrases or two clauses of equal rank that contain one or more verbs.

Like is a preposition and is used to introduce a comparison.

As is a conjunction and is used to introduce clauses of comparison.

EXAMPLES:

How would our language be today if Shakespeare had titled his play "**Like** You **Like** It" instead of "**As** You **Like** It" or an ad writer had written the slogan "Winstons taste good **as** (the way) a cigarette should," instead of "Winstons taste good **like** a cigarette should."? They can look **like** winners or losers, a person can suppose, depending upon the looseness of one's tongue and taste, or **as** one picks, pleases, or prefers.

likely See **liable / likely / apt.**

linage / lineage

The difference between these look-like words is marked by a number of things. When recognized, they can lead to the proper and not confused use of them as nouns. The first word has two syllables. The second has three. The first word has one **e**. The second has two. They are not pronounced alike, and their meanings, furthermore, are not even close. They are markedly separate.

Linage, two syllables, one **e**, is pronounced 'lī-nij. It means the number of lines of printed matter that appears in magazines, articles, newspapers, advertising, or the like; the amount paid, charged, or received for a printed line of advertising.

Lineage, three syllables, two **e**'s, is pronounced 'lin-ē-ij. It means descent in a line from a common ancestor or progenitor; a group of individuals tracing descent from a common ancestor; ancestry, derivation, or extraction. The word is given in some dictionaries as a variant for **linage**. Careful communicators avoid unneeded confusion by confining the use of **lineage** to what might be called "family matters."

EXAMPLES:

"How much **linage** do you want on the **lineage** of the Snobby family?" Fawn Features, the society writer, asked her editor. "No more than twenty lines," Quintus Quill replied. "That's all that conceited clan is worth!"

lineage See **linage / lineage.**

literally See **figuratively / literally.**

little / small

Some things are big. Some are not. These words, when used as adjectives, describe the latter, in one fashion or another, relative to their size in the scheme of things.

Little means not big, large, or much in amount, number, quantity, extent, degree, size, time, or duration.

Small has much the same meaning as **little**. The words frequently are used interchangeably. **Small**, however, applies more to relative size determined by capacity, number, or value.

EXAMPLES:

"I may be **small** in size," said Paula Petite as she opened a valentine, "but when it comes to affairs of the heart, I am far from being **little**."

livid / vivid / lurid

These adjectives have colorations in their meanings that should be noted carefully, for if misused, one could end up red-faced, betrayed by ignorance that one has come by unwittingly.

Livid, contrary to popular misunderstanding and misuse, does not mean red. It means black and blue, as discolored by bruising; ashen; the color of lead; deathly pale; extremely angry; enraged.

Vivid, not to be confused with **livid**, means strikingly bright or intense, as color, light, and the like; full of life; lively; animated; vivacious; spirited; strong, distinct, or clearly perceptible; evoking brilliant mental images; heard, seen, or felt as if lifelike or real.

Lurid, with its own coloration, means any of several light or medium grayish colors ranging in hue from yellow to orange; extravagently colored; lighted or shining with an unnatural, fiery glow; wildly or garishly red; glaringly sensational; startlingly; shocking; gruesome; causing horror or revulsion; horrifying or repellent in appearance; terrible in fiery intensity, fierce passion, or wild unrestraint.

EXAMPLES:

Molly Maligned, her face **livid**, thrust a copy of the *Sky Blue Bugle* under the editor's nose. "This story about me and my first marriage is **vivid** all right. It certainly evokes many memories, some of them even pleasurable. But couldn't you have omitted the **lurid** details?"

loan See **lend / loan.**

loath / loathe / loathing

These words are a good example how one letter, an **e**, can make a difference in their part of speech, meaning, and use. Careful communicators willingly entertain the differences and apply them with pleasure—perhaps affection?

Loath is an adjective. It means unwilling; reluctant; disinclined; averse; contrary to one's wishes.

Loathe is a verb. It means to hate; to dislike greatly; to abhor; to detest; to abominate; to feel disgust or intense aversion for; to dislike with utter disgust, contempt, or intolerance.

Loathing is a noun. It means strong dislike mingled with disgust; extreme disgust; intense aversion; great hatred; abhorence.

EXAMPLES:

Rhonda Reticent is **loath** to tell her husband that she has dented their car again for fear he will **loathe** her accidental ways even more than he does already. His **loathing**, it seems, is something she is not able to avoid any more than was the pole she backed into.

loathe See **loath / loathe / loathing.**

loathing See **loath / loathe / loathing.**

loose / lose

To use these words accurately, one needs to have a good hold on their parts of speech, spelling, pronunciation, and meaning. Otherwise, disregard of any, especially the letter **o**, could lead to unbridled and confused communication.

Loose is both a verb and an adjective. As a verb, it means to free from bonds or restraint, as from constraint, obligation, penalty, or the like; to unfasten, undo, or untie, as a tie, a knot, bond, or fetter; to make less tight; to slacken or relax. As an adjective, **loose** means free, unbound, untied, unfettered, unrestricted; slack; not firm, taut, or rigid; free from moral restraint; lax in principle or conduct; sexually promiscuous or wanton.

Lose is a verb only. It means to be deprived of; to mislay; to fail to win, get, or obtain; to forfeit; to miss; to waste, as time; to fail to keep control of; to suffer loss; to undergo deprivation of something of value; to fail to use or take advantage of; to wander or go astray; to free oneself from; to rid oneself of; to disappear or fade from view; to evade or outdistance someone or something.

EXAMPLES:

"**Loose** your **loose** fingers from that poker pot, bub," Sidney Stud snarled at Danny Draw, reaching for his switchblade, "or you'll sure find out what it means to **lose** them!"

lose See **loose / lose.**

lurid See **livid / lurid.**

luxuriant / luxurious

These adjectives, which commonly are confused in their adverbial forms of luxuriantly and luxuriously, stem from the Latin *luxur*, from which luxury is derived. Their meanings are quite different. With proper indulgence, they can be learned and be used precisely and perhaps with pleasure when needed.

Luxuriant means abundant or profuse in growth; dense or prolific, as in vegetation; producing abundantly, as in soil; fertile; suggestive of a rich and splendid abundance; superabundant; richly productive; growing profusely.

Luxurious means of, relating to, or marked by luxury; to what is expensive, choice or the like; marked by or given to self-indulgence of the senses; exceedingly choice and costly; sumptuous; opulent; excessively ornate.

EXAMPLES:

Growing a **luxuriant** beard doesn't always lead to a **luxurious** relationship with someone of the opposite sex as some men who can raise no more than a stubble soon find out.

luxurious See **luxuriant / luxurious.**

M

majority / plurality

These nouns usually add up to positive results. Knowing the differences in their meaning and in number is what truly counts in their use.

Majority means the greater part or number; the number larger than half the total, as opposed to the minority; a number of voters or votes, jurors, or others in agreement, constituting more than half of the total number. A **majority**, therefore, is one more than half. It also means the age at which full civil rights are accorded; the status of one who has attained this age; the group or political party whose votes preponderate. **Majority** is used in the singular or in the plural depending on the number of the subject of the verb that follows. When **majority** refers to a precise number, a singular verb is used. When **majority** refers to members of a group as individuals, a plural verb is used.

Plurality means the state or fact of being plural; the excess of votes over the next highest in which there are three or more candidates; more than the next highest number.

EXAMPLES:

"I win the election," said Foster Franchise to Brendon Bachelor. "My wife's vote gives me a **majority**." "You're the winner," Bachelor said, "but you're wrong about the balloting. Like most things about you, your arithmetic is screwy. You received 27 votes, I have 26, and Ollie Officeseeker got 12. That makes a total of 65 votes cast. You needed 33 for a **majority**, one more than half. What you received, thanks to your being married, was a **plurality** of the votes cast. Congratulations!"

marital / martial

"All's fair in love and war," so the saying goes, but the same cannot always be said for these two adjectives.

Marital means of or pertaining to marriage or the married state; of or relating to a husband and his role in marriage; of or between a husband and a wife; of married people.

Martial means inclined or disposed to war; warlike; military; pertaining to or connected with the armed forces; pertaining to or appropriate for war; of or befitting a warrior.

EXAMPLES:

Some couples begin their **marital** relations with love in the bedroom and, thanks to their **martial** acts, end their marriage with war in the courtroom.

marshal / marshall

The key to spelling these similar-looking words correctly is to use one **l** only in the first word and to add a second **l** in the second word in order to make the latter a proper noun.

Marshal is a noun and a verb. As a noun, it means a high official in the household of a medieval king, prince, or nobleman having charge of the cavalry but later usually in charge of the military forces; a person who arranges and directs the ceremonial aspects of a gathering or a concave; a general officer of the highest military rank; an officer having charge of prisoners; an officer appointed for a judicial district to execute the process of the courts and perform various duties similar to those of a sheriff. As a verb, **marshal** means to place in proper rank or position; to bring together and order in an appropriate or effective way; to lead ceremoniously or solicitously; to array, as for battle. (Note that the past tense of **marshal** is **marshaled.** The one **l** is in conformity with the rule in spelling that says in forming the past tense of a verb its final consonant is not doubled when the accent falls on the first syllable, as in **canceled**, for example.)

Marshall, as already stated, is a proper noun and is used to denote the name of people and places.

EXAMPLES:

"**Marshal** the troops for my inspection," the general ordered as he stepped ashore on the **Marshall** Islands during World War II. "And, oh yes, I want to meet the **marshal** who will lead them. Usher him in to me at once!"

marshall See **marshal / marshall.**

martial See **marital / martial.**

masterful / masterly

These words would not be interchanged, as the first often is for the second, if their misusers knew each word's meaning and also knew the difference between being dominating and being skillful, attributes to be found in some people but not in everyone.

Masterful is an adjective. It means compelling; domineering; imperious; strong-willed; fit to command. Its adverb form is **masterfully**.

Masterly is both an adjective and an adverb. As an adjective, it means very skillful; suitable to or resembling that, like or befitting a master, as in skill or art; worthy of a master. As an adverb, **masterly** means with the skill of a master.

EXAMPLES:

Masterful in appearance, Lee Saber is a **masterly** swordsman who struts and prances about, who feints, parries, and thrusts, and who yells "*touché* " at the top of his voice—with relish—much to his opponents' annoyance.

masterly See **masterful / masterly.**

material / materiel

These nouns differ not only in their final vowels, **a** and **e**, but also in the substance of their meaning, differences that have marked bearing on how they are used accurately.

Material is derived from the Latin *materia*, matter. It means the substance out of which something can be fashioned; the elements, constituents, or substances of which something is composed or can be made.

Materiel is the French word *materiél.* It means equipment, apparatus, and supplies used by an institution or an organization, such as the military.

EXAMPLES:

"This **material** will help The Cause of the South in some way, won't it, lieutenant?" Ali Bama asked the Confederate officer, pulling down the thick drapes from the parlor windows. "Yes, ma'am," Lou Siana replied as he bowed low to hide a smile. "It surely will. We'll put it with the other **materiel** we've collected to make us Boys in Gray look fit and trim for battle!"

materiel See **material / materiel.**

may See **can / may / might.**

mean / median / average

Each of these nouns, which have to do with numbers and statistics and the facts and information derived from them, clearly has an individual role to play in a world absorbed with precise knowledge and instant communication.

Mean may be the simple **average** of a set of figures, but it also may represent value midway between two extremes.

Median applies to the value that represents the point at which there are as many instances above as there are below.

Average is exactly or approximately the quotient obtained by dividing the sum total of a set of figures by the number of figures.

EXAMPLES:

Professor Grumble was overheard speaking to his class: "The temperatures registered a low of 40 degrees and a high of 80 degrees for a **mean** of 60 degrees for the day on which you took the exam. The **median** of your scores, from the top down and the bottom up, was 60. And the **average** of your scores, dividing a total of 1,800 by 30, was 60 also. Now that's something, isn't it? You, your brains, and the weather end up with the same score, a common statistic that marks an ordinary and undistinguished performance!"

meaningful

This adjective, which dates from the sixteenth century, has

become what H. W. Fowler characterizes in *A Dictionary of Modern English Usage* as a vogue word. "Every now & then," he says, "a word emerges from obscurity, or even from nothingness or a merely potential & not actual existence, into sudden popularity." Such seems to be the case with **meaningful**, for it apparently has replaced significant in many people's vocabularies at a point where it no longer is full of meaning. Thanks to its over and witless use, such as in "a **meaningful** conversation" or in "a **meaningful** look" or in other similar constructions in which **meaningful** is superfluous when applied to anything that has meaning already within it, the word has lost its worth.

Meaningful is defined as having meaning, function, or purpose; that thing which one intends to convey or express, especially by language; full of meaning, value, or significance; significant; having an assigned function in a language system.

EXAMPLES:

Meaningful has been so overused, misued, and abused as an adjective that it has become a meaningless word, one that deserves a much-needed respite. Better still, it is entitled to a **meaningful**, er, a merciful demise.

media See **medium / media / mediums.**

medium / media / mediums

These nouns frequently are confused and mixed in their use. In fact, they almost seem foreign to some people. The first two come directly from the Latin and remain unchanged in their singular and plural forms from Roman times. The third is an adaptation in English to provide **medium**, a singular noun, with a second plural form.

Medium has a variety of meanings. Its most common are: something in a middle position; a means of effecting or conducting something; a channel or system of entertainment, information, or communication; a go-between, an intermediary; an individual held to be a channel of communication between the earthly world and a world of spirits.

Media means, in the sense of mass communication, magazines, newspapers, the news services, and radio and television, and is plural in number. It is not a collective noun. In time the noun may become singular in usage. Until it does, a plural verb and the plural pronoun **they** should be used so that the three parts of speech—noun, verb, and pronoun—agree in number.

Mediums is the plural ending of **medium** when the word is used to mean two or more individuals held to be channels of communication between the earthly world and a world of spirits.

EXAMPLES:

If one suspects the news **media** latch on to every bizarre story they come upon, imagine what they would do should a **medium** announce that he or she has been in contact with the spirit of Elvis Presley. And were the **media** to pull all stops to cover numerous other **mediums** who say they, too, have "chatted" with the late rock 'n' roll singer, how long would the **media** and the **mediums** be for this world?

median See **mean / median / average.**

mediums See **medium / media / mediums.**

mendacity / mendicity

The truth about these two look-alike nouns is that their second vowel is not the same, and thus their meanings are not identical. The first word has to do with untruthfulness and the second with begging.

Mendacity, with an **a** in the middle, means untruthfulness; quality of being untruthful; tendency to lie; habitual lying; an instance of lying; falsehood; a lie; prevarication.

Mendicity, with an **i** in the middle, means the practice of begging; the condition of life of a begger.

EXAMPLES:

Could it be said that someone who practices **mendacity** and **mendicity** is a liar who goes a-begging?

mendicity See **mendacity / mendicity.**

men's / mens'

Men's is the correct possessive for men, a plural noun that means two or more male human beings.

Mens' is illiteracy, a nonword. See **children's / childrens'.**

mens' See **men's / mens'.**

metal / mettle

These nouns look so much alike that their use can be confused. Testing for their meaning discloses their difference and distinctiveness.

Metal means any of a class of mineral substances such as copper, gold, iron, silver, uranium, and so forth, or an alloy of any of these. As a verb, it means to cover with metal.

Mettle means courage or strength of character; characteristic disposition or temperament; spirit; staying quality.

EXAMPLES:

The Iron Maiden, an instrument of torture made of **metal** with spikes lining its interior and used in the Middle Ages, undoubtedly tested the **mettle** of anyone who was encased in it and compelled to feel its unladylike pressures.

mettle See **metal / mettle.**

might See **can / may / might.**

militate / mitigate

These verbs have a way of being interchanged when they need not be even though they look and are pronounced somewhat alike. Yet their meanings are about as different as two words can be. That is because they are derived from markedly different Latin words, the first having to do with weight, the second with softness.

Militate comes from the Latin word *militare*, meaning to serve as a soldier. Its English meaning is to have weight or effect; to be combative; to work or operate against; to have an adverse effect or influence on; to have force or influence; to serve or act as a strong influence.

Mitigate comes from the Latin word *mitis*, meaning gentle, soft, or kind. Its English meaning is to lessen in force or intensity, as wrath, grief, pain, harshness, and the like; to make less intense, serious, or severe; to temper; to soften; to ease; to make milder or gentler; to relieve; to alleviate.

EXAMPLES:

"The evidence and testimony presented in this trial," Judge I. M. Reasonable told the accused, "**militate** against your being cleared of the charges the state has brought against you. As for your sentence, I am going to **mitigate** its length because you are a first offender. Six months. Stay out of trouble!"

misdemeanor See **felony / misdemeanor.**

mitigate See **militate / mitigate.**

mobile / movable

These adjectives have to do with motion. The distinction in their meaning and use rests on the ease and frequency of movement each one describes.

Mobile means able to move or be moved easily, rapidly, or readily from one place to another; changeable in appearance, mood, or purpose; flowing freely.

Movable means capable of being moved; not fixed in one position, place, or posture; changing date from year to year.

EXAMPLES:

When Johannes Gutenberg created **movable** type and converted a wine press into a printing press in Mainz, Germany, in 1455, could he have envisioned that centuries later people would move about in **mobile** homes, a turn of events or movement that would rival his revolutionary invention?

moderate / modest

These adjectives have to do with limits, not extremes. Neither boldness nor timidity enters into their use—just the preciseness of meaning that marks their individuality.

Moderate means kept or keeping within reasonable or proper limits; not extreme, excessive, or intense; restrained; mediocre;

average; temperate; of medium amount, extent, quality, or the like; not violent; mild.

Modest means unassuming; unpretentious; not vain or boastful; placing a humble estimate on one's abilities or worth; neither bold nor assertive; having a shy and retiring nature; reserved; restrained; not excessive.

EXAMPLES:

A **moderate** drinker is one who does well in remaining **modest** about how much he or she has consumed.

modest See **moderate / modest.**

momentary / momentous

Brief or long-lasting consequences can follow the use of these adjectives, depending on how each one is employed, for the difference between them is that of time and importance.

Momentary means very brief; lasting or continuing but a moment; having a very brief life; occurring or present at any moment; transitory; short-lived.

Momentus means of great or far-reaching importance or consequence; very important; of utmost significance.

EXAMPLES:

"Let us take a **momentary** pause," Senator Simpson Scratchey said to his committee members, "before we continue with our **momentous** hearings on whether or not to recommend funding to save the mosquito from extinction."

momentous See **momentary / momentous.**

momentum / impetus

These nouns have to do with the force of bodies in motion and properly can be interchanged and not collide with each other. Substituting one for the other would be welcome in print and on the air, for when it comes to sports, **impetus** rarely is seen or heard. **Momentum** has it all on the field of play. To athletes and coaches and sportswriters and broadcasters, especially to those involved in or with football, **momentum** is the "in" word. They seldom, if ever, speak or write the word **impetus.** Why not? Why is the longer word overused and the shorter one underused or not used at all? **Impetus** means the same thing as **momentum**. So much for vogue words whose existence is short-lived and whose turnover rates have been known to outmatch those on gridirons and basketball courts—sportswriters and broadcasters and other followers of or participants in sports to the contrary not withstanding!

Momentum means the force or speed of motion; the **impetus** of a moving body; increasing motion or force; the quantity of motion in a body as measured by the product of its mass by its velocity; a property of a moving body that determines the length of time required to bring it to rest when under the action of a constant force or movement.

Impetus means energy of motion; a driving force; figuratively, any impulse or incentive; the force with which a moving body tends to maintain its velocity and overcome resistence; a stimulation or encouragement resulting in increased activity.

EXAMPLES:

"Coach," Sidney Scribe asked stiffly, "when did the **momentum** of the game shift your way?" "The same moment the **impetus** did," Pigskin snapped back.

moral / morale / morals

The right way to handle these words is to stick to their straight and narrow definitions, to note the difference in their parts of speech, and to treat each word with individual respect.

Moral is an adjective. It means ethical; chaste; virtuous; pertaining to right conduct, behavior, or duties; discriminating between right and wrong; hewing to established sanctioned codes or accepted notions of right and wrong. As a noun, it is the underlying meaning implied in a fable, allegory, or story.

Morale is a French word and is a noun. It means disposition or mental state with respect to cheerfulness, confidence, zeal, fortitude, well-being, and the like; a sense of common purpose with respect to a group.

Morals is a plural noun. It means the same as ethics; the principles, rules, standards, or habits of human behavior, particularly sexual conduct, as they relate to right and wrong.

EXAMPLES:

Dolly Dewright is a woman of **moral** uprightness whose **morale** is uplifted whenever she sees a rise in the **morals** in her community.

morale See **moral / morale / morals.**

morals See **moral / morale / morals.**

morays / mores

There is something fishy about one of these nouns and not the other even though the words are pronounced alike. To avoid slipping off the deep end when trying to use them, one needs to know their difference in meaning, which is a whale of a lot.

Morays are dangerous sharp-toothed, brightly colored eels that are capable of inflicting savage bites and that chiefly frequent tropical coastal waters.

Mores are the fixed morally binding customs, usages, or practices of a particular group of people; the customs, folkways, manners, or conventions regarded as essential to or characteristic of a community.

EXAMPLES:

Swimming in waters infested by **morays** is a practice not likely to be found in the **mores** of a people who value their lives.

more than See **over / above / more than.**

mores See **morays / mores.**

most See **all / any / most/ some.**

movable See **mobile / movable.**

mysterious / mystic / mystical

The accurate use of these adjectives should puzzle no one once any mystery or ''myst'' about their individual meanings has disappeared.

Mysterious means of, relating to, or forming mystery; exciting wonder, curiosity, surprise, amazement, awe; of obscure nature, meaning, origin, and the like; not easy to comprehend or to identify or to be understood; baffling; puzzling; inexplicable; strange; occult.

Mystic means of or relating to mysteries; having to do with religious, esoteric, or occult rites and or with mysticism or mystics; spiritually significant or symbolic or spiritual truth; having magical powers.

Mystical means of or pertaining to mystics or mysticism; having spiritual value, meaning, symbolism, or reality that is neither apparent nor obvious to the intelligence or senses.

EXAMPLES:

The **mysterious** ways of Madeleine Messmer, her **mystic** powers, and her **mystical** insights send shivers up and down the spines of those people who attend her seances.

mystic See **mysterious / mystic / mystical.**

mystical See **mysterious / mystic / mystical.**

N

nauseated / nauseous

A healthy understanding of the meaning of these adjectives, which look very much alike, can overcome any sickening thought one may have about their prescribed use. The words are not interchangeable, for **nauseated** has to do with effect and **nauseous** has to do with cause. Both words stem from *nausea*, which is the Latin form for the Greek word seasickness that, in turn, comes from *naus*, the Greek word for ship. To the ancient Greeks, who were poor sailors, being aboard a ship seemed cause enough to turn their stomachs.

Nauseated means to be affected with nausea, with seasickness, or with stomach distress; to be disgusted.

Nauseous means causing nausea or disgust; loathsome; disgusting. It does not mean to be seasick or to be disgusted.

EXAMPLES:

"I've had enough of your **nauseous** behavior and the rocking of this boat," Ursula Upsetta cried. "I'm **nauseated**, Sid Duction. Take your hands off me and row for shore this instant!"

nauseous See **nauseated / nauseous.**

naval / navel

These words look so much alike they often are pronounced the same. The **a** and **e** in the second syllable of each word, respectively, has its own sound. Further, the words are not interchangeable. The first is an adjective only, and the other is a noun, with two different meanings, and an adjective, with a single meaning. One way to keep the two words separate in thought and in use is to associate the words midship with **naval** and midsection with **navel**. That way one never need be at sea about how to pronounce, spell, and use each word in a suitable and shipshape manner.

Naval is an adjective only. It means of or pertaining to battleships or ships; belonging to, pertaining to, or connected with a navy.

Navel, as a noun, means a depression in the middle of the surface of the abdomen that marks the point of the former attachment of the umbilical cord or yolk stalk; the belly button. **Navel** also means a seedless orange having a pit at the narrow or pointed end where the fruit encloses a small secondary fruit. It is used also as an adjective to describe such an orange.

EXAMPLES:

"Now that **naval** maneuvers are over, Chief," Tommy Tarr asked, scratching his **navel**, "may I eat my **navel**?" "No," Beau Sun, the chief petty officer, replied with a twinkle in his eye as he glanced at Tommy's tummy, "you cannot eat your **navel**, but you're welcome to eat that **navel** orange you're holding in your other hand! "

navel See **naval / navel.**

nearest See **next / nearest.**

necessaries See **necessities / necessaries.**

necessities / necessaries

Some people may believe that these plural nouns are not interchangeable. But, as it says in George Gershwin's folk opera, *Porgy and Bess* , "It ain't necessarily so." In fact, the notion can be dispensed with. Their closeness in meaning, and not so much their look-alike appearance, accounts through longtime popular usage for their being regarded as synonyms for things that are indispensible. And of the two, **necessities** is far more popular in American usage, with the British still holding onto their **necessaries**.

Necessities means things that are necessary or indispensible; that which cannot be done without for maintaining life, comfort, or well-being; pressing needs and wants; a situation of difficulty or hardship.

Necessaries means things needed to maintain life or one's well-being or comfort, such as food, drink, or shelter; an indispensible item; essentials; a nonoffensive word used prior to modern indoor plumbing for identifying water closets, chamberpots, privies, and outhouses.

EXAMPLES:

When Indy Dispensible flies from New York to London, he finds that the **necessities** he takes with him, such as suits, shirts, socks, and underwear, have become **necessaries** by the time he gets there.

need See **lack/ need / want.**

neglect / negligence

These words and their meanings call for careful attention, not indifference or oversight. Although both words have to do with carelessness, failure, or some important omission in the performance of one's duty, their interchange is occasional, depending upon the context.

Neglect, the stronger of the two words, is both a noun and a verb. As a noun, it means the act, fault, or instance of neglecting something; disregard; careless treatment; omission; the state of being neglected; habitual lack of care. As a verb, it means to pay no attention or too little attention to; to slight; to disregard; to omit through carelessness, indifference, or oversight; to take no care of; to fail to do. **Neglect** ordinarily refers to the act.

Negligence is a noun and an adjective. As a noun, it means want of due care; carelessness; habitual neglect; failure to exercise care or to carry out one's duty; lack of proper care or attention. As an adjective, it is used in civil action to describe litigation in which **neglect** is charged or involved. **Negligence** ordinarily refers to the habit or trait of failing to attend to or to do what is expected or required.

EXAMPLES:

"You **neglect** another payment to me," Phil Landerer's former wife said to him, " and you'll be answering a **negligence** suit faster than you can say 'alimony'! Then you'll find out what your **negligence** will cost you because of your **neglect** of me!"

negligence See **neglect / negligence.**

neither See **each / either / neither.**

neither nor See **either or / neither nor.**

nerve See **verve / nerve.**

nevertheless / nonetheless

These words are synonyms—more or less. They are used either as adverbs or as conjunctions, depending on their functions as modifiers or as linking words. Even so, sentences become lighter when they are replaced as linking words by **but**, **still**, **yet**, and **however**.

Nevertheless means in spite of that; notwithstanding; however. It implies a concession, something that should not be lost to mind or forgotten.

Nonetheless comes from **none the less**, three words combined in modern times to one. It means all the same; however.

EXAMPLES:

The movie was sentimental and melodramatic; **nevertheless**, Felicia Flick enjoyed it. Her date, Bill Board, did not and tried, **nonetheless**, to look as though he had.

next / nearest

When one comes up against these words, one finds they are not synonyms. A difference in meaning separates them. The distance is not great, but it is sufficient to call for one's using each word in its precise context.

Next is an adjective and an adverb. As an adjective, it means immediately preceding or following in time, order, rank, sequence, place, importance, and the like. As an adverb, it means immediately after; on the first succeeding occasion; in a position of proximity; near to.

Nearest is the superlative of the adjective **near**. It also can function as an adverb. It means the closest in time, space, position, distance, degree, kinship, association, and so forth.

EXAMPLES:

The **nearest** Calvin Coldfeet gets to be close to girls is when one sits **next** to him in class or when the **next** one following him into the room takes the **nearest** seat to him.

night See **knight / night.**

noisome / noisy / noxious / obnoxious

These words have one thing in common. They are adjectives. Otherwise, each is distinct in its meaning. To distinguish among them, keep in mind the concepts of offensiveness, sound, poison, and unpleasantness.

Noisome comes from the Middle English word *noyesome* and is related to annoy. It means offensive or disgusting to the senses and especially to the sense of smell as an odor; evil or foul smelling; harmful; injurious; filthy. It does not mean **noisy**, for one smells odors but never hears them.

Noisy means making much noise, loud sound; abounding in and full of noise; clamorous; boisterous; tumultuous; uproarious.

Noxious has its origin in the Latin word *nocere*, to harm. It means harmful or injurious to health and well-being; constituting a harmful influence on mind or behavior; morally harmful; pernicious; unwholesome.

Obnoxious, like **noxious**, stems from the common Latin root *noxa*, meaning harm. The words sometimes are interchangeable. Even so, **obnoxious** has a derivation and meaning of its own. It comes from the Latin word *obnoxosus*: (*ob* + *noxosus*). It means exposed to something unpleasant, objectionable, odious, offensive; exposed or liable to harm, evil, or anything objectionable.

EXAMPLES:

The **noisome** fumes from the **noisy** gas stove were **noxious** to the late chef, Mal Odorous, whose **obnoxious** behavior, not to mention his cooking, had been known to leave a bad taste in the mouths of his diners.

noisy See **noisome / noisy / noxious / obnoxious.**

none

Like other indefinite pronouns, **none** can be troublesome in the matter of agreement between subject and verb if one does not know when to use it in the singular or when to use it in the plural. Contrary to long-held belief, **none** is not used exclusively in the singular. It is both singular and plural and is used more frequently in the plural because both the number and the sense of the construction in which it appears so dictate. In its singular use, **none** means "not one." In its plural use, it means "not any."

EXAMPLES:

Professor Grumble gazed at his class and mumbled to himself: "**None** (not one) of my students is eligible for a scholarship. What a pity! **None** (not any) of them have the brains and ambition, what more, the grades required for latching on to one and thus 'warm the cockles of this pedagogue's heart.' "

nonetheless See **nevertheless / nonetheless.**

normalcy / normality

These nouns are synonyms, for they mean the same thing: the state or fact of conforming to a type, standard, natural, or regular pattern. When President Warren G. Harding used **normalcy** in a speech in Boston in 1920, calling for a return to normal conditions in the United States, he was said to have coined a new word. He did not. **Normalcy** had been a rare, but legitimate, word in use before the Civil War. Its vogueness has waned, and **normality** has taken its place. Even so, **normal** is the "normal" word for expressing a state of naturalness or regularity.

EXAMPLES:

"When will the city be back to normal?" the reporter asked the mayor. "As soon as I declare a state of **normalcy** or **normality**," Nat U. Rally replied.

normality See **normalcy / normality.**

nostalgia / nostalgic

These words, the first a noun, the second its adjective form, are good examples of how the meanings of words can change almost completely and take on new connotations so that their original meanings seem archaic.

Nostalgia comes from the forming of two Greek words, *nostos* and *algia*. It originally meant acute or painful longing for home: homesickness. It now means a wistful or sentimental yearning or longing for a return to or of people, places, or events in some past period. Some dictionaries do not include the concept of homesickness in defining **nostalgia**. Others make it a second definition.

Nostalgic, instead of denoting from, in, or of homesickness, has taken on the meaning of yearning, longing, reminiscing.

EXAMPLES:

Tina Tempo grows **nostalgic** whenever she hears the music of the Big Band Era, for her heart beats with **nostalgia** for those days of "swing and sway."

nostalgic See **nostalgia / nostalgic.**

not See **knot / not.**

not only . . . but also

These words, like **either . . . or**, **neither . . . nor**, and **whether . . . or**, are called correlative conjunctions. They serve to indicate parallelism of thought and ideas. Logical and clear thinking is required for their correct use, for their purpose is to connect phrases of equal grammatical value. In short, correlatives join equal parts of speech, two of the same kind of thing, so that the elements being connected are given equal stress.

EXAMPLES:

Some men **not only** are eligible bachelors **but also** are vulnerable ones. That may be why some women **not only** like pursuing men **but also** enjoy overcoming them.

notable / noticeable / notorious

These adjectives are not to be tossed off lightly as being interchangeable because they start with the same first three letters. That is where their similarity ends. Each has its own meaning and therefore an individual role to play in the English language.

Notable means worthy of notice; noteworthy; prominent; remarkable. It implies commanding notice as standing out from background or surroundings.

Noticeable means such as to attract notice or attention; worthy or deserving of being noticed or being given attention. It implies an inability to escape notice.

Notorious means widely but unfavorably known; generally and publicly known and talked of unfavorably; infamous. It is not a synonym for **famous**, which conveys a positive and favorable meaning of being well-known.

EXAMPLES:

Renowned for his **notable** feats on the gridiron, Charley Chucker has become equally **noticeable** on another field of play because of his **notorious** reputation for throwing passes at women, with a completion rate that is the envy of his teammates.

noticeable See **notable / noticeable / notorious.**

notorious See **notable / noticeable / notorious.**

now See **present / presently / now / forthwith.**

noxious See **noisome / noisy / noxious / obnoxious.**

nozzle / nuzzle

Although these double **z** words are almost spelled alike and seem to have some kind of nose in common, they are far apart in their parts of speech and meaning, and should not, therefore, be confused.

N<u>o</u>zzle is a noun only. It means a projecting spout or vent; the outlet end of a pipe, hose, and the like. It is slang for the nose.

N<u>u</u>zzle is a noun and a verb. As a noun, it means an affectionate embrace or cuddle. As a verb, it means to rub, burrow, or root with the nose or snout, as animals do; to rub noses, as Eskimos do; to lie close to or cuddle or snuggle up with someone or something, as animals and human beings do.

EXAMPLES:

Washington Waters turned off the **nozzle** on the hose. "No need to rush the pup's first bath," he thought as he felt Barkis **nuzzle** him. "I'll turn it on and him off later!"

number

A common misuse of spoken and written English constantly occurs these days in the lack of agreement in number of the parts of speech. Agreement in number of subject, verb, and pronoun is a requirement in English syntax. When the subject of a verb is singular, each pronoun referring to that singular subject must be singular. The sentences that follow lack agreement in number of subject, verb, and pronoun. They express fuzzy, disjointed thinking, and smack of illiteracy.

- Each of the boys have their own toys
- Everyone is welcome to their dinners
- Minnesota has the ball on their 20-yard line

Truly caring communicators who wish to be precise and accurate in the use of spoken and written English would restate the above sentences as follows.

- Each boy has his own toy (or)
- Each of the boys has his own toy (or)
- All the boys have their own toys
- Everyone is welcome to his or her dinner (or)
- All are welcome to their dinners
- Minnesota has the ball on its 20-yard line (or)

- The Vikings have the ball on their 20-yard line

The same requirement holds true for both verbs and pronouns that relate to plural subjects. Both are plural in sentences such as these.

- All the boys have their own toys
- All are welcome to their dinners
- The Vikings have the ball on their 20-yard line

For further discussion of **number**, see **all / any / most / some; data and other Latin plurals**; **each / either / neither**; **every one / everyone**; **none**; and, in particular, **collective nouns**.

number of, a / number of, the

These combinations of words are nouns, prepositions, and articles. They can be thought of as meaning lot of, bunch of, heap of, few of. When used as the subject of verbs, they indicate whether a group of people, places, or things are singular or plural in number.

Number of, a (indefinite article) is a plural construction. It calls for the use of a plural verb.

Number of, the (definite article) is a singular construction. It requires the use of a singular verb.

EXAMPLES:

Although **a number of** people have asked Rachel Rapacious for money, **the number of** her favorable responses is unlikely to be ever known since the rates of interest she charges make those of credit cards pale in comparison.

number of, the See **number of, a / number of, the.**

nuzzle See **nozzle / nuzzle.**

O

obligate / oblige

Careful communicators do themselves a favor in observing the distinction in the meanings of these look-alike words and thus avoid getting into a bind by interchanging them indiscriminately.

Obligate is a verb and an adjective, and is restricted in its meanings. As a verb, it chiefly means to bind, compel, or constrain legally or morally, as under a contract. As an adjective, **obligate** is used in biology to mean able to survive in only one environment.

Oblige is a verb only and has wider meanings than **obligate**: to bind or constrain by physical, legal, social, or moral means; to make indebted or grateful by a service or favor; to do a service or favor for.

When constraint is from the outside, either **obligate** or **oblige** is used. When constraint is within one's mind, **oblige** is used.

EXAMPLES:

"The provisions of this policy would **obligate** me to pay premiums to Your Money or Your Life Insurance Company for forever," Edwin Erstwhile said to Fulton Fastbuck. "You will **oblige** me by changing them if you hope to get your first dime in commission!"

oblige See **obligate / oblige.**

oblique See **opaque / oblique.**

oblivious See **unaware / oblivious.**

obnoxious See **noisome / noisy / noxious / obnoxious.**

obscenity / profanity / vulgarity

One should tread carefully in using this trio of nouns, for each has to do with the less savory aspects of the human scene. Ordinarily, the words are not interchangeable, although something that is obscene can be vulgar also.

Obscenity is a strong word for an impropriety. It refers to those matters, epecially those having to do with excretion and reproduction, deemed to be offensive, disgusting, abhorrent, or repulsive to morality, virtue, or accepted standards of decency or modesty. **Obscenity** also means indecency or offensiveness in behavior, expression, or appearance; lewdness.

Profanity is religious in connotation. It means the quality or state of being not sacred or holy; of being unholy because impure, defiled, or unconsecrated; profane, irreverent, or unholy language; use or utterance of such language; an utterance of such language.

Vulgarity, which has a connotation of commonness or nongentility, means the quality or state of being crude, unrefined, or coarse; lack of refinement in manners; coarseness of ideas or language; something, such as a gesture, act, or expression, that offends good taste or propriety.

EXAMPLES:

The **obscenity** of the bedroom scenes, the **profanity** of the characters, and the **vulgarity** of the writing leave little doubt in some people's minds how and why some novels become best-sellers.

observance / observation

The difference between these two nouns is that of doing and seeing, so to speak, and accounts for why the words are not interchangeable.

Observance is the act or practice or an instance of following, obeying, or conforming to or with a law, custom, command, or rule; the act or custom of keeping or celebrating a holiday or other rite or event; a customary rite or celebration; a customary practice.

Observation is the act, faculty, habit, or instance of noticing or perceiving; the act, faculty, habit, or instance of regarding attentively or watching; notice; a comment; a remark; a statement; an inference or judgment drawn or made from or based on what one has noticed or seen.

EXAMPLES:

Observance of a new law often follows the **observation** of the need for it.

observation See **observance / observation.**

obsolescent See **obsolete / obsolescent.**

obsolete / obsolescent

These adjectives should not be, but sometimes are, confused in their use. They differ slightly, but importantly, in meaning in that one has to do with matters that are useless or dead and the other with things that are on their way of becoming so.

Obsolete means no longer in general use; fallen into disuse; outmoded in design, style, or construction; antiquated; out of date; dead.

Obsolescent means wearing out or going out of use; becoming outdated or outmoded, such as weapons, machinery, equipment, materials, systems, or the like; becoming or passing out of or fading from use, such as words or language or fashions.

EXAMPLES:

No wonder Johnny Jocular's days as a stand-up comedian are numbered. Most of his jokes are **obsolete** and the rest are **obsolescent**.

occur See **take place / happen / occur / transpire.**

odd / peculiar / quaint / queer

Isn't it strange how some words look to be interchangeable until we examine them and find each has an individual meaning that enables us to use each one accurately and precisely? That is why these adjectives are good examples of this fascinating fact.

Odd means differing in nature from what is ordinary, conventional, regular, usual, expected, or accepted; unconventional; fantastic; bizarre.

Peculiar means characteristic of only one person, group, or thing; different from the usual or normal; distinctive; particular; singular.

Quaint also conveys a suggestion of the unusual and means strange or odd in an interesting, pleasing, amusing, or picturesque way. Unlike **odd** and **queer**, **quaint** does not convey a sense of disparagement. In fact, pleasantness underscores its distinctiveness.

Queer and **odd** are synonyms in that both words mean differing from the ordinary. They are not alike otherwise, for **queer** means strange in a way that makes one uneasy. It also means slightly repellent; of questionable nature or character; suspicious; shady.

EXAMPLES:

Bo Hemian's **odd** behavior, **peculiar** views, and **quaint** sayings give some people a **queer** feeling.

odious / odorous

These adjectives have opposite meanings in that one has to do with what is unlikable and the other has to with what is pleasant. Exercising simple sense enables anyone to use this pair of words without a twitch of the nose.

Odious means deserving or causing hatred; hateful; repugnant; detestable; highly offensive; disgusting.

Odorous means yielding or diffusing a strong distinctive smell whether pleasant or unpleasant. It largely has come to mean emitting a distinctive and pleasant aroma, fragrance, or scent.

EXAMPLES:

Viewers who find television commercials promoting **odorous** deodorants to be **odious** should be grateful. They haven't been aired a scent's worth—yet!

odorous See **odious / odorous.**

official / officious

These words when used as adjectives hold no joint office as synonyms even though they look alike. Each has its distinctive meaning and its own mission to carry out. In fact, in one usage, they are antonymns or opposites.

Official means of or pertaining to an office, post, or position of duty, trust, or authority; holding office or serving in a public capacity; befitting or characteristic of a person in office or one in or of authority; prescribed or recognized as authorized.

Officious means objectionably forward in volunteering or offering one's unrequested or unwanted services or advice; meddlesome. In diplomacy, the word **officious** means of an informal nature; unofficial. When so used, it is the opposite of **official**.

EXAMPLES:

One thing Boris Buttinski did not need if he had any hope of being given a pay raise was to be handed an **official** reprimand for his **officious** behavior at the recent staff meeting.

officious See **official / officious.**

omission See **oversight / omission.**

on / onto / on to

These tiny words can be troublesome in their use if one does not know the difference between a preposition and an adverb, on the one hand, and position and location, on the other. **On** and **onto** are prepositions. **On to**, however, are two words, a combination of an adverb and a preposition.

On indicates position. It refers to something in contact with a surface. It also means time when or continued motion. One meets **on** Friday. One places a book **on** a table. One beats **on** a drum. One walks **on** the grass.

Onto indicates movement to a position on, not merely to a location on. One walks **onto** the grass. One climbs **onto** a table. In this usage, **onto** indicates that the motion was initiated from a point outside the grass or the table and that the movement was toward these surfaces. One can jump either **on** or **onto** a table, but if the motion is continuous (up and down) on the surface, then **on** is used to indicate such movement.

On to indicates continuing movement. It is written as two words and shows that **on** is a qualifying word, a full adverb, attached to a verb, and that **to** is a linking word, a preposition. One goes **on to** success. One moves **on to** a new job. One passes a book **on to** a friend.

EXAMPLES:

"We're late," Ima Impatient said to her husband, Seldom. "Step **on** the gas, hold **onto** that steering wheel and drive **on to** the party as if you'd been told there's no tomorrow, for you could be without one if you don't get me there **on** time!"

on to See **on / onto / on to.**

one another See **each other / one another.**

one of / only one of

To the eye and ear unskilled in seeing and hearing syntax precisely, these phrases can cause problems in agreement in number between subject and verb. Their exact, correct use calls for identifying the proper subject, which is either a noun or a pronoun and which is either singular or plural in number.

One of, for the most part, is plural. It almost always is followed by a plural noun, which becomes the subject of the verb that follows it.

Only one of is singular. The adjective **only** qualifies the pronoun **one** and emphasizes the singularness of the construction. When **only one of** is followed by a plural noun, the noun does not become the subject of the verb that follows. That is the function of **one**, the singular pronoun.

EXAMPLES:

Ben Byas is **one of** those people who have an opinion on every subject but is the **only one of** them, his wife says, who confines his oratory to 2 to 4 A.M.

only See **just / only.**

only one of See **one of / only one of.**

onto See **on / onto / on to.**

opaque / oblique

One can avoid confusing these adjectives by keeping one's thinking clear and by being straight to the point whenever speaking or writing them.

Opaque means not transparent; impenetrable to light; not allowing light to pass through; not shining or bright; dark; dull; not lucid or clear; hard to understand or explain; dull-witted; thick-headed; stupid or unintelligent.

Oblique means neither perpendicular nor parallel to a given line or surface; slanting; sloping; diverging from a straight line or course; indirectly stated or expressed; not going straight to the point; not straightforward; indirect or evasive; devious; misleading; underhand; dishonest.

EXAMPLES:

Isn't it a remarkable coincidence, one could ask, how often it is that **opaque** statements stem from **oblique** thinking? But then that's looking at the dark and slanted sides of things, isn't it?

optimist / pessimist

These nouns are antonymns, for they have opposite meanings. They are used to identify a person who has either a bright or a dark perspective of things.

An **optimist** is a person who tends to look on the more favorable side of events or on the bright side of life, who is hopeful of good results, who believes the existing world is the best of all possible worlds, who believes that good ultimately triumphs over evil.

A **pessimist** is a person who habitually sees or expects the worst, who is disposed to be gloomy, who tends to look on the dark side of things, who expects the worst possible outcome, who believes the world fundamentally is evil and is the worst of all possible worlds, who believes that the evil in the world outweighs the good.

EXAMPLES:

"Isn't it wonderful that the sun is shining brightly?" Sherwood Smiley, the **optimist**, asked. "I suppose so," replied Gordon Grouchy, the **pessimist**, "but I see a cloud on the horizon."

oral See **verbal / oral / written.**

ordinance / ordnance / ordonnance

When these look-alike nouns are used and regulated rightly, and their parts arranged correctly, no one has cause to get up in arms over their usage.

Ordinance means an authoritative rule or law; a decree or command; a public injunction, or regulation, usually issued by a municipal government; a religious rite or ceremony.

Ordnance means cannon or artillery; armament; military weapons of all kinds with their equipment and ammunition; the branch of a military unit that procures, stores, maintains, and issues weapons and munitions.

Ordonnance means the ordering, arrangement, or disposition of parts, as of a building, a picture, or a literary composition.

EXAMPLES:

When a municipal council issues an **ordinance** prohibiting the storage of **ordnance** within the city limits, firearm fanciers are dismayed, but when the same council approves an **ordonnance** that is favorable to the public library, literature lovers are delighted.

ordnance See **ordinance / ordnance / ordonnance.**

ordonnance See **ordinance / ordnance / ordonnance.**

oscillate / osculate

These verbs are so clearly different in meaning that one need not wobble over their use but simply kiss one's vacillation goodbye.

Oscillate means to swing, move, or travel back and forth, as a pendulum or a fan does; to vibrate; to vary between extremes or two opposite points; to waver between differing beliefs, theories, opinions, feelings, conditions, or the like; to be indecisive or uncertain; to vacillate.

Osculate means to kiss. It also means to come into close contact or union; to touch, as two curves; to have characteristics in common, as two genera, two species, or two families.

EXAMPLES:

"Stop tinkering with that fan, Freddy Fixit, and come over here and **osculate** me," Rosie Receptive said, puckering her lips. "You can try getting that thing to **oscillate** later."

osculate See **oscillate / osculate.**

ought / should

Both these auxiliary verbs have a duty to perform in conveying a sense of obligation. In doing so they have become so interchangeable that for all practical purposes they are synonyms. Even so, discriminating speakers and writers know that each word has its own purpose, and so they try to use each auxiliary in separate context with other words, phrases, and sentences.

Ought is used to express duty or moral obligation, and has a sense of both desirability and necessity. It is always used as an auxiliary and usually is followed by a **to** infinitive to complete its meaning.

Should is used to express obligation, propriety, expediency, expectation, probability, or condition. It also is used to soften a direct statement or to express a request in a polite manner.

EXAMPLES:

Even Buck Wheat has enough sense to realize what makes a good marriage. That is why he knows he **ought** to eat—or, at the very least, **should** taste —the pancakes his perspiring and petulant wife says she "stood and sweated over a hot grill" to make for his breakfast.

over / above / more than

The war about the use of two of these three words is about over, for it has passed the height of its intensity. **Over** has taken **over** from **more than**. Even so, some grammarians still argue that **over** should be used only when referring to spatial relationships and not in colloquial reference to numbers. **More than**, some purists contend, are the proper words to use for such indication. But popular usage seems to have had its say and way, for the use of **over** and **more than** as prepositions has become a matter of individual preference rather than one of a hard-and-fast rule. As for **above**, it is beyond the fray and lives and moves and has its being mostly in the grammatical realm of the adverb. Some people, however, condescend to using it as a noun rather than confining its usage to the above.

EXAMPLES:

''The tide had risen **over** six feet **above** the high-water mark.'' Del Aware was reading aloud the essay he had written on what he had done last summer when Ms. Souri, the geography teacher, interrupted him. ''That's not proper English, Del,'' she said. ''You should say, 'The tide had risen **more than** six feet **above** the high water mark.' '' She turned to Ken Tucky, who was spaced out **over** a comic book, and asked. ''Would you agree, Ken, that **more than** is proper usage and **over** is not?'' ''**More than** or **over**? What's the difference? It's all **above** me!'' Tucky said with a chuckle as he flipped **over** a page.

overlay See **underlay / underlie.**

overlie See **underlay / underlie.**

overlook / oversee

These verbs, when ignored and undirected, can lead to confusion on the part of ill-informed users.

Overlook means to fail to notice, perceive, or consider; to miss; to excuse, pardon, ignore, or disregard indulgently, as someone's faults, misconduct, and the like. It also means to look over or at from a higher place, such as a wall or a balcony; to rise above or afford a view of.

Oversee means to direct, manage, or supervise, such as workers, students, or other people, or programs, projects, or other activities; to scrutinize; to examine or inspect; to survey; to watch.

EXAMPLES:

"I'll **overlook** your mistake this time," Christopher Cyclops said to Peter Prone, "but you can be sure I'll **oversee** your work with two eyes hereafter!"

oversee See **overlook / oversee.**

oversight / omission

Carefulness and carelessness are words that underscore the meaning and use of these nouns, for if care is not exercised, one can communicate the very opposite idea of what one intends to express.

Oversight has two opposite definitions. The first means failure to notice or consider; an inadvertent omission, error, or mistake; unintended neglect; an omission, error, or mistake due to carelessness. The second, which is not widely used, means watchful or responsible care or management; supervision.

Omission means the act of leaving out, not mentioning, not including; the state of being left out, not mentioned, not included; something neglected, left out, or left undone. An **omission** can be unintentional or deliberate, or it can be due to carelessness or to calculation.

EXAMPLES:

Lawrence Leftout handed the engraved card to his fiancée and asked, "I can understand the **oversight** of not including the date of our wedding in this announcement, but how do you explain the **omission** of my name?"

P

palate / palette / pallet

These nouns look and sound so much alike that they are easily confused. Attentiveness to their spellings and to their definitions enables one to keep each word separate in thought and in use according to taste, coloration, and movement, as the case may be.

The **palate** is the roof of the mouth, which consists of a bony front, the hard palate, backed by the fleshy soft palate, and separates the mouth from the nasal cavity. **Palate** also is the sense of taste, which can be physical, intellectual, or aesthetic.

A **palette** is a thin oval or rectangular board, with a hole for the thumb, that a painter holds and on which he or she mixes pigments. A **palette** is the set of colors put on the **palette** or board. It also is a particular range of quality or use of colors.

Pallet has three definitions whose meanings are apart. The first is that a **pallet** is a straw-filled tick or mattress; a small, hard temporary bed. The second is that a **pallet** is a wooden flat-bladed instrument; a lever or surface in a timepiece for converting reciprocating motion to rotary motion or vice versa. The third is that a **pallet** is a portable platform for storing, handling, or moving materials and packages, such as books in a warehouse.

EXAMPLES:

Percy Painter, a promising but penniless portraitist, might possibly profit were he to pick up, perhaps procure, (1) a plentiful patron with a **palate** for portraiture, (2) a **palette** with pigments properly primed, and (3) a pretty person pleasingly prepared to pose pleasantly on his paltry **pallet**.

palette See **palate / palette / pallet**.

pallet See **palate / palette / pallet**.

pardon / parole / probation

Legal words, such as these three, can be confused. Even though all are nouns and verbs, they are not interchangeable. Still one need not court trouble over their use. Just confine each word to its own special meaning. Then it can serve its proper purpose within phrases, clauses, or sentences.

A **pardon** is an action taken by an executive, such as a president or a governor, that forgives an offense or an offender and releases a person from further punishment. A general **pardon**, usually for political offenses, is called amnesty. The conviction, if it exists, is not removed from the record, nor are a person's civil rights restored because of a **pardon** in itself.

Parole is an action taken by a parole board, part of the executive branch of government, that releases a prisoner before his or her sentence has expired, on condition of good behavior. A **parole** can be revoked only by the board and is done so when the parolee violates the conditions of his or her **parole**.

Probation is an action taken by a judge that suspends the sentence of a person convicted, but not yet imprisoned, on condition of good behavior. It can be revoked only by the judge and is done so when he or she finds that the terms of **probation** have been violated.

EXAMPLES:

The governor would **pardon** his close friend, Clem Mency, who was convicted of perjury, were it not for the political firestorm that undoubtedly would follow such executive action. Whereas, the state parole board revoked Pete Placebettor's **parole** when it found he had been seen hanging around the racetrack and playing the horses. And Judge Justus Juvenilus suspended Sandy Snitchem's sentence and placed him on one year's **probation** with two conditions: (1) that he steal no more hubcaps and (2) that he obey his mother.

parole See **pardon / parole / probation**.

partially / partly

Confusion arises over the use of these adverbs because both mean in part, in some measure, not wholly. As a result, some people overuse **partially**, thinking it the more elegant word, and disdain **partly**, when in most cases the latter is the appropriate word to use.

Partially has a sense of incompleteness to it; unfinished; not total or general; imperfect; limited. It emphasizes the whole of which the action or condition is a part. In addition it means with prejudice or bias in favor of a person, group, or side; unjustly; unfairly.

Partly means in some part; to some extent; in some measure or degree; not wholly. It emphasizes the part of which the action or condition is a part.

EXAMPLES:

When Natalie Nimbus, the television weather person, forecasts **partially** clearing skies, not **partly** clearing ones, and says it is going to be **partly** cloudy, not **partially** cloudy, she shines in her ability not only to interpret weather fronts capably but also to speak English correctly.

partly See **partially / partly**.

peak / peep / peek

These tiny words, because they look and sound almost alike, would appear to be simple enough to use, yet they are not. Each has more than one definition, and each is at least two parts of speech. A close look at the differences in these four-letter words shows how each is a distinctive and individual one.

Peak is a noun, a verb, and an adjective. As a noun, it means a pointed or projecting part of a garment, such as a cap or hat; the bill or visor. It also is a promontory or the top of a hill or mountain ending in a point. It is the upper aftermost corner of a fore-and-aft sail. It is a point formed by the hair on the forehead or on the chin. And it means the highest level or degree. **Peak**, as a transitive verb, means to reach a maximum; to cause to come to a peak, point, head, or maximum. As an intransitive verb, it means to grow thin, pale, wan, or sickly; to dwindle away. As an adjective, **peak** means being at, or nearing, approaching, or reaching the maximum.

Peep is a noun and a verb, both of which have a variety of meanings. As a noun, **peep** means a feeble, shrill sound, such as that made by a bird or a baby. A **peep** is a slight utterance or complaint. It is a first glimpse or faint appearance; a brief look or glance, as well as a furtive look. And it is any of several small sandpipers, a North American bird. As a verb, **peep** means to utter a feeble, shrill sound as that of a bird or a baby; to utter the slightest sound. It also means to look at or peer through a small opening or crevice; to look furtively, cautiously, or slyly; to become visible or to begin to emerge from a place of concealment or hiding.

Peek, a noun and a verb, has the slightest of meanings and use of these tiny words. As a noun, **peek** means a furtive, slow, deliberate, brief look; a glance. As a verb, it means to take a brief look; to look furtively as from a place of concealment or hiding.

EXAMPLES:

The **peak** moment in Sylvia Scaler's ascent was when she was able to peer through the mist and see the mountain's **peak**. ''I guess this is where I **peak** in my climb,'' she thought as she touched the **peak** of her cap. Then, uttering an almost inaudible **peep** of delight, she tried one more time to **peep** at the mountain top, but the mist had closed in again. ''It was worth the one **peek**,'' she told reporters upon her descent, ''even if I had only one brief moment to **peek** at what I had climbed all that way to see. And no matter what anyone chooses to say, at least I rose to my **peak**, **peep**, and **peek**'s worth, didn't I?''

peculiar See **odd / peculiar / quaint / queer**.

pedal / peddle

These same-sounding verbs have to do with propulsion on the one hand and with promotion on the other. They should never be confused but are, thanks to the indifference some people pay to the differences in the meanings of words that make the English language rich in its variety of expression and rewarding to those who use it precisely. In the case of **pedal** and **peddle** it is a pedantic matter actually, for they stem from different roots.

Pedal is from the Latin *pedalis*, of the foot. It means to work a **pedal**, a foot-operated lever that is used to control certain mechanisms, such as powered vehicles, musical instruments, or bicycles.

Peddle is an unexplained derivation of *ped*, basket, from the Middle English *pedlere*. It means to travel about with goods and wares for sale; to be busy with trifles; to deal out, distribute, or dispense in small quantities; to hawk.

EXAMPLES:

Chief of Police Thornton Thuggrabber caught Hubie Hustler by the arm and growled: "**Pedal** your bike and **peddle** your stuff somewhere else, but not in this mall! It's off limits to wheeler dealers like you!"

peddle See **pedal / peddle**.

peek See **peak / peep / peek**.

peep See **peak / peep / peak**.

penetrate / permeate / pervade

To use these verbs precisely, since they appear to be somewhat similar, one needs to look straight in, through, and at their definitions to determine how narrow or widespread they are in their meanings.

Penetrate, a transitive and an intransitive verb, is derived indirectly from the Latin *penitus*, inward. In its transitive use, **penetrate** means to pierce or pass into or through; to diffuse; to gain entrance to; to enter or force a way into; to touch, affect, or impress deeply (the heart or mind); to arrive at, discover, or understand the truth, the inner meaning, or contents of. **Penetrate**, in its intransitive form, means to pierce, pass, extend, or diffuse into or through something; to understand or read the meaning of something; to have a profound effect or impact upon the senses and feelings.

Permeate is a transitive and an intransitive verb also. It comes from the Latin word *permeare*, to go, to pass. In its transitive form, it means to pass, diffuse, flow, or spread through or into every part of something; to saturate; to pass through the openings, pores, or interstices of. In its intransitive form, **permeate** means to become diffused; to spread throughout. It is used in a concrete sense, such as summer rains **permeate** dry soils.

Pervade is a transitive verb only. It stems from the Latin *pervadere*, to go through. It means to extend, pass, spread its presence, activities, influence throughout; to become diffused throughout every part. It is employed in an abstract sense, such as good feelings **pervade** the White House depending upon the president's mood.

EXAMPLES:

Mal Content, a calloused and cynical critic of our times, was heard to say recently: "The mass media are determined to **penetrate** the thinking and feelings of vulnerable audiences; to **permeate** these people's waking and sleeping hours with ceaseless images and messages; and, with the exception of anchorites, recluses, hermits, cave-dwellers, and other seclusionists or isolationists, to **pervade** the minds of every man, woman, and child in America with relentless dissemination of junk, waste, rubbish, and garbage. And they've barely done a tiddly tad to tidy up their act. Man, I'm turned off!"

percent / percentage / proportion

One's knowledge of arithmetic need be simple, not profound, for figuring out how to use these three words in expressing the relationships of numbers or things. What is required is the ability to define each word precisely, to determine when the word is singular or plural in its usage, and to add, subtract, multiply, and divide numbers accurately.

Percent is a noun. It means one one-hundreth part; one part in a hundred. Most dictionaries list its spelling as a single word, although for years it was spelled as two words, **per cent**, the second being the abbreviation of the Latin *centum*. As an adjective, **percent** means reckoned on the basis of a whole divided into one hundred parts; out of each hundred; paying interest at a specified percentage. Because **percent** is specific, it requires being used with numbers, preferably figures.

Percentage is a noun. It means a rate or proportion per hundred; a part of a whole expressed in hundredths; the result obtained by multiplying a number by a percent; a share of winnings, earnings, sales, profits, allowance, duty, commission, and the like. Because it means "a part of a whole," it must be used with a qualifying word. **Percentage** is used with numbers or figures depending upon whether it is specific or modified in general terms.

Proportion is a noun. It means comparative relationships between things or magnitudes as to size, quantity, number, degree, and so forth; a part considered in relation to the whole; proper relation between things or parts; relative size or extent; ratio; a proper or equal share.

When **percent**, **percentage**, and **proportion** stand alone, a singular verb is used.

- Thaddeus Tester said 65 **percent** was passing
- Thaddeus Tester said the **percentage** was high
- Thaddeus Tester said the **proportion** was large enough

When a singular word follows an **of** construction, a singular verb is used.

- Tess Teach said 98 **percent of** the class was present
- Tess Teach said the **percentage of** increase was high
- Tess Teach said the **proportion of** the work was small

And when a plural word follows an **of** construction, a plural verb is used.

- Tester and Teach agree that 98 **percent of** the students were present

- Tester and Teach agree that a tiny **percentage of** the students were absent
- Tester and Teach agree that a **proportion of** the grades were below normal

Note that when **the** precedes **percentage** or **proportion**, a singular verb is used, and when **a** precedes either word, a singular or plural verb is used, depending on the number of the noun in the **of** phrase that follows.

EXAMPLES:

"Your 30-**percent** pay increase," Walton Wantmore said to Elton Elated, "is way off. Such a **percentage** is much higher than that of our top employees. Besides, your **proportion** of the company's profits far exceeds mine. I'd best look into the matter right away! Hand me the phone and I'll call payroll!"

percentage See **percent / percentage / proportion**.

permeate See **penetrate / permeate / pervade**.

persecute See **prosecute / persecute**.

persuade See **convince / persuade**.

pervade See **penetrate / permeate / pervade**.

pessimist See **optimist / pessimist**.

phase See **faze / phase**.

plurality See **majority / plurality**.

podium See **lectern / podium / pulpit / rostrum**.

poor / pore / pour

These words, pronounced the same way, can be confused and be confusing. All are nouns, a coincidence that doesn't help in sorting them out. Even so, their similarity ends with that part of speech, for one is an adjective and the other two are verbs. Furthermore, they mean three different things.

Poor, as an adjective, means deficient or lacking in something; having little or no money, goods, or other means of support; lacking in skill, ability, or training; less than adequate; inferior in quality and value; meager; scanty. As a noun, it is used in the plural, as **the poor**, and is the term for the condition of people lacking the means to obtain the comforts of life.

Pore, as a noun, means a minute opening or orifice, as in the skin or a leaf, for perspiration, absorption, or the like. As a verb, **pore** means to meditate or ponder intently; to gaze earnestly or steadfastly; to read or study with steady attention or application.

Pour, as a noun, means the act of pouring; an abundant or continuous flow or stream; a heavy fall of rain. As a verb, **pour** means to cause to flow in a stream; to give full expression to; to dispense from a container; to supply or produce freely or copiously; to move with a continuous flow; to emit in rapid succession; to rain hard.

EXAMPLES:

Have you noticed how some students who get **poor** grades seldom **pore** over their books but still find time to **pour** beer or stronger stuff in themselves?

pore See **poor / pore / pour**.

possible See **practicable / practical / possible**.

pour See **poor / pore / pour**.

practicable / practical / possible

These adjectives, which have to do with what can or is capable of being done, can cause confusion if they are not used clearly in the situations to which they are applied. A close look at their definitions helps place their meanings in proper perspective and thus helps lead to their respectable use.

Practicable means feasible, capable of being done, effected, or put into practice with the means available; capable of being used. **Practicable** applies to that which can be done with the means at one's disposal and with the conditions as they are.

Practical means capable of being put to use or into practice; pertaining to or governed by actual use or experience or action, as contrasted with ideals and speculations. It applies to things and people, and implies proven success in meeting the demands made by actual living or use.

Possible means what may or can be, exist, happen, be done, be used; being something that may or may not occur; being something that may or may not be true. It indicates that something can exist, happen, be done, or be used or may occur or be true, given the proper conditions.

EXAMPLES:

"How **practicable** is your invention?" Professor Tinkerer was asked. "I'm a **practical** person," he responded. "I know what is **possible** and what is not. Just ask my students. When it come to exams, they know whose feet are on the ground and whose heads are in a cloud!"

practical See **practicable / practical / possible**.

practically / virtually

For all practical purposes, thanks to widespread popular use, these adverbs are virtual synonyms. A shade of difference in meaning exists between them that is worth noting and applying whenever they are spoken or written.

Practically is used when contrasts are being made. It means in practice; in effect; for practical purposes; in a practical manner. In informal usage, it means almost; nearly.

Virtually means for the most part; almost wholly or entirely; just about; as good as; in essence; in effect. In everyday usage, **virtually** has come, like **practically**, to mean almost or nearly.

EXAMPLES:

"We're **practically** out of pop," Stewart Slurps said as he took a can from the six pack. "In effect, you're right, ole buddy," Galen Guzzler rejoined, "but you should say **virtually**, 'cause one can's left. How about tossin' it to me?"

precede / proceed

These verbs need not be troublesome because of their closeness in spelling and pronunciation. Their prefixes are the key to their meaning and use, for one has to do with going before and the other with going ahead.

Precede, as a transitive verb, means to go before, as in order, place, rank, importance, or time; to introduce by something preliminary; preface. As an intransitive verb, it means to go or to come before.

Proceed is an intransitive verb only. It means to move or go forward or onward, especially after stopping; to carry on or to continue any action or process; to go in an orderly and regulated way; to go on to do something.

EXAMPLES:

"I would **precede** you into the water," Debbie Dipper announced to the other swimmers, "but my halter is slipping. Please **proceed** without me. That is, if you have a good grip on things!"

precipitate / precipitous

Confusion can and does rise over the use of these look-alike adjectives that stem from the same Latin word, *praecipitatus*, meaning headlong. Even so, they are not synonyms, for they fulfill separate functions. It might be said **precipitate** rushes into its job, while **precipitous** has a steep one.

Precipitate has retained the meaning of its root, headlong. It is applied to actions and means rushing headlong or rapidly onward; proceeding rapidly or with great haste; lack of due deliberation; acting with excessive haste or impulse; acting prematurely; rash; overhasty.

Precipitous usually, but not always, is applied to physical things. It means steep; extremely or impassably steep; perpendicular or overhanging in rise and fall; like a precipice; abrupt; sheer.

EXAMPLES:

As some students sadly have found, **precipitate** answering of questions on an examination can lead to a **precipitous** decline in one's grade.

precipitous See **precipitate / precipitous**.

presage / prophesy

These words have to do with what lies ahead. In the case of **presage**, there is a dire or dangerous outlook to things, while in **prophesy's** case things are foreseen as neither good nor bad. They are just predicted in a neutral way.

Presage is a noun and a verb. As a noun, it means a foreboding; an omen; an intuition, feeling, or indication of what is going to happen in the future; something that foreshadows or foretells future events; foresight; a warning.

As a transitive verb, **presage** means to forebode, portend, foretell, predict, foreshadow; to give an omen or warning of in advance. As an intransitive verb, it means to make or utter a prediction. Through usage, the words have taken on the meaning of the prediction of ill or evil events or foretelling portending dire things.

Prophesy is a verb. Its transitive form means to foretell or predict; to indicate before hand; to declare or foretell as if by divine inspiration; to reveal by divine inspiration; to predict with assurance or on the basis of mystic knowledge. In its intransitive form, it means to utter predictions. Note that prophe**c**y, a noun meaning a prediction, the inspired declaration of divine will or purpose, is spelled with a **c** and not with an **s**.

EXAMPLES:

''Oh, my!'' Claire Voyant exclaimed as she gazed at the young man seated across the table from her. ''I **presage** only dire days ahead in your romantic life.'' ''Thanks for the **presage**, ma'am, but you're wrong and so's your crystal ball,'' Lowe Thario quipped. ''In fact it's so cloudy, I **prophesy** that you'll start polishing it the moment I'm gone!''

prescribe / proscribe

These look-alike verbs often get confused when they should not. They mean two different things, for one accents the positive, the other the negative.

Prescribe has a positive tone to it. In its transitive form, it means to set or lay down a rule, guide, or course to be followed; to enjoin, appoint, or ordain; to order or recommend the use of something, such as a drug or treatment; to write or give medical precriptions. In its intransitive form, it means to lay down rules, laws, or directions; to direct; to dictate.

Proscribe has a negative aspect to it. A transitive verb only, it means to put outside the protection of the law; to outlaw; to banish or exile; to prohibit; to denounce, condemn, or forbid something as harmful, dangerous, or unlawful; to publish the name of a person outlawed; to announce the name of a person as condemned to death and his or her property to confiscation.

EXAMPLES:

When doctors **prescribe** drugs that have met with approved governmental standards, all goes well. In fact, many patients have been known to get well. But when governments **proscribe** drugs that have yet to be found to be safe and doctors would like to recommend their use, well, that is a medicinal matter of a nonprescriptive nature.

present / presently / now / forthwith

Time is of the essence in dealing with these four words, for three have to do with the moment and the other with the future.

Present, when used as an adjective, means at this time; here or at hand; existing or occurring now; now existing or in progress; being in a certain place; being in the place in question.

Presently is an adverb. Since the seventeenth century the word has meant in a little while; soon; without undue delay. Its original meaning was at the present time or now. A trend has developed in recent times to return to the word's original meaning, a practice that has led to confusion when it is so used since the word acquires double meaning. The way to handle this adverb and keep its meaning clear is to use it in the context of soon or in a little while. To indicate matters of the moment, use **at present**, **currently**, or the simple three-letter word **now**.

Now is an adverb. It means at the present time or moment; of or relating to the present time; without further delay; at the moment or time only just past; immediately; at once; in these present times.

Forthwith is an adverb. It means right now; at this moment; immediately; without delay; at once.

EXAMPLES:

"All **present** and accounted for, suh!" Sgt. Barton Barker called out, saluting his commanding officer. He turned smartly on his heel and faced his platoon. "At ease," he said in a growling voice. "**Presently**, youse recruits is gonna go on a twenty-mile hike. For **now**, ya gonna police this here area. If somethin' ain't nailed down, youse pick it up! That's it! Start picking! **Forthwith**!"

presently See **present / presently / now / forthwith**.

prestigious

Everything is described as **prestigious** these days: from the cars we drive, to the places where we dine, to the communities in which we live, to all sorts of awards and prizes that are given. This once honorable adjective has been so overworked and so freely used that it has become an ordinary, commonplace word and its meaning has been weakened. **Prestigious** means having a high reputation; honored; esteemed. But its value as a word has been so cheapened that when it is used randomly it no longer really characterizes something of unusual prominence or distinction. **Prestigious** deserves to be retired and used on the rarest of occasions to describe only those things that truly can be called "of high reputation; honored; esteemed."

presumptive / presumptuous

One may be tempted to jump to the conclusion that these two adjectives are synonyms because they look alike. Not so. Each is distinctive in meaning.

Presumptive, largely used in legal terminology, means affording grounds for presumption, the act of presuming or taking for granted; giving grounds or basis for reasonable opinion, belief, or acceptance; assuming something to be true based on presumption, probability, or inference.

Presumptuous has a derogatory sense to it in that it means behaving in a bold manner; acting without authority; overstepping due bounds; excessively forward or confident; taking liberties; forward; arrogant.

EXAMPLES:

Ivan of Craven, younger brother of the **presumptive** heir to the throne, covets the royal crown in a manner so blatant that in the days of powdered wigs and blade-wielding monarchs a **presumptuous** prince soon would have found himself separated from his place in court—and at a loss for his head.

presumptuous See **presumptive / presumptuous**.

pretense / pretext

The one thing these nouns have in common is that neither deals with what is on the up-and-up. Nonetheless, they are not synonyms and should not be so confused or be interchanged.

Pretense means pretending or feigning: make-believe; an act of pretending or alleging falsely; a false show of something; insincere or false profession.

Pretext means that which is put forward to hide or conceal a true purpose or object; a purpose or a motive alleged or an appearance that is assumed in order to cloak the real intention or state of affairs.

EXAMPLES:

Critics of E. Van Gelical believe that when he appears on television he makes a **pretense** about family values when actually his messages, they charge, are a **pretext** for eliciting dollars from his audiences.

pretext See **pretense / pretext**.

pretty / rather / very

These words are used to intensify or tone down statements. They appear more in informal than in formal speaking and writing. They have been abused to the point where their effectiveness as modifiers has been almost lost. Even so, each word has a rightful role to perform in communicating ideas and thoughts in understandable English once its part of speech is identified.

Pretty, as an adjective, means pleasing or attractive to the eye, in a feminine or childlike way, as by delicacy, gracefulness, and the like. It is used informally to mean considerable, fairly great, moderately large.

Rather is an adverb. It means with better reason or more propriety; more readily or willingly; to the contrary; instead; in some degree; somewhat.

Very, as an adjective, means precise; mere; sheer; utter; being exactly as stated; actual. As an adverb, it means to a high degree; extremely; truly.

EXAMPLES:

Had Irving Berlin been fond of adverbs, he could have written, "A **very pretty** girl is **rather** like a melody." Had he done so, the words would not have fit his music. And that would have been one heck of a note—or lyric—wouldn't it?

principal / principle

These words may sound alike, but that is all they have in common. The main thing about them is to keep their final syllables separate in one's head and to hold to whatever rules there are regarding their usage as parts of speech.

Principal is both a noun and an adjective. As a noun, it means a person who has controlling authority or is in a leading position; a chief or a head. In finance, it means a capital sum distinguished from interest or profit.

Principal, as an adjective, means first or highest in rank, importance, value; chief; foremost; most important, consequential, or influential; of the nature of or constituting principal or capital.

Principle, on the other hand, is a noun only. It means a comprehensive or fundamental law, doctrine, or assumption; an accepted or professed rule of action or conduct.

EXAMPLES:

The **principal** thing students first learn when their teachers send them to Harrison Hardrule's office is that the **principal** is a man of **principle** who knows that the **principle** of discipline comes before all else in education if everyone involved is to have a school worthy of the community's respect.

principle See **principal / principle**.

prison See **jail / prison**.

probation See **pardon / parole / probation**.

proceed See **precede / proceed**.

prodigal See **lavish / prodigal / profuse**.

profanity See **obscenity / profanity / vulgarity**.

profuse See **lavish / prodigal / profuse**.

prophesy See **presage / prophesy**.

proportion See **percent / percentage / proportion**.

prosecute / persecute

These verbs sometimes get confused in their use and should not. Other than that both words have two things in common—the same last syllable (**cute**) and a connotation of pursuit—they are not alike, for their definitions are quite different.

Prosecute means to seek to enforce or obtain by legal process; to institute legal proceedings against a person for redress or punishment of a crime or violation of law; to follow or pursue with a view to reaching or accomplishing something; to follow to the end; to pursue until finished. In its intransitive form, **prosecute** means to initiate and conduct legal proceedings or to carry on a legal suit or prosecution; to act as a prosecutor.

Persecute is transitive only. It means to pursue and to subject someone or something to persistent ill-treatment; to harass in a manner designed to injure, grieve, or afflict; to bother; to pester; to annoy persistently; to cause to suffer because of belief; to subject to constant hostility or cruel treatment, especially because of religious or political beliefs.

EXAMPLES:

"You **persecute** my tabby one more time, Tommy Tormentor," Kitty Katz shouted across her backyard fence, "and I'll call the police and have them **prosecute** you! Then we'll see whose hair it is that really flies!"

proscribe See **prescribe / proscribe**.

proved / proven

"The proof of the pudding is in the eating," Miguel de Cervantes Saavedra wrote in *Don Quixote*. The same can be said about these two words. Thanks to popular consumption, they have become interchangeable. Yet at one time they were regarded and strictly used as different parts of speech. Some people continue to make the distinction when the need for clarity so dictates.

Proved is the past participle of the verb **prove**. It stems from the Latin *probare* and means to test the truth or genuineness of; to test the worth or quality; to establish the existence, truth, or validity of; to show (oneself) to be worthy or capable.

Proven stems from the past participle of the Middle English verb *preve*. For the most part, it is used as an attributive adjective before nouns. It is widely used in legal terminology and is found in some literary works as a substitute for **proved**.

EXAMPLES:

"Ladies and gentlemen, Ferdinand Fabricator's own words and the testimony of several witnesses have **proved** that he is not telling the truth," Mordecai Mandamus, the state's attorney said, addressing the jury. "In fact, he is a **proven** liar and that is what the state has **proved**—or is it **proven**? Mm! Let me check my Gladstone to be sure I have used the correct legal word here."

proven See **proved / proven**.

provided / providing

These two words have the same meaning: on the condition that or with the understanding that. Both are conjunctions. Why, therefore, should there be any question about the provisions for their use? Are they not synonyms? Not all grammarians agree that **provided** and **providing** are subordinating conjunctions and may be so used to introduce a clause that contains a stipulation or a demand. Some purists insist that **providing** is a participle and, therefore, cannot serve such a syntactical function. Thanks to modern usage, most dictionaries list the words as conjunctions and as synonyms when used to mean "on condition that." One can use **provided** exclusively and still be on safe grammatical ground, and please the purists! Since both words imply a stipulation or condition of some kind, they are not a mere synonym for the more general word **if**. This conjunction merely indicates that the following clause contains a condition, not a stipulation or demand. A simple possibility can be stated, of course, by introducing it with **if**.

EXAMPLES:

"I'll move my car **provided** you move yours first!" yelled Grid Lock. "No way, turkey!" Ob Durate shouted back. "I'll move mine **providing** you move yours first!" They, their cars, and the traffic didn't budge. Now wouldn't you think there would be a provision in common law or in common courtesy or in the common tongue **if** that is all it takes to deal with such a stupid stalemate?

providing See **provided / providing**.

puerile See **juvenile / puerile / infantile**.

pulpit See **lectern / podium / pulpit / rostrum**.

pupil / student / scholar

The question about these three common nouns is not which one is the name for a person who learns the best. Rather, it is a way of indicating the level in education at which someone is a learner and the nature of the learning.

A **pupil** is a child in elementary school or a person under close supervision of a teacher, either because of his or her youth or because of specialization in some branch of study. A **pupil** also is a part of the eye.

A **student** is a person attending either high school or college, or one who devotes much attention to a particular subject.

A **scholar** once meant the same as **pupil**. Today a **scholar** is considered to be a person who has done advanced study in a special field or who is a learned person or who is a holder of a scholarship.

EXAMPLES:

What do a seventh-grade **pupil**, a college **student**, and a Rhodes **scholar** have in common? An education that can be measured in, with, or by degrees.

purposefully / purposely

Aimless speakers and writers probably would miss the target if they were asked why and how these two adverbs are not interchangeable. Not so for one whose purpose is to express ideas clearly and accurately. Suffixes (the endings of words) can make a difference in the meaning and pronunciation of similar-looking words. Such is the situation with this pair.

Purposefully has a sense of determination in its meaning, such as infused with purpose or having a definite goal in mind.

Purposely has a sense of intention in its meaning, such as by design, aim, or goal; not accidentally.

EXAMPLES:

While other reporters worked **purposefully** to meet the 10 P.M. deadline, Abe Amorist **purposely** missed it. He already had taken off for a late date.

purposely See **purposefully / purposely**.

puzzle See **enigma / puzzle / riddle**.

Q

quaint See **odd / quaint / queer**.

queenly See **kingly / queenly / regal / royal**.

queer See **odd / quaint / queer**.

quota / quotient

One need not be a whiz in mathematics to use these nouns correctly when speaking and writing them, even though the words relate to mathematical matters. One does need to know, however, the differences in their meanings, their Latin origins, and their roles having to do with numbers, for the words are not interchangeable and therefore not synonyms.

Quota, from the Latin *quota pars*, how great a part, means a proportional part or share, such as goods or items assigned to a group or to each member of a group; the number of people who may be admitted to or who may enter a nation, organization, or institution.

Quotient, from the Latin *quotiens*, how many times, means the number of times one quantity is contained in another; the quantity resulting from the division of one number by another.

EXAMPLES:

"Do you have a **quota** for passing grades, professor?" Gasper Grasper asked. "No, I don't," replied Samuel Savant. "I find that you students usually manage to establish a **quotient** of failures from within your own numbers."

quotation / quote

These two words are interchangeable nouns in casual communication, with **quote** serving as a diminutive of **quotation.** Otherwise, **quote** is confined in formal writing to its true part of speech, a verb.

Quotation is almost exclusively a noun. It means that which is cited, such as a passage from a book, article, speech, and the like; the statement of the current or marked price, bid, or offer of a commodity or security; the price, bid, or offer so stated. The word also serves as an adjective to describe a mark used in punctuation.

Quote, as a noun, is a colloquialism, an "inside word" used in journalistic writing that should be confined to that kind of communication. It means a quotation, a citing, of a person's or persons' words. A **quote** can be direct or indirect. A direct **quote** is used to state a speaker's actual words, whereas an indirect **quote** is used to paraphrase what a speaker says. **Quote**, as a verb, means several things: to cite; to copy or repeat a passage from; to reproduce the actual words of a speaker; to state a price, bid, or offer for.

EXAMPLES:

"Do you think you might use a **quotation** or two?" Val E. Dictory asked Benny Byline. "I might," the reporter responded. "If I **quote** from your commencement talk, I'll put **quotation** marks around anything I use. After all, I know what makes a good **quote**, kid, even if it's only that of a high school graduate!"

quotation marks

Increasingly these punctuation marks have fallen into misuse thanks largely to the ignorance and/or the "cuteness" of some communicators who place them around single words or phrases as if they were scattering chocolate bits on ice cream cones. To use **quotation marks** properly, one needs to learn and adhere to their rules, which are relatively few, although a bit (pardon the redundacy) complicated. Once the rules are learned, they should be applied uniformly and consistently. After all, the purpose of punctuation is to provide clarity for one's readers.

The function of **quotation marks** primarily is to indicate the beginning and end of a quotation of another person, text, or source, and repeated word for word. They are used also to set off the titles of short poems, lectures, talks, and speeches, and radio and television programs; to mark a word that is being used in an unusual way or colorful way; and to indicate a word or words that have not come into widespread use and are considered to be jargon.

Quotation marks come in pairs, double (" ") and single (' '). In American punctuation, the single pair is confined to one use: to indicate a quotation within a quotation (" '—' "). Double **quotation marks** are used to set off partial quotations, such as one or two or more words. Single **quotation marks** are used to set off one or two or more words only when the word or words are within the full matter that is being quoted.

American and British punctuation differs in the use of other punctuation marks with **quotation marks**. In American punctuation, the period and the comma are placed always within the end quotation mark: (." ,"). Not so in British punctuation, which requires the period to be placed within or outside the end quotation mark depending on whether the period marks the end of the sentence or the end of the quotation. The placement of question marks and exclamation points within or outside **quotation marks** depends on the meaning and on whether these punctuation marks are or are not part of the quoted material.

EXAMPLES:

"Did you know that Fred and Fern Familia saw the television program, 'Facts of Life,' and after that had four children of their own?" Sybil Smalltalk asked.

"Fred and Fern Familia saw the television program, 'Facts of Life,' and said, 'After that, we had four children of our own,' " Sybil Smalltalk remarked.

"A couple watched a television program about about the facts of life and after that had four children of their own!" Sybil Smalltalk exclaimed.

A couple watched "Facts of Life" on television and after that had four children of their own. Wow! That series must have been a real "zinger"!

quote See **quotation / quote**.

quotient See **quota / quotient**.

R

rack / wrack / wreck

These words can be troublesome, for they look and sound alike. Yet they are not totally interchangeable. They have distinctions in meanings and in parts of speech that call for individual, not blended or bended, use.

Rack is both a noun and a verb, and has a variety of meanings. As a noun, it means a framework of bars, wires, or pegs on which clothes, hats, books, bottles, or other items are placed, displayed, or hung; a frame or instrument for stretching; an instrument of torture on which the limbs of the body are stretched to the point of dislocating; a framework in which hay is placed; a cause of anguish or pain; acute suffering; a triangular frame used in the game of pool within which balls are arranged before play; a straight cogged bar or gear with a toothed wheel for producing linear motion from rotary motion or vice versa; a group of drifting clouds; the fast pace of a horse whose legs move in lateral pairs but not at the same time; the neck of pork, mutton, or veal. As a transitive verb, it means to stretch almost to the breaking point; to overstrain; to torture; to distress acutely; to torment; to strain in mental effort; to strain by physical force or violence; to place in a rack; in pool, followed by **up**, to place balls in a rack or to score points; to draw off wine, cider, or like liquids from the lees, sediment, or dregs of grapes, apples, or other fruits. As an intransitive verb, **rack** means to drive or move, as clouds, before the wind; to move, as horses, in a rack.

Wrack is also a noun and a verb. It has fewer meanings and is used less than **rack**, although, in part, the two words are interchangeable. As a noun, **wrack** also means seaweed or other marine vegetation thrown ashore by waves, such as kelp; wreck or wreckage; shipwreck; ruin or destruction; a remnant of something destroyed. As a transitive verb, **wrack** means to utterly ruin; to cause the ruin of; to **wreck.** As an intransitive verb, **wrack**, means to be wrecked. It also is a variant of **rack**.

Wreck, a noun and verb, is closer in meaning with **wrack** than with **rack**, inasmuch as both words have to do with ruin or destruction, whereas **rack** has to do with pain or suffering. As a noun, **wreck** means the remains of anything ruined or destroyed, such as a ship, plane, vehicle, structure, or building; desolation; dilapidation; a person in ruined health, in bad shape physically or mentally, or in a shattered, broken-down, or worn-out state. As a verb, **wreck** means to cause the ruin or destruction of; to bring ruin on or reduce to a state of ruin; to undermine; to upset completely; to tear down or dismantle; to demolish.

EXAMPLES:

Faced with the prospect of **rack** and ruin, Captain Keel Haul thought again of his ship, a **wrack** or **wreck** on the shoals. To **rack** his brains over how he had let it **wrack** or **wreck** would leave him a nervous **wreck**. So he hung his cap, and perhaps his thoughts, on a **rack** in the tavern's cloakroom and headed for the bar and a drink.

racket / racquet

It does not take a stroke of genius to see that these words, although they look alike, are spelled differently. And if one is on the ball, he or she would know that the first word has many different meanings and that the second word comes from the French.

Racket, as a noun, has a number of disparate meanings: a loud, clattering noise, usually of a disturbing and confusing nature; din; uproar; clamor; a social whirl, excitement, gaiety, or dissipation; the strain of exciting or trying experiences; a fraudulent scheme; an illegitimate business, activity, or enterprise, such as bootlegging or the extortion of money from legitimate business people by threat or violence; an easy and lucrative means of livelihood; a lightweight, oval-shaped bat with netting stretched across it that is used to strike a ball in tennis or a shuttlecock in badminton; a flat, oval paddle used to strike a ball in table tennis. As an intransitive verb, **racket** means to make a loud noise, din, or uproar, such as a racket; to engage in wild social life or activities.

Racquet comes from the French *raquette*. It is an acceptable variant of the noun, **racket**. When spelled **racquets**, it is singular and means a game played with rackets and a ball by two or four people on a four-walled court.

EXAMPLES:

Armand Le Bounce leaned on his **racquet** and shouted, "Your serve, *mon ami*?" Frankie Forecourt raised his **racket** and smashed the ball across the net. The game went well until a neighbor leaned out a bedroom window and yelled: "Hey, you guys! Cool that **racket**! Don't you know it isn't 6 A.M. yet?"

racquet See **racket / racquet.**

raise / rear / rise

Confusion over the use of these verbs stems from the upward connotation each word suggests. A careful look at their definitions shows that they are close but distinct in meaning and should be used accordingly.

Raise, a transitive verb, takes a direct object. Its principal parts are **raise**, **raised**, **raising**. It has many, many meanings, chief of which are: to move to a higher position; to elevate; to increase in height; to set upright by lifting or building; to help or cause to rise to a standing position; to awaken; to arouse; to care for and promote the growth of; to bring up.

Rear is both a transitive and intransitive verb. Its principal parts are **rear**, **reared**, **rearing**. In its transitive form, **rear** means to care for or attend to in the early stages of life; to bring up. In this meaning, **rear** and **raise** are acceptable for interchangeable use even though some people continue to use **raise** when referring to animals and plant life, and **rear** when referring to human beings. **Rear** also means to erect; to build; to lift upright. In its intransitive form, it means to rise on the hind legs, as a horse or other animal; to rise high in the air; to tower.

Rise, an intransitive verb, does not take a direct object. Its principal parts are **rise**, **rose**, **risen**, **rising**. It has numerous meanings: to get up from a lying, kneeling, or prone position, as from the ground, floor, bed, and the like; to move upward; to ascend; to increase in size, height, or volume; to increase in number, amount, or value; to extend above other objects.

EXAMPLES:

Some fathers are known to **rear** their offspring with the rule that they don't mind if their children **raise** the roof at home so long as when they are in public they **rise** to the occasion and do not embarrass their mothers.

rare / scarce

A casual look at these adjectives would suggest that they are synonyms. In some respects they are inasmuch as they have to do with matters that are in short supply. A close examination of their meanings shows, however, that the words are not totally interchangeable.

Rare means uncommon, few, and far between; seldom occurring; infrequently found; marked by unusual quality, merit, or appeal; superlative or extreme of its kind; of the highest excellence; extremely valuable; thin, not dense, as air or gases. **Rare** describes things that are infrequent at all times and that have superior qualities, such as precious stones or great men and women.

Scarce means not abundant; insufficient in supply, numbers, and quantities; insufficient to meet a demand or requirement; deficient; wanting. **Scarce** describes things that are insufficient in supply and implies a previous or usual condition of greater abundance, such as rain or food.

EXAMPLES:

A **rare** gem sometimes is **scarce** to come by.

rather See **pretty / rather / very.**

ravage / ravish

Because these words look alike and have to do with violence does not mean they are synonyms. They are not. The aggressiveness each verb connotes is entirely individual and notably different from the other.

Ravage means to devastate; to despoil; to lay waste; to do ruinous damage; to plunder, pillage, or sack; to work havoc.

Ravish means to seize and carry away by force or violence; to rape. It also means to enrapture; to fill or overcome with strong emotion, especially joy or delight.

EXAMPLES:

"**Ravage** my house," the maiden screamed at the raider, "but **ravish** me not!"

ravish See **ravage / ravish.**

real / really

These two words are good examples of how spoken and written English part company, one resorting to nonstandard or informal usage, the other adhering to standard, general, or formal expression. Competent communicators know the difference and speak and write accordingly. They also know that both words are greatly overused and oftentimes can be omitted from what is spoken or written without impairing clear, coherent communication.

Real primarily is an adjective. It means true; existing or occurring as fact; not fictitious or imaginary; genuine; not counterfeit, artificial, or imitation; not sham; actual. When **real** is used to modify or qualify a noun, it refers to facts rooted in nature, actual things with objective existence, rather than imaginary. Progressively, **real** has come into colloquial use as an adverb. In such usage, it means actually; very; indeed. It is not so used in formal or impersonal writing but is confined to spoken expression. As an adverb, **real** modifies adjectives and other adverbs but not verbs.

Really is an adverb only. It means very; truly; in fact; in reality; actually; in actual truth or fact; indeed; unquestionably; positively.

EXAMPLES:

Real champions know for themselves when they have played **really** or very well, and so they smile modestly and agreeably when others tell them that they have played, ugh, "real good."

really See **real / really.**

rear See **raise / rear / rise.**

rebuff / reject

These words, which relate in one way or another to hurt feelings, or to the causing of them, should not be passed over on the assumption that they are synonyms. Not so. Each has its own way of being pushy.

Rebuff is a noun and a verb. As a noun, it means a contemptuous, blunt, or abrupt refusal; a check or abrupt setback to action or progress; a repulse; a snub. As a verb, **rebuff** means to refuse bluntly, contemptuously; to beat back; to check; to snub; to repel; to drive away.

Reject is a noun and a verb. As a noun, it means a person or thing that is tossed aside or that is discarded as not meeting a required standard or as being imperfect. As a verb, **reject** means to refuse to accept, make use of, take, or recognize someone or something; to refuse to grant; to refuse to accept; to refuse affection to a person or persons; to throw away or discard as useless or unsatisfactory; to cast out or eject; to spit out or vomit.

EXAMPLES:

"I understand why you **rebuff** my kisses, "Al Liaceous said to Suzannah Sweetbreath, "but do not **reject** me. Your **rebuff** surely has to do with the garlic that I've eaten. Let it, not me, be the **reject** you disdain."

rebut / refute

When it comes to debate and argumentation, as well as courts of law, there is no question about these verbs. They are not synonyms. True, they score a lot of points when they are used inasmuch as both deal with contradiction. Proof of their nonalikeness, nonetheless, is to be found in their definitions that show **refute** to be a stronger and more decisive word than **rebut**.

Rebut means to reply in contradiction but not necessarily effective enough to prove wrong; to argue or oppose to the contrary; to contradict; to deny; to present opposing evidence or argument.

Refute means to disprove; to prove to be false, erroneous, or incorrect, such as an opinion, a charge, or a statement; to prove a person or a statement or charge to be in error.

EXAMPLES:

"You are welcome to **rebut** my arguments," Tess Timony said to Dee Fender, "but I challenge you to **refute** the evidence against your client that I, on behalf of the state, have presented in this courtroom!"

recalcitrant See **intractable / intransigent / recalcitrant.**

recall See **remember / recollect / recall.**

receipt / recipe

These nouns, which come from the same Latin root *recipere*, to receive or take, once were commonly substituted for the other. Not so in modern times. Each has taken on a particular meaning and thus gone its independent way.

A **receipt** is a written acknowledgement of receiving money, goods, or the like. It also means the act of receiving something.

A **recipe** is a set of instructions or directions with a list of ingredients for making or preparing something, such as food. It means a formula for doing or attaining something. And it means a medical prescription.

EXAMPLES:

"I am acknowledging **receipt** of your **recipe** for fig-mint cookies," Betsy Blender wrote Cynthia Cutter, "but with the kind of directions you sent me I'll need to sprinkle my imagination in with your ingredients to make certain my batches turn out right!"

recipe See **receipt / recipe.**

recollect See **remember / recollect / recall.**

refute See **rebut / refute.**

regardless / irregardless

Some people confuse these words as opposites and should not. **Irregardless** is a nonword. It is a superfluous and needless repetition of **regardless**, which is both an adjective and an adverb. As an adjective, it means heedless; careless; unmindful; without regard for. As an adverb, it means without concern as to advice, warning, hardship, and the like; without regard for; in spite of; despite; irrespective.

EXAMPLES:

Despite, contrary to, irrespective, and **regardless** of what some misusers of the English language say and write, **irregardless** is as real as a seven-dollar bill.

regal See **kingly / regal / royal.**

regretful / regrettable

A sense of sadness underlies these adjectives. It is expressed differently in keeping with each word's distinctive meaning.

Regretful means full of regret, sorrow, disappointment, remorse. Its use is applied to people only.

Regrettable means deserving or worthy of regret, sorrow, disappointment, remorse; causing, admitting of, or calling for regret. It is used to refer to a happening, condition, or situation.

EXAMPLES:

When one is truly **regretful**, a **regrettable** error is overlooked sometimes.

regrettable See **regretful / regrettable.**

reign / rein

As all of us have learned, not all words in the English language that are pronounced alike are synonyms. Their meanings, as a general rule, often are very different. Such is the case with this pair of identical-sounding words.

Reign is a noun and a verb. As a noun, it means the exercise of possession of supreme or sovereign power, such as royal power; dominance or widespread influence; sovereignty; dominion; rule; sway; kingdom. As a verb, **reign** means to hold, exercise, or possess supreme or sovereign power; to hold royal office; to be a monarch; to be predominant; to prevail; to hold sway.

Rein is also a noun and a verb. As a noun, usually in the plural, it means a long, narrow leather strap used by a rider or driver to control a horse or other animal; any means for restraining, checking, curbing, or governing. As a verb, **rein** means to halt, check, hold back, restrain, curb, guide, or govern.

EXAMPLES:

Known as "The **Reign** of the Rain," the multitudinous months of moisture did not dampen the dry humor of King Ribaldo, for even though he could not **rein** the rain, he was able to **reign** with relaxed **rein** much to the merriment of his oftentimes soaked, saturated, and satisfied subjects.

rein See **reign / rein.**

reject See **rebuff / reject.**

reluctant / reticent

"He who hesitates is lost," goes the old saying. Such could be the case with these two adjectives if one is not careful in using them. Confusion need not arise over their possible interchanging, once their origins and meanings are learned. In fact, the second word has a sense almost of being speechless.

Reluctant comes from the Latin *reluctans*, to struggle against. It means unwilling; averse; marked by unwillingness; disinclined to yield to some requirement; hesitant; indisposed; loath; struggling; resisting.

Reticent stems from the Latin *reticens*, to be silent. It means disposed to keep silent; not given to speaking freely; uncommunicative; quiet, reserved in manner, appearance, style, and the like.

EXAMPLES:

Reticent romanticists sometimes are **reluctant** to express their feelings openly, out loud, or in public.

remainder See **balance / remainder.**

remember / recollect / recall

These three verbs, in varying degrees, have to do with memory. Yet each has its own individual meaning that should not be lost to mind. In fact, each word has its own definition that distinguishes it from the others and that calls for its distinctive and individual use.

Remember means to bring back or call again to mind, thought, or memory; to keep in mind carefully, as for a purpose; to bear in mind, with affection, awe, or the like; to bear in mind as worthy of reward, gift, or the like; not to forget. The word denotes what is effortless or spontaneous.

Recollect means to call or call back to mind; to remember, especially by effort; to succeed in remembering. It implies that the act of recollecting requires considerable effort.

Recall, the middle word of the trio, means to call back, summon, command, or order to return; to call back in awareness or attention; to cancel; to take back or revoke; to serve as a reminder; to call back to mind. The word implies an effort but not a great one.

EXAMPLES:

"Would you please **recall** for the jury the events of the night of July 13?" Quenton Quibble, the prosecutor, asked. "I don't **remember** them," Sylvester Skipover responded. "I suggest you **recollect** them promptly," Judge Maggie Straight interjected, "or I may be obliged to hold you in contempt of court!"

repel / repulse

Some dictionaries list these verbs as synonyms. A careful examination of their meanings shows that the words are not exactly alike. They should be used, therefore, with their individual definitions in mind and not be forced back or driven off because of indifference or indolence.

Repel means to force or drive back; to ward off; to hold off; to keep away; to reject; to refuse, as a suggestion or an idea; to turn away from; to spurn. It also means to cause to feel distaste or aversion.

Repulse, the stronger of the two words, means to drive back, as an attacking force; to drive off; to reject or turn away with denial, rudeness, discourtesy, or the like; to rebuff. It does not have a connotation of distaste or aversion.

EXAMPLES:

"Dear John: You say you don't understand why I **repulse** your advances. Would you prefer that I **repel** them and thus reveal my true feelings toward you? Sincerely yours, Mary."

replace See **substitute / replace.**

repulse See **repel / repulse.**

reputation See **character / reputation.**

restive / restless

Popular usage, along with some dictionary listings, has led to the belief that these adjectives are synonyms. Careful users of the two words know they are not and, therefore, have not laid to rest the precise differences in the words' meanings. To the contrary, they express both words distinctively in their spoken and written communication.

Restive means stubbornly resisting control; balky; marked by restlessness; impatient of control; unruly; fidgety; nervous or impatient under pressure or restraint; unsettled; contrary; obstinate; as if ready to break from control.

Restless means having no rest; without quiet, repose, or rest; never still or motionless; unable or disinclined to rest; sleeplessness; obtaining no rest or sleep; constantly seeking change; unceasingly active; unquiet or uneasy as a person, the heart, the mind, or the like; discontented; impatient.

EXAMPLES:

Restive in his attitude toward women and their relentless desire to marry him, Al Legro, nonetheless, was **restless** in his pursuit of them.

restless See **restive / restless.**

reticent See **reluctant / reticent.**

reversal / reversion

These nouns should not be turned about in their meanings, as some inept communicators do in their zealousness to make the words synonyms. Each has a distinctive definition that calls for its individual expression and use.

Reversal means an act or instance of turning backward or reversing in position, direction, or order; the state of being turned back or reversed; a change in fortune, usually for the worse. In law, the word means annulment, setting aside, change, or revocation, as of a lower court's decision.

Reversion means a return to some form or condition; opposite direction; the act of reversion; a reverting; a throwback. In biology, the word means a return to a former or primitive type; atavism. In law, reversion means the right of succession, future possession, or enjoyment; the return of an estate to the grantor or his or her estate after the grant has expired.

EXAMPLES:

"Cheer up, Lowbucks!" Benton Brokeridge said to his change-counting client. "A **reversal** of twenty points in the stock market doesn't mean a **reversion** to the poverty level, not for an old skinflint like you!"

reversion See **reversal / reversion.**

riddle See **enigma / puzzle / riddle.**

right See **wright / write / right.**

rise See **raise / rear / rise.**

robbery See **burglary / larceny / robbery / thievery.**

role / roll

The similar pronunciation of these two words 'rōl leads to their confused use. Yet they are different in other ways. The first word has only one part of speech to perform, that of a noun, with limited meaning. The second word is more expansive in that it is a noun and a verb, and has many meanings.

Role comes from the French *rôle*. It means a character assigned or assumed; a socially expected behavior pattern; a part played by an actor or singer; a function or position.

Roll, as a noun, means anything rolled up in a cylindrical or spiral form. A **roll** can be a list of names, a roster; a strip of material wound on a core; any food rolled up in its preparation; a rapid succession of light blows or taps on a drum; the motion of a vessal or craft on water or land, or in the air, and so on. As a verb, **roll** means to cause to drive or move forward or backward; to rotate; to press, flatten, or spead out, thin, or smooth with a roller; to beat rapidly on a drum; to rumble; to trill; to peal; to pour in waves; to cause a swaying motion; and so on.

EXAMPLES:

Brill Yant downed a **roll** for breakfast, paused to **roll** on his drum, went to school, saw his name on the honor **roll**, attended classes, and practiced the lead **role** in the senior play. Now there's one kid, you could say, who's on some kind of a **roll**!

roll See **role / roll.**

root / rout / route

This trio is troublesome, because the words can be pronounced ′rüt or ′rüt depending upon where in the United States they are spoken. As a result, confusion can arise over their spellings and hence which word is intended. As long as regional differences continue over how the words are pronounced, care should be taken with their spellings and meanings to assure their correct use.

Root is a noun and a verb. As a noun, it means the underground part of a plant or a tree; the source, cause, basis, foundation, or occasion of anything; an essential or basic part; the embedded part of an organ or structure, such as a hair, tooth, nail, nerve, or the like; any base of support; a primary source or origin; an antecedent; an ancestor. As a verb, **root** is both transitive and intransitive. In its transitive form, **root** means to furnish with or enable to develop roots; to fix or implant by or as if by roots; to grow roots or to take root; to have an origin or base. It also means to turn over, dig up, or discover and bring to light. In its intransitive form, **root** means to turn up or dig the earth or other matter with the snout; to grub; to police about; to noisily applaud or encourage a contestant or team.

Rout also is a noun and a verb. As a noun, it means a state of wild confusion or disorderly retreat, a disastrous defeat; a debacle; a precipitate flight.

Rout is a transitive and an intransitive verb. In its transitive form, it means to disorganize completely; to demoralize; to put to precipitate flight; to drive out; to defeat decisively or disastrously; to dispel. In its intransitive form, **rout** means to grub with the snout; to search haphazardly.

Route is the simplest of the three words. It, too, is a noun and a verb, but its meanings are limited. As a noun, it means a traveled way; a highway; a means of access; a channel; a line of travel; an assigned territory to be systematically covered, as by a sales or delivery person. As a verb, **route** is transitive only. It means to direct, send, dispatch, commission, forward, or transport by a specified way; to fix the order or sequence of procedures or steps to be followed.

EXAMPLES:

"The **root** of my concern," said Warren Worrisome to Ernest Expediter, "is that the **route** you present passes too near the scene of the **rout**. I'd gladly **root** for the victors if you'd **route** me anew so I can **rout** my fears."

rostrum See **lectern / podium / pulpit / rostrum.**

rout See **root / rout / route.**

route See **root / route.**

royal See **kingly / regal / royal.**

S

scarce See **rare / scarce**.

scarcely See **barely / hardly / scarcely**.

scholar See **pupil / student / scholar**.

seasonable / seasonal

These look-alike adjectives require a sense of time and a knowledge of their individual meanings in order for them to be used correctly. One could say it is a matter of choosing or seasoning one's words carefully.

Seasonable stresses appropriateness to season. It means suitable or usual to the time of year or to the season of circumstances; coming, occurring, or done at the right time or in good and proper time; opportune; timely.

Seasonal applies mainly to what depends on, and is controlled by, seasons or a particular time of year. It means of, relating, or varying in happening or occurrence according to the season or time of year; characteristic of the season, seasons, or time of year.

EXAMPLES:

Thanks to domed stadiums, baseball, which once was strictly a **seasonable** sport, no longer is totally governed by **seasonal** conditions in the areas in which it is played, a turn of circumstances that gives meteorologists peace of mind and fans something to cheer about even when their teams are losing.

seasonal See **seasonable / seasonal**.

semi See **bi / semi**.

senate See **collective nouns**.

sensual / sensuous

One might sense, and correctly, that these adjectives have to do with the senses. To make sense of them and to use them correctly, one needs to choose between what is considered coarse and what is regarded as refined.

Sensual has a coarse connotation. It has to do with bodily, sexual, and physical pleasures and gratification of the senses. It means lewd, full of lust, lascivious, licentious. It suggests indulgence in the senses of physical appetites as ends in themselves.

Sensuous has a refined and intellectual connotation. It has to do with the physical senses, but it also has to do with what is readily susceptible through the senses that is pleasing to the eye, ear, touch, and so forth. It implies gratification of the senses for the sake of aesthetic pleasure.

EXAMPLES:

Some artists pursue **sensual** models; others paint **sensuous** masterpieces.

sensuous See **sensual / sensuous**.

separate

This popularly mispronounced and, therefore, misspelled word is a verb and an adjective. Its equality of vowels governs its proper pronunciation and spelling. It has two **e**'s and two **a**'s, not three **e**'s and one **a**. And it has a **par** and not a **per** sound in it when pronounced properly and perfectly. As a verb, it means to set or keep apart. As an adjective, it means set or kept apart; detached; individual.

EXAMPLES:

Golfers sometimes **separate** themselves from the other players and hold **separate** consultations with their caddies to determine how they managed to miss what everyone thought was an easy piddley putt for **par**.

set / sit

Use of these verbs can be confusing and unsettling if one does not know which one of them takes an object and which does not, and how each verb is used sometimes in the opposite form to its customary one.

Set, for the most part, is a transitive verb. Its action goes to an object. The word has numerous meanings, some of which are: to place in or on a seat; to cause to sit; to put; to place; to make ready, as a trap or snare, to catch prey; to put aside; to appoint or assign; to fix. **Set** is an intransitive verb when it is used in such constructions as: "The sun and moon **set**. "Hens **set**." "People's manners **set** well."

Sit, for the most part, is an intransitive verb. It does not have an object, because it has no action. It, too, has many meanings, some of which are: to rest upon the buttocks or haunches; to perch; to roost; to occupy a place as a member of an official body; to hold a session; to cover eggs for hatching; to serve as a model for an artist; to remain inactive or quiescent. **Sit** is used as a transitive verb in such constructions as: ''Hens **sit** on eggs.'' ''Riders **sit** on horses or bicycles.'' ''Cars **sit** two or more people.''

EXAMPLES:

''I'll **set** the hen on the table,'' the giant said to his wife, ''and let her **sit** until the sun and moon have **set** twice. If she doesn't lay a golden egg and **sit** on it by then, we'll forget all about this fairy tale!''

sewage / sewerage

These words have to do with waste materials and their means of disposal. Some dictionaries list them as synonyms, indicating apparently that popular usage has made them inseparable. Caring communicators know that the words have precise meanings, and so they do not substitute or waste one for the other. Rather, they make productive use of such knowledge and speak and write each word accurately.

Sewage is both a noun and an adjective. As a noun, it means the waste materials that are passed through or carried off by sewers or drains. As an adjective, it means to describe such a process: **sewage** system.

Sewerage, a noun only, means a system of sewers by or through which waste materials are passed or carried off. The word **sewerage** is falling off, wasting away, in disuse and is being replaced by **sewage** even though the words clearly do not mean the same thing.

EXAMPLES:

"Have you noticed how the **sewage** has improved since the city installed new **sewerage**?" Var Mint, the sewer rat, asked Roe Dent, his subterranean mate, as they merrily munched away on a morsel or two.

sewerage See **sewage / sewerage**.

shall / will

Where there is a **will** there is a way, especially among Americans. Such has become the case with these verbs that refer to the future. The rule once was, and still is in British usage, that **shall** should be used in the first person and **will** in the second and third persons: "I or we **shall** go; you, he, she, or they **will** go." To state determination or emphasis, the words should be reversed: "I or we **will** go; you, he, she, or they **shall** go." Such distinction seldom is observed in American usage. In most instances, **will** is used in declarative sentences. As for **shall**, the distinction has been retained in rhetorical questions, and in contracts and other legal documents.

EXAMPLES:

"**Shall** we dance?" Willard Waltzer asked with a gallant bow. "We **will**," Rita Rhumba replied with a grimace, "once you get your big foot off my toe!"

ship See **boat / ship**.

shortfall See **windfall / shortfall**.

should See **ought / should** and **should / would**.

should / would

These verbs, the past tense for **shall** and **will**, have varied uses and are governed less by strict rules than in the past. Most people do what comes naturally in using either word and no longer make a distinction between the first person and the second and third persons. **Should**, for the most part, is used for all persons when condition or obligation is being expressed: "I, you, he, she, or they **should** go." **Would** is used for all persons to state a wish or a customary action. "**Would** that I, you, he, she, or they had gone."

EXAMPLES:

"**Should** we dance?" Rita Rumba asked rosily. "We **would**," Willard Waltzer responded wistfully, "if I could remember which foot to put forward first!"

sight / site / cite

Although these words are pronounced alike, ′sīt, and get confused, they have to do with separate things: vision, place, and communication, respectively.

Sight, as a noun, means something that is seen. It also means the process of seeing. As a verb, it means to catch sight of or to view an object.

Site, as a noun, means the place, location, scene, or point of something. As a verb, it means to place on a site or in position.

Cite is a verb only. It means to summon, call upon, or refer to; to bring forward or to call attention to.

EXAMPLES:

When Wilber Wanderabout caught **sight** of the police, he fled the construction **site** before they could **sight** and seize him, and **cite** him for vagrancy.

sit See **set / sit**.

site See **sight / site / cite**.

skeptic See **cynic / skeptic**.

slander See **libel / slander**.

slothful See **idle / indolent / lazy / slothful**.

small See **little / small**.

so / however / therefore

These words, which are called conjunctive adverbs, call for the use of particular punctuation, when written, to mark their syntactical function of connecting independent clauses. Unlike **and**, **but**, and **for**, which are pure conjunctions, these words require stronger punctuation than a comma for joining clauses. One should use either a semicolon or a period, or the word **and**. The same requirements apply to other conjunctive adverbs, such as **moreover**, **accordingly**, **consequently**, and **furthermore**.

EXAMPLES:

- Sandra Stylish liked the sweater; **so** she bought it
- Sandra Stylish liked the sweater. **So** she bought it
- Sandra Stylish liked the sweater, and **so** she bought it
- Sandra Stylish liked the sweater; **therefore**, she bought it
- Sandra Stylish liked the sweater. **Therefore**, she bought it
- Sandra Stylish liked the sweater, and, **therefore**, she bought it
- Sandra Stylish liked the sweater; **however**, she had no money
- Sandra Stylish liked the sweater. She had no money, **however**

Some further words about **so**: It is not an appropriate substitute for **very** in a construction such as "Graham Goodhealth felt **very** well." And when **so** is used to express purpose or result, it is followed by **that** as in a construction such as "Reginald Rigorous lifts weights **so that** his body will remain firm."

solid / stolid

These words get confused sometimes when they should not. One has to do with dimensions and substance. The other does not. One has many meanings. The other has only one. One functions as more than one part of speech. The other is one part of speech only.

Solid is both a noun and an adjective. As a noun, it means a geometrical figure, such as a cube or a sphere, having three dimensions; a substance that is neither liquid nor gaseous. As an adjective, **solid** means having three dimensions, without an interior cavity; not hollow; of definite shape and volume; not liquid or gaseous; without gaps or breaks; well-made; of good quality or substance; substantial; complete; sound; reliable; dependable; strong; concrete.

Stolid is an adjective only. It comes from the Latin *stolidus*, immovable, dull, stupid. It means not easily moved or stirred mentally; dull; stupid; having or expressing little or no feeling or emotion, sensitivity, sensibility, or perception; unexcitable; unemotional; impassive.

EXAMPLES:

Moe T. Vator pointed to the **solid** in the form of a cube on the blackboard, hoping that for just once one of the **stolid** students in front of him would have a **solid** answer to his oft-asked question, "What is this I have drawn?"

some See **all / any / most / some**.

sort of See **kind of / sort of**.

specie / species

A specious glance at these collective nouns would have one believe that the second is the plural of the first. Not so. The first has no plural. In fact, it has a single meaning that was coined exclusively for it.

Specie is singular only. It has one simple meaning: money in coin, as distinguished from paper money.

Species is singular and plural. It means a distinct kind, sort, or variety; a class or group of individuals or objects agreeing in some common attribute or attributes and designated by a common name. In biology, **species** means a scientific category of animal or plant.

EXAMPLES:

"Sorry," Garson Greenback said to Nathan Nickles. "I refuse to accept **specie** in payment for something that is worth more than a dollar. I'm a **species** of businessman who likes having folding money in his wallet and not change in his pocket."

species See **specie / species**.

stanch / staunch

One should not have to stop, even pause perhaps, to consider whether these words are interchangeable or not. For the most part, they are. Through the years they have been steadfastly used one for the other even though they stem from different roots and have different meanings.

Stanch generally is used in its verb form, which comes from the Latin *stanticare*, to stop or stand. As a verb, it means to check or stop the flowing of; to stop the flow of blood or other liquid. As an adjective, it is a variant of **staunch**.

Staunch generally is used in its adjective form, which comes from the French *estranche*, firm or strong. As an adjective, it means dependable; constant; steadfast; loyal; faithful; true; substantial; strongly built; stout. As a verb, it is a variant of **stanch**.

EXAMPLES:

It is a **staunch** friend who will **stanch** a buddy's wound, just as it is a **stanch** buddy who will **staunch** a friend's wound.

stationary / stationery

These words can be troublesome. They are pronounced alike but are spelled slightly differently, are two different parts of speech, and have different meanings. Yet when each word is spelled and defined correctly, and its part of speech identified, its proper use, so to speak, spews from the lips or flows from the fingertips in unchanging, clear communication.

Stationary is a noun, meaning one who or that which is not moving; fixed; unchanging. As an adjective, it means not moving or movable; fixed; still; unchanging in condition, position, or value.

Stationery is a noun. It means writing paper and envelopes; materials used in writing, such as notebooks, pens, pencils, and the like. It also is used as an adjective to describe a store that sells such materials: **stationery** store.

EXAMPLES:

One thing is on the level: **Stationary** surfaces can serve evenly whether you write on the finest **stationery** or you scribble on the poorest scratch paper.

stationery See **stationary / stationery**.

staunch See **stanch / staunch**.

stolid See **solid / stolid**.

straight / strait

Misuse of homophones—words that are pronounced alike but have different meanings and spellings—can be avoided if one is aware of and attentive to their differences. Such is the case with this pair.

Most dictionaries show **straight** and **strait** as variants. In time the words undoubtedly will be commonly interchanged as their users discriminate no longer between them when writing them. So may be the case, and the English language will have lost a bit more of its preciseness. Yet the words, as their definitions indicate, have distinctive meanings that provide a reason and a basis for spelling and writing each one separately and in its own right.

Straight generally is used as an adjective, meaning without a bend, angle, curve, or irregularity; direct; unswerving; uninterrupted; consecutive; frank; candid; honest; not evasive; marked by no exceptions or deviations; unmixed; regular; conventional. It also is a noun and means the condition of being **straight**. And, as an adverb, it means in a direct or frank manner.

Strait, as a noun, is the singular of **straits**, and is used in either number. It means a narrow passage of water connecting two large bodies of water; a situation, a state of affairs, or position of difficulty, distress, perplexity, or need. It also is an adjective that some people regard as being archaic. It means narrow; limited in space or time; constricted in area; tight; affording little room; closely fitting; strict, rigid, or righteous, such as in principles or requirements.

EXAMPLES:

"I want a **straight** answer to this question. So give it to me **straight**," the **strait**laced woman said to the man in the **strait**jacket seated in the deck chair next to her as their cruise ship passed through the **strait** or **straits**. "Is it proper for me to conclude that you are in **strait**ened circumstances because you have failed to walk a **straight** and narrow path in life?"

strait See **straight / strait**.

strategy See **tactics / strategy**.

strided / strode

One needs to watch one's step with these words. They appear to be synonyms and the past tense of the verb **stride,** meaning to walk or move with long steps, especially in a hasty, vigorous, impatient, or arrogant way; to take a long step. The words are not interchangeable, although **strided** is used in ignorance in some parts of the United States ostensibly as a colloquialism.

Strided is a nonword. It is not the past tense of **stride**.

Strode is the correct past tense of **stride**, whose principal parts are **stride**, **strode**, **stridden**.

EXAMPLES:

Most human beings and some animals can **stride**, they can have **strode**, and they can have **stridden**, but when it comes to **strided** it is something good English usage says two- or four-legged creatures cannot have done.

strode See **strided / strode**.

student See **pupil / student / scholar**.

subjunctive mood

This verb form progressively is disappearing from the spoken and written English used by many educated and literate speakers and writers. Even so, the need continues for it to be used for stating conditions contrary to fact and expressions of doubt, possibility, request, command, recommendation, wish, regret, and the like. The indicative mood, on the other hand, is used to express a contingency or hypothesis unless there is little likelihood the continuency might come true. In which case, the **subjunctive** is used.

EXAMPLES:

''If I **were** your wife, sir,'' the shrew sneered, ''I **would** shoot you!'' ''And if I **were** your husband,'' the rogue retorted, ''I **would** hand you the gun!'' ''**Were** I to shoot you, what **would** you do?'' she asked. ''I **would** roll over and play dead,'' he said. ''**Could** you forgive me **were** I to say I was sorry for all that I **had** spoken?'' ''Yes,'' he replied, ''**were** it to be the last thing you say to me!''

subpoena See **warrant / summons / subpoena**.

substitute / replace

These verbs cannot do the work of the other. Each calls for the idiomatic use of a different preposition in fulfilling its function. Thus the words are not interchangeable as their definitions clearly indicate.

Substitute is followed by the preposition **for** and means to put or use in the place or position of another person, construction, or thing; to exchange.

Replace is followed by the prepositions **by** or **with** and means to take or fill the place or position of another person, construction, or thing; to put back in a former position or place; to succeed; to restore; to return.

EXAMPLES:

"I want you to go in and **substitute** for Danny Dropsem at wide receiver," Coach Sherman Scrimmager said, patting Randy Resin on the back. "We need to **replace** him with someone with sticky fingers who can catch a pass for a change. So get a good grip on yourself and the ball when it's thrown to you!"

successfully / successively

Keeping these adverbs separate in thought and in use calls for making a distinction in how matters are accomplished.

Successfully means in a manner desired or favored as to outcome, such as favorable or prosperous conclusion of attempts or endeavors.

Successively means in a manner following in order; in a manner following each other without interruption.

EXAMPLES:

Dee Cathlon **successfully** won the track and field events **successively** one after another. Then she rested on her laurels and on the infield grass when she was done.

successively See **successfully / successively**.

suit / suite

These nouns get confused sometimes because some people are set in their ways and others are not. Both words come from the French word, *suivre*, to follow, but are pronounced differently and have widely different meanings. Even so, **suit** is used for **suite** in spoken and written advertising messages and in the furniture trade, much to the dire dismay of those people who believe in absolute purity of language. Yet one need not get upset over or annoyed at the seeming misuse of these two words. In most instances, one can speak and write **set** for **suit** or **suite**. Such a simple substitution ends any dilemma over which of the two words to use, dispels any confusion over what is intended or meant to be said, and enables purists to live one more day, at least, in peace.

Suit, pronounced ′süt, has numerous meanings, some of which are: a set of clothes of the same color and fabric; an outfit of armor worn by a warrior; a complete group of sails on a boat or ship; one of four sets of playing cards; the act, process, or an instance of suing in a court of law; the wooing and courting of a woman; the act of petitioning an authority.

Suite, pronounced ′swēt, means a number of things forming a series or set; a connecting series of offices, rooms, or apartments that are used together; a set of furniture, especially a set making up the basic furniture necessary for one room, such as a bedroom **suite**; a train or retinue of followers or attendants; a modern instrumental piece of music in several movements of different character, such as Ferde Grofé's "Grand Canyon **Suite**."

EXAMPLES:

One can have a **suit** or **set** of clothes, and one can have a **suite** or **set** of furniture, but one cannot have a **suit** or **suite** of dishes, only a **set** of them.

suite See **suit / suite**.

summons See **warrant / summons / subpoena**.

superlatives See **adjectives**.

supersede / surpass

These verbs have separate roots and different meanings, and should not be confused nor interchanged even though, in a sense, they have to do with one thing coming after another.

Supersede comes from the Latin *supersedere*, to sit. It means to set aside; to replace by another person or thing; to force out of use as inferior; to take the place, room, or position of; to supplant. Its correct spelling is with two **s**'s, **supersede**. Some dictionaries list supercede, with a **c** as a variant, on the illogical grounds that its constant misspelling has made it acceptable, a myth that merits dispelling.

Surpass comes from the French *surpasser*, to pass. It means to go beyond; to outstrip; to outdo; to exceed; to go beyond in amount, extent, or degree; to transcend; to go beyond the limit, powers, or extent of; to become better, greater, or stronger than; to go beyond in excellence or achievement; to excel.

EXAMPLES:

"You may **supersede** me in the chow line," the private said to the sergeant, "but when it comes to having an appetite you'll never **surpass** mine!"

suppose See **guess / suppose / surmise**.

surmise See **guess / suppose / surmise**.

surpass See **supersede / surpass**.

T

tactics / strategy

These nouns, for the most part, are associated with and used in military matters, although they do have their applications in civilian affairs as well. They are not synonyms by any means, for the difference in their meanings is distinguishable and distinctive between doing something and planning it.

Tactics ordinarily is used in the singular. It means the art and science of deploying military, naval, or air forces in battle or in maneuvers; the art, technique, or skill of employing available means to accomplish an end. In its plural use, it means the maneuvers or methods of operations themselves.

Strategy means generalship; the art and science of planning and conducting military, naval, air, or operations; the art of devising and employing plans and stratagems to achieve goals; a careful plan or method; skillful management in getting the advantage over an adversary.

EXAMPLES:

Colonel Patrick Plotter's **strategy** for seizing the hill seemed flawless, but his **tactics** for doing so were quickly found to be far from perfect when, to his dismay, his regiment retreated resolutelessly in a rain of enemy gunfire.

take See **bring / take.**

take place / occur / happen / transpire

This quartet of verbs has led to much discussion and controversy among linguists, grammarians, and other overseers of language. They differ over whether the words are synonyms and, therefore, interchangeable. Purists say they are not, insisting that the words' definitions govern their strict and individual use. Compilers of dictionaries and other scholars say they are interchangeable words, pointing to such usage by noted speakers and writers through the years. What is one to do then in using these words? The answer is twofold: to study their definitions and to decide which word best conveys the idea one is seeking to express, keeping in mind that the English language can be spoken or written informally or formally and that, like the age in which we live, it is in a constant state of change.

Take place means to come to pass; to come about. It refers to a planned or scheduled event. In such connotation it is not a synonym for **happen** or **occur**.

Happen means to come to pass by chance; to come about without apparent reason or design; to come into being; to meet or discover by chance. It is the most general word used for coming to pass.

Occur also means to come to pass; to come about. It has these additional meanings: to be met with or found; to present itself; to appear; to come into existence or being as an event or a process; to suggest itself in thought. **Occur** is often interchanged with **happen**, but it is more formal and is usually more specific as to time and event.

Transpire has two definitions that are quite different from those of the other verbs. The first means to be revealed; to become known or apparent; to come to light. The second means to emit or give off waste matter, as through the body; to escape, as moisture, odor, and the like, through the pores, such as the surface of a leaf. **Transpire** is not considered a proper synonym for **take place**, **happen**, or **occur**, even though sometimes it is so used, for it tends to be a formal word and to some people seems pretentious.

EXAMPLES:

"Will the wedding **take place** as scheduled?" Gwendolyn Gossiper asked. "Yes," replied Margery Magpie, "and it couldn't **happen** to a nicer couple." "Let's hope that no disruptions **occur** to spoil their nuptials," Gossiper said. "Yeah," Magpie quipped, her eyes twinkling. "It's where they go on their honeymoon that I'm waiting to see **transpire**!" "Do you mean come to pass or come to light?" Gossiper asked. "Take your choice," Magpie replied. "I had both in mind!"

talent See **genius / talent.**

team See **collective nouns.**

temerity / timidity

Why these nouns become confused, and they do, is a mystery to those who know their meanings. They are virtual antonymns, in that their definitions are about as opposite as any two words can be, for the rashness of the first word and the shyness of the second mark how they are distinctly different.

Temerity means recklessness, boldness, rashness; disregard, unreasoning contempt or heedlessness of danger or opposition; foolhardiness; audacity; effrontery; gall; nerve.

Timidity means lack of courage or self-confidence; shyness; lacking in boldness or determination, in forcefulness or aggressiveness; hesitancy; fearfulness; cowardliness.

EXAMPLES:

In olden days when a knight-errant sallied forth to slay the red dragon, his **temerity** was roundly praised. When another cowered within the castle, his **timidity** was widely scorned but not, perhaps, by a maid in waiting for him.

temporal / temporary

Even though these adjectives are involved with time in some manner and measure, they do not do so in the same way.

Temporal means of or pertaining to time rather than to eternity; enduring for a short or brief time; pertaining to or concerned with the present life, to earthly rather than to clerical or sacred life; secular; worldly.

Temporary means lasting, existing, serving effective for a time only; not permanent; lasting for a limited time; fleeting.

EXAMPLES:

Novices in religious orders whose thoughts dwell inordinately on **temporal** matters soon discover their novitiates, much to their dismay, have become **temporary** ones that are about to run out of time.

temporary See **temporal / temporary.**

than / then

These words get confused because they look alike and because they sound the same when they are not pronounced clearly. Yet the words are different, as their parts of speech indicate.

Than is a conjunction. It introduces an adverbial clause of comparison and occurs after the comparative form of an adjective or an adverb. It introduces the second member of a comparison in which a person, place, or thing is greater or lesser **than** the other, such as "He is taller **than** she is." or "She is shorter **than** he is." or "He likes her better **than** she does him." When a verb does not follow that which is being compared, **than** functions as a preposition, as in "He is taller **than** her." or "She is shorter **than** him." or "He likes her better **than** him." Note the use of the objective case.

Then is an adverb of time. It means at that time; immediately afterward; soon after that; thereupon; next in order of time, order, or space; in addition; that being so; for this reason. It also is an adjective, meaning of that time, as in "the **then** president."

EXAMPLES:

"I love this great state more **than** words can say, and I don't want to see it divided by greedy politicians," Gerry Mander said, as the debate on proposed changes in congressional district lines grew heated. "State no more **then**," an opportunistic opponent yelled from across the aisle, "and sit down!"

that / which / who

These relative pronouns, which are used to introduce essential (restricted) or nonessential (nonrestricted) phrases and clauses, have a reputation for being troublesome when it comes to deciding which one to use in a given construction. Yet the selection of each pronoun need not be difficult, once its purpose and function are understood, for there are guidelines one can follow with relative ease.

That is used to restrict meaning. It introduces a defining clause, as in "This is the house of cards **that** Ernie Erecto built." The words following "cards" are essential for completing the sentence. The clause is not set off by a comma, because the clause defines or limits the meaning of the words preceding it and is needed to complete the sentence.

Which is used when meaning is not restricted. It introduces a nondefining clause, as in "This house, **which** Ernie Erecto built, is made of cards." The words between "house" and "is" are not essential for completing the sentence. Without the nonessential clause, the sentence reads, "The house is made of cards." Commas are used to set off the clause and to show its words are parenthetical and can be omitted without changing the meaning of the simple or basic sentence. Or one could say, "Ernie Erecto built this house, **which** is made of cards." The words following "house" are not essential for completing the sentence. It reads, "Ernie Erecto built this house." A comma is used to set off the clause to show that it is nonessential and that its words can be omitted. For further discussion on the proper use of **that** and **which**, one should consult a grammar, several of which are listed in the Bibliography.

Who can introduce both essential and nonessential clauses, for it follows the same guidelines as those for using **that** and **which**. Therefore, **who** requires no comma preceding it when it is part of an essential clause, as in "Ernie Erecto is the one **who** bragged about building a house of cards." When **who** is part of a nonessential clause, a comma is used preceding or following the clause, as in "Ernie Erecto, **who** is a clever fellow, built this house of cards" or in "This house of cards was built by Ernie Erecto, **who** is a clever fellow."

Some further words about these relative pronouns. **That** refers to people, animals, and things, **which** to things and inanimate objects (not to people), and **who** to people and to animals with names. In spoken English with its tendency to be informal, these distinctions are not always made. In written English, however, in which formal expression often is desired or required, these distinctions are and should be observed. Some authorities favor using **who** when referring to people for designating the individual or for distinguishing each member of a group, as in "Ernie Erecto is the one **who** built the house of cards." And they favor using **that** for identifying the group or class itself, as in "Clever people are ones **that** can build houses of cards." Yet "Clever people are the ones **who** can build houses of cards" expresses the thought just as clearly, if not better.

Some speakers and writers prefer using **who** only and not **that** when referring to human beings, a practice this book endorses because such usage simplifies choosing between the two pronouns and allows each one to function in its own right.

their / there / there're / they're

These words, because each one is pronounced exactly like the others, can be troublesome to anyone who is not versed in each word's part of speech, meaning, and use, for, as Shakespeare has Hamlet exclaim in the oft-quoted soliloquy, "**there**'s the rub."

Their is a possessive pronoun. It means of those ones. It functions like an adjective in that it modifies nouns (people, places, and things}, as in **"their** kings, **their** kingdoms, **their** thrones."

There is three parts of speech. It functions as: an adjective, as in "that jester **there"**; a noun, as in "the jester from **there**"; an adverb, as in "the jester right **there**." **There** also functions as a pronoun—or an expletive, a word that is used to start a sentence whose subject appears later, as in "**There** are few jesters around these days." In the preceding sentence, **there** is called a false subject. The real subject is the plural noun "jesters." The simple and tidy way for expressing the thought is to say, "Few jesters are around these days." **There** is a weak means for starting a sentence. With adroitness and care, one can avoid its use easily and still communicate effectively.

There're is a contraction. It consists of two words that are two different parts of speech: **there**, a pronoun—or an expletive, and **are**, a plural verb, as in "**There're** few jesters around these days."

They're also is a contraction that consists of two words and two different parts of speech: **they**, a plural pronoun, and **are**, a plural verb, as in "As for the jokes, **they're** fewer, too."

then See **than / then.**

there See **their / there / there're / they're** and **there is / there are.**

there are See **there is / there are.**

therefore See **so / however / therefore.**

there is / there are

These words, which are called expletives or anticipatory subjects, serve as a means for starting a sentence but have no grammatical function. They can be troublesome when it comes to determining whether to use the singular or the plural form since the true subject appears later in the sentence. In some sentences, expletives are mandatory for making sense. In others, they can be eliminated and the sentences reworded.

There is is singular and is used with that noun which is the true subject of the sentence, as in "**There is** no homework tonight." In such a sentence the expletive is needed, for one would not say, "No homework is tonight." But in a sentence such as "**There is** no homework for us to do tonight" the expletive is not essential. It can be eliminated and the sentence recast to read, "We have no homework to do tonight." The result is a strengthened and polished sentence. And if its words were true, students affected by them would dance nearly all night with delight!

There is sometimes is used colloquially with a plural noun or nouns that are the true subject of the sentence, as in "**There is** a magazine, four books, and three newspapers on the table." Some authorities defend the mixing of the number of the verb and the subject on the grounds that "magazine," a singular noun, is closest to the expletive. Others insist that the sentence should read, "**There are** a magazine, four books, and three newspapers on the table." Whereas, a clear-minded communicator would say, "A magazine, four books, and three newspapers are on the table." And then would read them!

One more thing about **there is**. When the words are contracted to **there's**, one should be alert and should determine whether or not the expletive has to do with a singular noun. One would not say, even if one were singularly hungry, "Mmm, **there's** five pieces of cake left." One would control one's appetite, as well as one's syntax, and say, "Mmm, **there're** five pieces of cake left." And then devour the largest!

There are, the plural expletive, has guidelines for its usage comparable to those for **there is**. The difference, of course, is that **there are** is used with a plural noun or nouns that are the true subject of a sentence, as in "**There are** two flies in my soup." As with its singular counterpart, the plural expletive can be deleted and a stronger sentence formed, as in "Two flies are in my soup." And, if one is truly conceited, one can always write or say, "I have two flies in my soup!"

As for the use of **there are** with a singular noun, it rarely occurs. When it does, it is made through ignorance or oversight. A careful look at both the verb and the noun should be sufficient to keep their number in agreement. For a discussion of **there're**, the contraction of **there are**, see **their / there / there're / they're.**

Some final words about **there is** and **there are**. Feeling and instinct for language should guide one. Whenever a sentence reads unevenly or sounds awkward, rework it, as can be done by eliminating these expletives, so that words flow smoothly and express ideas accurately. After all, agreement in number does mean making sentences agreeable!

there're See **their / there / there're / they're.**

they're See **there / their / there're / they're.**

thievery See **burglary / larceny / robbery / thievery.**

though / although

These words, which suggest a sense of doubt or hesitancy, mean the same thing: in spite of the fact; regardless of the fact. As conjunctions, they are interchangeable and are commonly so used. Even so, they differ in how each is positioned in sentences. And one of the words is two parts of speech.

Though, the more popular of the pair, is the shortened version of **although**. It has double duty, for it is both a conjunction and an adverb. It can be used anywhere in a sentence, as in "**Though** Otto Octogenarius is old, he still runs ten miles a day." "Otto Octogenarius still runs ten miles a day, **though** he is old." "Otto Octogenarius still runs ten miles a day. He is old, **though**." Notice in the third example **though** is used adverbially. **Though** also is used in these ways: "**Even though** Otto Octogenarius is old, he still runs ten miles a day **as though** he were many years younger."

Although has fewer uses. It can begin a sentence as the first word in a subordinate clause that introduces the main clause, and usually does, as in "**Although** Otto Octogenarius is old, he still runs ten miles a day." It always begins a subordinate clause, as in "Otto Octogenarius still runs ten miles a day, **although** he is older than most people believe him to be." **Although** never ends a clause or sentence, **though** (however), for it does not have the adverbial right to do so!

titillate / titivate

A passing glance at this pair of verbs might lead one to believe they are interchangeable. Not so. The words have to do with being made pleasurable and looking good, two conditions that for some people are not simultaneous.

Titillate, which comes from the Latin *titillare*, to tickle, means just that: to tickle pleasurably; to arouse or excite by touching or stroking lightly; to excite agreeably.

Titivate is listed in some dictionaries as an informal word whose origin is unclear. It stems perhaps from tidy + elevate, tidivate, or it may be a blend of **titillate** and cultivate. Either way, **titivate** means to put on decorative touches; to dress up; to make smart or spruce; to smarten; to spruce.

EXAMPLES:

"So long as you **titillate** me, Frankie Fingers," Bea Bonnet said, giggling with pleasure, "I can't **titivate** myself and get ready for the Easter parade. You do want me to be decorative, don't you, and spruce up Fifth Avenue a bit?"

timidity See **temerity / timidity.**

titivate See **titillate / titivate.**

to / too / two

Unlike the days of the weeks, these words are pronounced alike, 'tü, even though, like the days of the week, they are spelled differently and have their own purposes and meanings. That is why they are called homophones.

To is a function word that is used both as a preposition and as an adverb for indicating movement or an action, or direction or place, or purpose or intention, and so on. It also is used for forming infinitives.

Too is an adverb. It means also; to or in an excessive degree.

Two, an adjective, a noun, and a pronoun, means being one more than one in number.

EXAMPLES:

Once there was a woman named Dorinda Doublesome who went **to** a discount store **to** buy **two** appliances, only **to** find that the **two** items were sold out. She was told **to** come back on Tuesday and **to** bring her rain check, **too**. Now the delay wasn't **too** troublesome for Doublesome, for she could have been told **to** return in **two** weeks or in **two** months or in **two** years—a wait that could really amount **to** something or **two**.

too See **to / too / two.**

tortuous / torturous

A single letter can and does make a difference in how two words that look alike are spelled and defined, as these adjectives certainly attest. A close look at them shows that the **r** in the second one accounts for the difference between that which twists and bends and that which inflicts or causes pain.

Tortuous means marked or having twists, bends, turns; full of twists and turns; twisting, winding, crooked; not straightforward; deceitful; devious.

Torturous means inflicting or causing excruciating pain particularly from cruelty, hatred, revenge, or the like; causing torture; cruelly painful.

EXAMPLES:

Instructors who deliberately drop **torturous** questions into exams and then rub their hands in delight as they watch their students grimace while trying to figure out what the questions mean should not be surprised to get back **tortuous** responses that are less than straightforward answers.

torturous See **tortuous / torturous.**

trace See **vestige / trace.**

transpire See **take place / happen / occur / transpire.**

translucent / transparent

These adjectives offer no mental block to their use if one distinguishes between "shining through" and "being seen through," for the distinctiveness of each adjective clearly is apparent when both are defined accurately.

Translucent comes from the Latin *translucere*, to shine through. It means permitting the passage of light; diffusing light so that the objects beyond are not clearly visible or cannot be seen clearly; free from disguise or falseness; easily understandable; lucid.

Transparent, which comes from the Latin *transparere*, to be seen through, means permitting the passage of light so that objects beyond are clearly visible; fine or sheer enough to be seen through or to be clearly seen; honest, open; free from pretense or deceit; easily understood; obvious.

EXAMPLES:

The difference between frosted window glasses and clear ones is that the frosted are **translucent** while the clear are **transparent.** No difference exists between them, however, when the clear panes are smeared by muddy hands whose owners' parents leave them and the windows utterly unwashed.

transparent See **translucent / transparent.**

trip See **journey / voyage / trip.**

triumphal / triumphant

The late Vince Lombardi, the famed professional football coach, who was reputed to have said winning is the only thing that counts, may have had these two adjectives in mind when thinking about his teams and players, and their many triumphs, for he undoubtedly knew the distinction between the two words, savoring what each meant to him during his brilliant career.

Triumphal means of, pertaining to, celebrating, or commemorating a victory or a triumph. It is applied to the objects and activities, such as processions or celebrations, but not to people, for one cannot be **triumphal**.

Triumphant means having gained victory or success; victorious; exultant; a feeling of triumph; exulting over victory; rejoicing over success. It can be applied to successes—and to successful people, for one can be **triumphant**.

EXAMPLES:

Flashing a **triumphant** grin he had not displayed in nearly ten years, Coach Puntus Pigskin relished the **triumphal** rally that celebrated, his wife said, his football team's "one-game winning streak" following seventy-two losses in a row.

triumphant See **triumphal / triumphant.**

troops See **troup / troupe / troops.**

troup / troupe / troops

Some people band these three words together, thinking incorrectly that they mean the same thing, when actually each noun has its own definition and, therefore, its own use in denoting an assemblage of persons or things.

Troup is singular in number. It means a large assemby of people; a group or company of people, animals, or things; a group of soldiers; a body of cavalry; the basic organizational unit of the Boy Scouts or the Girl Scouts under the guidance of an adult leader.

Troupe also is singular in number. It is used exclusively to mean a company, group, or band of actors, singers, dancers, acrobats, other entertainers, especially one that travels about.

Troops is plural in number. It means several bodies of soldiers or men. It is used when referring to a large body of soldiers or men in terms of them as individuals. One can speak or write of three thousand **troops**, meaning three thousand soldiers, but one would not say three thousand **troops** of soldiers nor two **troops** of soldiers.

EXAMPLES:

An encamped Boy Scout **troop** wanted to watch and hear a **troupe** perform at a nearby military base. When informed that the show was for the **troops** only, the boys had to entertain themselves by working on their merit badges.

troupe See **troup / troupe / troops.**

try and See **try to / try and.**

try to / try and

These words are an interesting pair that point up how spoken and written English differ especially when it comes to logic and intent. The formal and proper literary form is **try to**. It means to attempt to and is used to show one action, such as "Let us **try to** be quiet." On the other hand, one might speak or write, "Let's **try and** be quiet." Even though only one action is involved, the words are used to express intention and emphasis rather than to reflect logic.

The British do not get hung up over the use of **try to** and **try and**. They use **try and** all the time and consider it standard English. In American usage, **try to** is preferred, especially in written expression. **Try and** can be used and justified in both oral and written sentences such as these: "**Try and** cheer up," Nurse Pillgiver said (a tone of encouragement); "**Try and** make me stay at home," Tyrone Takeoff cried (a note of determination); "Just you **try and** stop me!" Robin Resolute shouted (a note of defiance). But, for the most part, **try to** is the correct and proper form. So **try to** use **try to** logically, especially when you intend to express one action.

EXAMPLES:

"Will you **try to** remember me?" the American sailor pleaded as he hugged and kissed the British girl goodbye. "I'll **try and** do so," she replied, her eyes drifting along the pier, looking for a seaman who might be remaining in port.

turbid / turgid

These look-alike adjectives often get confused, muddled, mixed, and even distended and overblown in their use, and should not, for they stem from two different Latin words whose meanings clearly are not the same.

Turbid comes from the Latin *turbidus*, disturbed. It means clouded, opaque, obscured; confused, unclear, muddled; disturbed; thick, heavy, dark, or dense, as smoke or clouds or the like.

Turgid comes from the Latin *turgidus*, swollen. It means swollen; bloated; tumid; bulging; distended; inflated, overblown, grandiloquent, or pompous in use of language; bombastic; not flowing easily.

EXAMPLES:

A **turbid** letter is one that is filled with muddled thinking, while a **turgid** one bulges with undisciplined use of language. A letter that is both **turbid** and **turgid** is not too likely to be understood even by someone who has the patience to try reading it.

turgid See **turbid / turgid.**

two See **to / too / two.**

U

unaware / oblivious / unawares

In some marriages, whether they are good or bad, matters become confused, some go unnoticed and unobserved, and others are filled with surprises. So it is with these two noninterchangeable adjectives and with this adverb that works by itself.

Unaware is an adjective. It means not conscious of; not cognizant; having or showing no realization, perception, or knowledge; not aware; unmindful of; inperceptive; ignorant; uninformed.

Oblivious is an adjective also. It means forgetful; lacking all memory; lacking active conscious knowledge or awareness; without remembrance, memory or mindful attention; unaware or unconscious of something.

Unawares is an adverb exclusively. It means without warning; suddenly; unexpectedly; without design, attention, preparation, or premeditation.

EXAMPLES:

"I was **unaware** it was your birthday," Ossie Oversight said to his weeping wife. "Hah!" she sobbed. "**Unaware**? Baloney! You're **oblivious** of me and to what goes on around here!" "I'm sorry, honey," Oversight said, "but can't you see that sometimes a woman's age has a way of catching a man **unawares**?"

unawares See **unaware / oblivious / unawares.**

underlay / underlie

How strange the English language can be. On the surface one would assume that these verbs, like **lay** and **lie**, their root words, would be transitive and intransitive, respectively. Not so, oddly enough, for when **lie** is prefixed by **under** or **over** it becomes exclusively transitive. And, oddly too, when **lie** is made into **underlie** and **overlie**, its meanings, for the most part, become interchangeable with **underlay** and **overlay**. Yet one would not say or write, "The rules that **underlay** the referees' decisions." One would use **underlie**, for the sentence does not contain a direct object. Therefore, an intransitive verb is needed. A way to determine when to use **underlay** or **underlie** is to place **under**, the preposition, after **lay** or **lie**. Thus, in the absence of a direct object, one would use **lie**, the intransitive verb, and would say or write, "The rules that **lie under** the referees' decisions."

Underlay means to lay under or beneath; to support by something put below or underneath; to cover, line, or extend across the bottom of.

Underlie means to lie under or beneath; to be the basis of; to account for.

EXAMPLES:

"Before you try to **underlay** the linoleum with that sealer," Herb Headlong's wife asked him, "don't you think you should read the instructions on the can to see what steps **underlie** such an undertaking?"

underlie See **underlay / underlie.**

uninterested See **disinterested / uninterested.**

unique See **unusual / unique.**

unlawful See **illegal / illegitimate / unlawful.**

unusual / unique

In an age in which hyperbole and exaggeration play a prominent part in how people think, behave, and communicate, one can well understand how these adjectives are used unsparingly. It is the use of the second one, however, that has led to a difference of viewpoint among grammarians.

Unusual means not usual, common, or ordinary; rare; uncommon in amount or degree; exceptional; singular; remarkable; extraordinary; strange; curious; odd; queer. Its comparative form is **more unusual** and its superlative form is **most unusual**.

Unique means being the only one; being the only one of its kind; existing as the only one or as the sole example; having no like, equal, or equivalent; unequaled; incomparable; unparalleled; standing alone in quality; single in kind; solitary.

Many grammarians insist that **unique** is an absolute term, an incomparable adjective that cannot be qualified. They contend that something cannot be very or more **unique** or most **unique**. Yet other grammarians endorse the comparative and superlative forms, pointing to what they say is increased and widespread comparing of **unique** by reputable speakers and writers. In time common usage probably will settle the argument, and purity in the use of **unique** will disappear. Meanwhile, those communicators who choose to keep **unique** pure can say something is almost or nearly **unique** or they can say something is most **unusual** or most distinctive and have solid grounds for stating such a high sense of things!

EXAMPLES:

"What an **unusual** dress you're wearing!" exclaimed Hermonie Handmedown. "I've never seen a **more unusual** one. It has to be **unique.**" "Thank you," Gloria Gladrags said with a smile. "I'm glad you like my dress, Hermonie, but it's not **unique**, though it is **very unusual** or **most unusual** and almost **unique** or nearly **unique**. My twin sister has one just like it."

unwanted / unwonted

A lapse in spelling or a lisp or a slip in pronunciation can lead to undesired misuse of these adjectives, for they have very different meanings, thanks to an **a** in the first one and an **o** in the second.

Unwanted means not wanted; not needed; not desired.

Unwonted means not customary, habitual, or usual; being out of the ordinary; unaccustomed; unusual; rare.

EXAMPLES:

''How come I don't seem to be getting rid of these **unwanted** pounds?'' Frieda Flabbie asked sadly as she stepped from the scales. ''It's fondness for food and **unwonted** exercise,'' replied Tanya Trim. ''That's 'how come'!''

unwonted See **unwanted / unwonted.**

usage / use / utilize

These words, which have to do with the act of employing and putting into service, should not be regarded as altogether interchangeable. Some people like to think they are, for they often employ **usage** and **utilize** in place of **use**. They assume apparently that the longer a word is the fancier it must be. Yet **use**, a simple three-letter word, in most instances is the precise one to put into service.

Usage is a noun only. It means customary way of doing things; the manner of using or treating something; the customary or accepted manner in which language or a form of language is spoken or written; accepted manner of procedure; long-established custom; mode of using; treatment.

Use is a noun and a verb, both of which have a variety of meanings. As a noun, it means the act of employing, using, or putting into service; the fact or state of being used; the privilege or benefit of using something; a method or manner of employing or applying something; a particular service or end; accustomed practice or procedure; custom; habitual practice. As a verb, **use** means to employ; to make use of; to practice habitually; to put into action or service; to avail oneself of; to exploit for one's advantage or gain; to take or partake of; to treat or behave toward; to consume or expend; to habituate or accustom.

Utilize is a verb only. It means to turn or put to profitable use; to put to use for a certain purpose; to turn to practical use or account of; to find a use for; to make useful of.

EXAMPLES:

"I'll never learn proper English **usage**!" exclaimed Polly Sybil. "It's just too darn difficult, when you consider the way people speak these days." "Sure, you can," Ellie Mentary, her English teacher, assured her, "but it takes more than a dictionary and a good handbook to **use** words precisely. It requires caring and intelligence. You surely must have some of both within you that you can **utilize** and turn to profitable expression and **use**!"

use See **usage / use / utilize.**

usual See **habitual / usual.**

utilize See **usage / use / utilize.**

V

vacant See **empty / vacant.**

vacillate / hesitate

Any indecision or irresolution one may have over the use of these verbs, any moving back and forth between them, disappears once one recognizes and understands the distinction in their meanings.

Vacillate means to sway unsteadily; waver; totter; stagger; to oscillate or fluctuate; to move to and fro; to waver in mind or opinion; to be indecisive; irresolute or hesitant; to keep changing one's mind. It implies a prolonged pause from inability to reach a firm decision.

Hesitate means to be reluctant or to wait to act because of indecision or doubt; to pause; to delay momentarily; to hold back; to be slow to decide; to falter in speech; to stammer. It implies a pause before deciding or choosing.

EXAMPLES:

"I can't understand why you **hesitate** about trying the cake," Susan Sweetly said to Orville Overwait, "considering the size dinner you've managed to put away so far. Furthermore, I don't see why there's need for you to **vacillate** between picking up a little piece and the big one!"

vapid / insipid

Even though these adjectives deal with matters of taste and flavor, each has its refinements in meanings that indicate each word is palatable in an individual way and, therefore, not altogether interchangeable with the other.

Vapid comes from the Latin *vapidus*, savourless. It means flavorless or savourless; lacking or having lost life, spirit, sharpness, briskness, zest, interest, force, tang, or flavor; without liveliness or spirit; lifeless; flat, bland, dull, or tedious. It has a suggestion of stupidness to it.

Insipid comes from the Latin *insipidus*, tasteless. It means lacking taste; tasteless; unpalatable; flavorless; without sufficient taste to be pleasing, such as food or drink; bland; lacking in qualities that interest, stimulate, or challenge. It simply means without distinction, interest, or attractive traits or qualities.

EXAMPLES:

"I can handle an **insipid** meal now and then, no matter how tasteless and flavorless it may be," Ellsworth Eligible said to Monique Monologue, "but not when **vapid** talk blandly and blindly goes with it! So do me a favor please and don't ask me to be 'the extra man' at your dinner parties again!"

venal / venial

One can confuse these adjectives, and understandably so, because they look and are pronounced somewhat alike. What adds to the confusion in their use is that each word stems from the same Latin root, *venum*, for sale. Yet the words, as used in English, have opposite meanings.

Venal is an ugly word, for it means capable of being bought or purchased for money or other valuable consideration; corruptly open or susceptible to or prepared to take bribes; capable of betraying one's trust, honor, good name, or scruples for a price; capable of being obtained for money; mercenary.

Venial has a redeeming sense to it, for it means capable of being forgiven, excused, or pardoned (of a sin or fault); easily excused or forgiven; minor; not serious; trifling; forgivable; excusable; pardonable.

EXAMPLES:

The difference between **venal** politicians and **venial** sinners is that the former stick out their palms, expecting them to be crossed with currency, while the latter cross their hearts, hoping their errancy will be forgiven.

venial See **venal / venial.**

verbal / oral / written

The first of these adjectives is used so indiscriminately these days that its users fail to be precise in indicating, for example, how an agreement has been made. A **verbal** agreement is one that has to do with words. An **oral** agreement is one spoken with the mouth. A **written** agreement is one that is committed to paper. Nonetheless, through centuries of common usage, the term **verbal** agreement has come to mean an **oral** but not a **written** one. Yet uncertainty can occur when it is not clear whether an agreement results from conversation or is one set down on paper. The use of the words **oral** or **written** in such a situation not only would clarify matters but also would express preciseness of thought, a prerequisite of competent communication. In any event, **verbal** agreements, despite popular misbelief and misuse, are not reached by gestures or with body or sign language, with handshakes, or through other physical means. **Verbal** agreements exist only when words someway, somehow are used, for the way they are employed marks the difference between **oral** and **written** ones.

Verbal comes from the Latin, *verbum*, word. It means of or consisting of or pertaining to words; consisting of or pertaining to words only, rather than with ideas, facts, or realities or emotions, actions, or images.

Oral comes from the Latin *os*, *oris*, the mouth. It means of or pertaining to the mouth; uttered or spoken by the mouth in words; of or using speech, that is, the faculty, art, or ability of expressing or describing thoughts, feelings, or perceptions by the articulation of words; spoken not **written**.

Written comes from the Old English *writan*, to inscribe. It means that which is formed in visible letters or characters, which serve as visible signs of ideas, words, or symbols, and is committed to or put down on paper.

EXAMPLES:

"You say you've come to a **verbal** agreement with Wilburn Welsher?" Manny Makedeals asked Al Ledged. "That's right, Boss," Ledged replied. "Is it an **oral** one you two talked over or is it a **written** one you've put on paper?" Manny shot back. "**Oral** or **written**, what difference does it make, Boss, as long as it's **verbal**?" "It makes a big difference to me! You don't think I'm going to count on that clown's mouth, do you?"

verve / nerve

These look-alike nouns, thanks to the possible juxtaposition of their first letters, can become confused in their meaning and use. Yet they are far from being synonyms or being alike in any way, as their definitions reveal.

Verve, which stems from *verba*, the Latin plural of *verbum*, meaning mere words, talk, has come into English by way of the

French for fantasy, caprice, animation. It means the enthusiasm, vigor, energy, vitality, spirit animating artistic or literary composition or performance; vivaciousness; liveliness.

Nerve, which comes from the Latin *nervus*, sinew, means one of the bundle of fibers that convey impulses either from the brain to muscles, producing motion, or from the skin, eyes, nose, and the like, producing sensation. It also means fortitude; boldness; courage; coolness in danger; cool assurance; power of endurance or control. And it means, informally, impertinence; gall; presumptuous audacity; effrontery; impudence.

EXAMPLES:

"I like the **verve** in this essay," Professor Literatus said, handing back the unmarked paper to Dustin Drags after having given it a cursory reading, "but I am uncertain what kind of **nerve** it took on your part to turn it in late: cool assurance or abject gall."

very See **pretty / rather / very.**

vestige / trace

These nouns are an interesting pair that not always are, but should be, kept separate in thought. They have to do with things that are left, slightly more or less. Because of the coincidence, the words appear to be synonyms, which in most, but not all instances, they are.

Vestige is the more limited of the two words in that it refers to the last, usually slight, remains of something that no longer exists. It means a slight, though actual, visible, or discernible mark, sign, evidence, or remains of something that no longer is present, that does not exist or no more appears.

Trace is more general in its use. It means a surviving, continuing, or present mark, sign, or evidence of the former existence, influence, passage, or action of a person, thing, or event; a barely perceptible sign or evidence of some past or present thing; a suggestion of any mark, line, or discernible effect; a tangible mark or line left by something that has passed, such as a footprint; a track, or mark left, such as a path; a fragment; a very small quantity.

EXAMPLES:

"We searched the desolate planet Earth and found no **trace** of our missing galaxyliner," said the Martian, "but we found this." "How so," mused Lazoriux, studying the small object the Martian placed on his upright palm. "Ah, yes! I believe it is a compact disc, a **vestige** of the Rock 'n' Roll Era centuries ago when children had their parents going round in circles."

viable / vibrant

These adjectives have a sense of activity about them that would have one believe they are interchangeable words. Not so. They lead independent lives.

Viable, which comes from the Latin *vita*, life, and from the equivalent of the French *vie*, life, means capable of living; capable of surviving outside the mother's womb without artificial support; having the capacity and ability to grow, develop, expand, or mature; capable of succeeding or gaining success.

Vibrant comes from a different Latin root, *vibrans*, shake, move to and fro. It means moving to and fro rapidly; pulsating or throbbing with energy, life, activity, or vigor; vibrating; resonant; thrilling with energy or activity.

EXAMPLES:

Viable from birth and active thereafter, Vi Vacious was named "The Girl With the Most **Vibrant** Personality" her high school senior year, a selection, some classmates said, was made in recognition of her capacity to move rapidly from one crush to the next.

vibrant See **viable / vibrant.**

vice / vise / visa

Other than their somewhat similar pronunciation, their same first and second letters, and their equal four-letter length, these nouns have nothing in common. The first has to do with sin and wrongdoing, the second with a device for keeping things tightly together, and the third with endorsement of a passport. So why are the words confused? It must have something to do with how they are spelled—or misspelled!

Vice comes from the Latin *vitium*, fault, defect, vice. It means a degrading, immoral, or evil habit or practice; depraved or degrading behavior; a blemish or defect in character; wicked conduct; a physical defect, flaw, or infirmity.

Vise, which comes from a different Latin word, *vitis* , vine, spiral, means a device with two jaws that can be brought together with screws, for holding firm or steady anything that needs to be worked on; something like a **vise**, a tight bind.

Visa is derived from a third Latin word, *visera*, look into. It means a stamp or mark placed on a passport by officials of a foreign country to show that the holder may enter their country.

EXAMPLES:

Bernie Bind stared glumly at his unstamped passport. Denial of a **visa** for what the official called his ''well-known role in American **vice**'' had him caught in a **vise:** between the jaws of a waspish wife and persistent police.

visa See **vice / vise / visa.**

vise See **vice / vise / visa.**

virtually See **practically / virtually.**

vital See **essential / indispensible / vital.**

vivid See **livid / vivid / lurid.**

vociferous / voracious

These adjectives bear curbing, for they often are confused, thanks to their exuberant misuse.

Vociferous means vehement deafening shouting or calling out; making loud outcry; expressing one's views forcibly and insistently; crying out loudly; clamorous; loud; noisy; vocal; loudmouthed; strident; uproarious; boisterous.

Voracious means having a huge or enormous appetite, especially for food; greedy or gluttonous in eating; having an insatiable appetite for an activity or pursuit; eager to devour; ravenous; exceedingly eager; rapacious.

EXAMPLES:

Sheldon Stuffer's **voracious** appetite was appeased somewhat after he told Harlan Heaper, the waiter, in a **vociferous** voice that was heard throughout the restaurant, to keep piling the food in front of him.

voracious See **vociferous / voracious.**

voyage See **journey / trip / voyage.**

voyageur / voyeur

Once these nouns are defined, one should clearly see there is no reason for misusing them even though the words have been transported from the French to English.

Voyageur means one who works in the woods, operates a boat, or acts as a guide, especially one hired by fur companies to transport furs, supplies, and people to and from remote areas, trading posts, and stations in the United States and the Canadian Northwest.

Voyeur means one who derives sexual satisfaction from seeing or watching sexual objects or acts, especially secretively. Broadly, **voyeur** means one who derives pleasure from secretly observing others. In recent years the word has taken on the meaning of one who observes, and thus loosely it has become a synoynm for observer.

EXAMPLES:

Pierre Le Peep loved the rigorous outdoor life of a **voyageur** in the Canadian Northwest, but at times, especially when he was all alone, he longed for the old days and the stimulating indoor life of a **voyeur** secretly and sometimes openly taking in the "sights" of Paris.

voyeaur See **voyageur / voyeur.**

vulgarity See **obscenity / profanity / vulgarity.**

W

waist / waste

These words, like other pairs that begin with the letter **w**, are pronounced the same way, ′wāst. Yet they are greatly different in their meaning and in their use, for one has to do with the middle of things, so to speak, while the other pertains to desolate, unused, or worthless places or matters.

Waist is a noun only. It means the part of the human body between the ribs and the hips, usually the narrowest part of the torso; the part of a garment that covers this part of the body; a blouse; a child's undergarment; a ship's center or middle; that part of a ship's upper deck which lies between the quarter-deck and the forecastle; the middle of anything.

Waste is three parts of speech: a noun, a verb, and an adjective. As a noun, it means a sparsely inhabited, barren, or uncultivated place, region, or land; useless consumption or expenditure; gradual loss or decrease by use, wear, or decay; refuse from places of human and animal habitation: garbage, rubbish, trash, sewage; the undigested residue of food eliminated from the body; ruin or devastation, as from war, pillage, fire, and the like; anything that is leftover or is not used in the manufacturing process; remnants. As a verb, **waste** means to expend uselessly; to use extravagantly; to neglect; to spoil; to squander; to wear away or diminish gradually; to exhaust, tire, or enfeeble; to cause to lose energy, strength, vigor. As an adjective, it means not cultivated, not productive; wild; barren; desolate; uninhabited; being in a ruined or devastated condition; discarded as worthless, defective, or of no use; lying unused; of no worth; excreted from the body as useless.

EXAMPLES:

"Remove your hand from around my **waist**," Karen Kool said to Alan Ardent. "It's a **waste** of effort on your part to think you can entice me to go to the dance with you. Besides, I hate to **waste** time straightening out or changing my blouse when I haven't a **waist** or a **waste** moment to spare!"

waive / wave

Despite popular misbelief, these two verbs are not interchangeable, nor are they variants in spelling, even though, in a sense, they have to do with letting or seeing things go by—or bye bye.

Waive means to give up claim to; to forgo; to relinquish; to put aside or off for the time; to put aside for consideration or discussion; to postpone; to defer. In law, it means to relinquish voluntarily a known right or interest.

Wave in its transitive form means to cause to move back and forth or up and down; to cause to flutter; to move or swing as in giving a signal; to signal; to arrange into curls, curves, or undulations; to gesture with the hand in greeting, farewell, or homage; to dismiss or put out of mind; to disregard. In its intransitive form, **wave** means to motion with the hands; to signal; to flap; to undulate; to curl; to curve; to float, move, or shake in an air current, such as a flag; to move or sway or bend back and forth or up and down, as branches of a tree.

EXAMPLES:

Despite his jubilation, Felix Flippant gripped his hands and did not **wave** at Judge Lewis Lighttouch when the latter decided to

waive a stiff fine and place him on probation. One **wave**, he sensed, could lead to one "**waive**" less.

wale / whale

These words are about alike as a gnat and an elephant. Yet, oddly enough, they are pronounced the same way, 'wā(ə)l. The difference between them, like that of a tiny insect and a huge animal, is one of definition and dimension of major proportion.

Wale is both a noun and a verb. As a noun, it means a mark or a welt left on the flesh by a rod or a whip; a narrow raised surface; a lengthwise ridge on woven or knitted fabric, especially on corduroy; any of certain strakes of thick outside planking on the sides of wooden ships; the gunwale, ship's rail. As a verb, it means to mark with wales.

Whale also is both a noun and a verb. As a noun, it means a large fishlike mammal; any of the larger marine mammals of the order of Cetacea that lack hind limbs, have front limbs modified as flippers, and have a head that is horizontally flattened, especially as distinguished from smaller whales, such as dolphins and porpoises. **Whale** also is slang for something enormous or huge. As a verb, it means to hunt for whales; to lash; to thrash; to strike or hit vigorously; to attack vehemently; to defeat soundly.

EXAMPLES:

"Man, that's some **wale** on your forearm," Moby said to Dick as they stood at the ship's gunwale. "Does it hurt?" "Naw, not much," Dick replied, "but if you want to see a **whale**, take a look at that huge white fish out there in the water spouting off air. Now, that's some **whale**! It makes my **wale** pale—almost disappear—in comparison!"

wane / wax

Like the phases of the moon that are known to **wane** and **wax**, and vice versa, things and events can diminish or increase, as these antonymous or opposite meaning verbs indicate in their definitions.

Wane means to decline, dwindle, or decrease gradually in size, intensity, extent, amount, degree, power, strength, importance, or prosperity; to draw to a close; to diminish; to fail; to sink. **Wane** stands alone and ordinarily is used without modifiers, such as "energies **wane**."

Wax means to increase in size, quantity, numbers, intensity, power, extent, degree, and the like; to grow or become as specified. It also means to treat, coat, or rub with wax, usually for polishing or stiffening. **Wax** does not stand alone. It is used with modifiers, most of which are adjectives, as in "People **wax** enthusiastic." Some homemakers, on the other hand, have been known to **wax** enthusiastically when they polish furniture, an adverbial modification that delights manufacturers and finds favor with grammarians!

EXAMPLES:

When it comes to Professor Evan Essay, some students sadly learn that their scores on his exams **wane** proportionately to how poetic they **wax** on them.

want See **lack / need / want**.

warrant / summons / subpoena

One shouldn't need a lawyer to mark the distinction in the meanings of these commonly known and used nouns. Yet if a person were to be served with any or all of them, a lawyer's assistance could well make his or her day in court.

A **warrant** is an instrument issued by a judge or magistrate authorizing an officer to make a search, seizure, or arrest or to carry a judgment or a court order into execution.

A **summons** is a call or notice issued by a judge or magistrate ordering a defendant to appear in court or a person to appear in court as a juror or as a witness. The word **summons** is singular. Its plural is **summonses**.

A **subpoena** is a writ commanding a person to appear in court or before a governmental body or other authority, under penalty for nonappearance.

EXAMPLES:

Mal E. Factor had the kind of day he would like to forget. He was shown a **warrant** authorizing the repossession of his car. He was issued a **summons** for jury duty. He was handed a **subpoena** ordering him to testify before the crime commission. And when he tried telephoning his lawyer, all he got was a recorded message: "Sorry, Mal E. Factor, should you call, but I'm out of town indefinitely."

warranty See **guarantee / guaranty / warranty**.

waste See **waist / waste**.

wave See **waive / wave**.

wax See **wane / wax**.

way / weigh

These same-sounding words when used are not interchangeable, not even in nautical terms, contrary to some ill-informed misappliers.

Way, when used as an adverb, as in **under way**, means in motion or moving along; in progress; not at anchor, moored to a fixed object, or aground.

Weigh, when used as a verb, as in **weigh** anchor, means to lift, raise, or heave up a ship's anchor in preparation for the vessel's getting under **way**. **Weigh**, when used as an adverb, as in **under weigh**, despite its popularity among sailors, is not, strictly speaking, correct. **Under way** is the preferred and proper usage.

EXAMPLES:

"**Weigh** anchor, lads!" Horatio Heaveho shouted to his ship's crew. "We can't get under **way** till you do. Even lamebrained landlubbers ought to know that!"

weather / whether

Even though these words are pronounced alike, there are no ifs, ands, or buts about them. They are not variants in spelling nor are they interchangeable, for one has to do with climate and the other with matters of choice.

Weather is a noun, a verb, and an adjective. As a noun, it means the state or condition of the atmospshere relative to temperature, barometric pressure, sunshine, cloudiness, moisture, precipitation, wind, and so on; a strong wind or storm or strong winds or strong storms collectively; state of life or fortune. As a verb, **weather** means to expose to the open air; to season by exposure to open air; to sail or pass to the windward of; to bear up against and come through safely; to endure. As an adjective, it means windward, on the **weather** side. It is used as an adjective, in such terms as **weather** vane, **weather** bureau, **weather** forecast, and so forth.

Whether is a conjunction. It is used in indirect questions to introduce one alternative, such as in "Primo Pugnacious should find out **whether** he is in fighting condition.'' **Whether** also is used to introduce the first of two or more alternatives, the others being connected by **or**, such as in ''**Whether** Primo Pugnacious wins **or** draws **or** loses, it will be his last fight.'' **If** can be used in place of **whether**, as in ''Primo Pugnacious should find out **if** he is in fighting condition.'' Such usage is considered standard English and has been so regarded for many years. The use of **or not** following **whether** to indicate a second alternative when it is simply the negative of the one stated largely appears in formal usage, as in ''Primo Pugnacious couldn't decide **whether** to fight **or not**.'' **Or not** frequently is omitted in informal usage. Thus one could say, ''Primo Pugnacious couldn't decide **whether** to fight.'' And **or not** can and should be omitted in both formal and informal usage when its use would be awkward, as in ''It's a sorry situation when Primo Pugnacious can't decide **whether (or not)** he is fit to fight.'' Or ''It's a sorry situation when Primo Pugnacious can't decide **whether** he is fit to fight **(or not)**.''

EXAMPLES:

''I'll **weather** the **weather**, **whether** anyone likes it **or not**,'' Sigrid Slicker yelled as she fumbled with the zipper on her **weather**-beaten raincoat and stepped out the door.

weigh See **way / weigh**.

well See **good / well**.

whale See **wale / whale**.

what ever See **whatever / what ever**.

whatever / what ever

At one time grammarians insisted that a strict distinction be made between the use of **whatever** as one word and **what ever** as two words in dealing with what is declared and what is asked. **What-**

ever, they contended, clearly is one part of speech, a pronoun or adjective, and should be spelled as one word when used in declarative sentences. As for **what ever**, they argued that the two-word spelling was permissible only in interrogative sentences, for the words, when so used, are two parts of speech, a pronoun and an adverb. The distinction in spelling and use between **whatever** and **what ever**, just as with whoever and who ever and whenever and when ever, in keeping with modern English usage, has just about disappeared from formal and informal communication. **Whatever**, like the other ever words, is used in both declarative and interrogative sentences, thus eliminating what some people considered to have been an unnecessary distinction in the first place.

EXAMPLES:

"**Whatever** others say and **whatever** opinion they may have of me will not deter me from using **what ever** as two words in interrogative sentences even if people think I am some reluctant rhetorician from a bygone century," Percival Primmer said to himself smugly as he turned on his microcomputer.

when / where

These versatile words and their several parts of speech often are confused and misused, and should not be. They are distinctive in use and meaning, for one has to do entirely with time and the other with place, location, or occasion.

When is an adverb, meaning at what time or at which time, as in " '**When** will lunch be ready?' Vore Racious asked." It is a conjunction, meaning at or during that time, at any time, while, as in, "Homer Hooker went fishing **when** he was a boy." It is a pronoun, meaning what time, as in " 'Since **when** do I have to go to bed before dark?' Bea Wildered asked her mother." And it is a noun, meaning the time of anything, as in "Orr Fan knows the **when** of many events but not that of his birth."

Where also is an adverb, meaning in, at, or to what place, situation, source, position, direction, circumstance, respect, as in " '**Where** is my lunch?' Vore Racious asked." It is a conjunction, meaning in or at which or what place, as in "Homer Hooker liked to go **where** he knew the fish were biting." It is a pronoun, meaning the place in or at which, the point at which, as in " 'Bed is **where** you are going and not another word,' Bea Wildered's mother snapped." And it is a noun, meaning location or occasion, that place in which something is located or occurs, as in "Orr Fan knows the **where** of many events but not that of his birth."

EXAMPLES:

When children quarrel, wise parents know **where** to put them: rooms apart, just as smart parents know **where** to put children **when** they have behaved: in kitchens, parlors, and places **where** ice cream abounds in many flavors.

where See **when / where**.

whether See **weather / whether**.

which See **that / which / who**.

who See **that / which / who.**

who / whom / whoever / whomever

The problems that occur in the use of these four pronouns result from two main causes: the hastiness with which we speak our thoughts and the lack of preciseness we use in uttering them. In an age of instant communication, one in which oral rather than written expression is on the rise, it is little wonder that we do not want to or do not take the time to deal with the niceties of language and its proper usage, and to figure out how and when to use the subjective and objective case of these seemingly complex pronouns.

Thus Theodore N. Bernstein and other scholars of English usage have astutely predicted the oblivion of two of the pronouns in this foursome, **whom** and **whomever**. Their days are numbered, these savants say, and in time they will be used no more. Relatively few people, even the most learned, seldom speak the words **whom** and **whomever**. Unwittingly, or otherwise, they no longer distinguish between the subjective and objective case. Instead, they utter **who** and **whoever** indiscriminately, leaving it to those caring communicators who cherish precise syntax to speak and write **whom** and **whomever** and thus preserve the use of the objective case awhile longer.

Who is a relative pronoun in the subjective case. It means what person. It has two functions: to serve as the subject of verbs and to refer to nouns or other pronouns that are the subjects of verbs. Through subterfuge and substitution, it has become a replacement for **whom**.

Whom is a relative pronoun, the objective case of **who**. Its functions are twofold: to serve as the object of verbs and the object of prepositions, and to refer to nouns and other pronouns that are the objects of verbs or prepositions. Most authorities agree that **whom** should be used when it follows a preposition, as in John Donne's ". . . for **whom** the bell tolls. . . ." Otherwise, there is no consensus on its use as an objective pronoun. Thus **whom** appears to be spoken or not spoken, written or not written, thanks to whim, fancy, ignorance, or indifference and not because of any restrictive or hard-and-fast rules. And so a solecism, an ungrammatical combination of words, such as "**Whom** did Tammy Talebearer say the culprit was?" goes unchallenged and uncorrected even though properly the words should read, "**Who** did Tammy Talebearer say the culprit was?" For not even Talebearer would say, "**Him** is the culprit"!

Whoever, an indefinite pronoun in the subjective case, means whatever person. Its functions are like those of **who**. Indiscriminate use, nonetheless, has led to its acting as a substitute or replacement for **whomever**.

Whomever, an indefinite pronoun, is the objective case of **whoever**. Its functions are like those of **whom**.

A pitfall to avoid in using these indefinite pronouns after prepositions is the assumption that they always are in the objective case. Not so. They can be the subject of a verb, as in "Toss the ball to **who** is nearest you." Or "Toss the ball to **whoever** wants to catch it." In the first sentence, "**who**" is the subject of the verb "is." In the second sentence, "**whoever**" is the subject of the verb "wants." In both sentences all the words that follow the word "ball" combine as the object of the verb "toss." Keep in mind that all verbs must have a subject or an implied one. In both example sentences, "you" is the implied subject of the imperative verb "toss."

EXAMPLES:

"Are we going to sell all these potatoes to **whom**—or is it to **whomever**—we please?" Ida Hoe asked her husband, Hy, uncertain of her syntax. "To both and to **whoever** will pay our price, naturally," he replied, eyeing profitably the bulging sacks piled high in front of them. **Who** else is worth selling to?"

whom See **who / whom**.

who's / whose

These words often become confused, misused, and transposed when they are written, not because their users are careless, necessarily, but because the words are pronounced alike: 'hüz. The way to keep them separate in thought and use is to recognize and observe their differences in parts of speech and meaning, just as one does with **it's** and **its**.

Who's is a contraction of the two words, who is, a pronoun and a verb, or a contraction of two words, who has, a pronoun and a verb. Because **who's** is a contraction for either who is or who has, generally it is best not to contract the two words but to spell them out and thus avoid confusion.

Whose is a pronoun only. The possessive case of who, it functions as an adjective and means belonging to what person, place, or thing.

EXAMPLES:

A student **who's** (who is or who has) prepared for an exam is one **whose** grade will, and usually does, reflect how well he or she has done so.

whose See **who's / whose**.

will See **shall / will**.

windfall / shortfall

These nouns have to do with what might be considered good and bad luck. One means an unexpected advantage, the other a shortage. And, because of their opposite meanings, these antonyms obviously are not interchangeable.

Windfall is a word of long duration. It stems from medieval England when commoners were not allowed to cut down trees but could gather branches blown down by the wind and use them for firewood. Hence it has acquired the concept of good luck or good fortune that is associated with the word. **Windfall** means something blown down by the wind, such as wood or fruit; an unexpected or sudden gain, good fortune, advantage, legacy, piece of good luck, or the like. One can enjoy a **windfall** profit, but one would not call it "an unexpected **windfall** profit." That would be a redundancy, for the word **windfall** implies that the profit was unexpected.

Shortfall, like other fad words, falls short in effectiveness because of its overuse. It dates from the late nineteenth century and means a failure of something or a supply to attain a specified level or need; the quantity or extent by which something or a supply falls short of expectation, need, or demand; the amount of such failure; a deficiency in funds or money.

EXAMPLES:

Autumn winds that blow branches to the ground for easy collecting can be a **windfall** that warms one in winter, while a **shortfall** in dollars can spring forth a chilling effect in summer or any other season.

-wise

A word to the wise (or is it to the unwise?) should be sufficient in dealing with this four-letter adverb-forming suffix, for as William Strunk Jr. and E. B. White state in *The Elements of Style*: "There is not a noun in the language to which -wise cannot be added if the spirit moves one to add to it. The sober writer will abstain from the use of this wild additive." These renowned authorities on English usage are right. There are writers and speakers, especially the latter, these days who not only are intoxicated with **-wise** but also are addicted to its use. One has only to watch, read in, and listen to the media or to observe elsewhere, to realize how mindless, unlimited, and seemingly endless are ways these faddists somehow manage to tack the suffix on to another noun.

Most authorities agree that **-wise** has three distinct meanings: The first denotes manner, position, direction, reference, as in clock**wise** (the manner in which a clock turns); or in length**wise** or coast**wise** (in the direction of); or in like**wise** or other**wise** (in reference to). The second meaning deals with wisdom and knowledge and knowledgeability, as in weather**wise** (knowledgeable of or about weather); or in money**wise** (knowledgeable of or wise in the use of money); or in city**wise** (wise in or knowledgeable of the ways of city life). The third, the meaning that lends itself to tacking-on tactics and whose use is frowned upon by purists of language, except in limited instances, denotes with regard to, in respect of, concerning, as in

- "Percentage**wise** (with regard to percentage) Influx Company's profits rose in the fourth quarter."
- "Banking**wise** (in respect to banking) Dee Posit knows very little."
- "Speech**wise** (concerning speech) Orr A. Torr is brilliant."

These sentences can, and should, be revised, "de-wised," and presented in a simple, direct, nonfaddish manner, as in

- "The percentage of Influx Company's profits rose in the fourth quarter."
- "Dee Posit knows very little about banking."
- "Orr A. Torr is a brilliant speaker."

In its third meaning (with regard to, in respect of, concerning), **-wise** does lend itself to quick communication, to economy in the use of language, but it also is a shortcut, a kind of shorthand, that encourages the caring less about precise and direct expression. Its use is widespread, with new combinations appearing almost overnight. Fad**wise**, maybe this popularized practice will abate. But, breath**wise**—bated or other**wise**—don't hold or count on it!

women's / womens'

Women's is the correct possessive for women, a plural noun that means two or more female human beings.

Womens' is illiteracy, a nonword. See **children's / childrens'**.

womens' See **women's / womens'**.

would See **should / would**.

would have

These two words, used in conditional sentences, are an excellent example of how spoken and written English can be confused and be confusing. When the words **would have** are contracted to and spoken "would've," and they often are, they can sound like "would of." When they are so written, the words form an illiteracy that betrays the user's ignorance and makes possible his or her admission to the ranks of the functional illiterate.

A further misuse of **would have** is its substitution for had in an **if** clause that expresses an imagined condition. It is what is called a plupluperfect, the supplying of an auxiliary to the pluperfect tense of a verb. Such usage appears to be characteristic not only of informal speech, in which **would have** is contracted to "would've" and when pronounced sounds like "would of," but also of written expression in which the plupluperfect is spelled any one of three ways. The point is that none of these three versions, regardless of its spelling, is a proper substitution for the pluperfect **had**.

EXAMPLES:

The tasteful and proper usage of the well-known saying, "If I had known you were coming, I **would have** baked a cake," certainly would be lost were the sentence to be recast to read, "If I would have known you were coming, I would of baked a cake." So why tamper with the original recipe?

wrack See **rack / wrack / wreck**.

wrath / wrathful / wrathy / wroth

These four words, the first a noun and the others adjectives, have one thing in common. They all have to do with the same human emotion: anger. How each word deals with this temperamental trait marks its individuality.

Wrath is used as a noun only. It means an intense emotional state induced by displeasure; strong, stern, fierce, resentful, or violent anger; resentful indignation; fury; rage; ire; choler; resentment; vengeance or punishment as a consequence of anger.

Wrathful, the most common of the three adjectives, means very angry; ireful; full of anger or indignation; characterized by or showing wrath; full of wrath; irate.

Wrathy is an adjective that means wrathful, angry, or irate. It is used in informal expression. Originally an early nineteenth-century word and chiefly American, it is falling into disuse.

Wroth is largely a literary word that is used as a predicate adjective. It, too, means wrathful, angry, or irate.

EXAMPLES:

Wrathful because his wife had burned his breakfast, Chester Chafing came upon a bull while wearing a red shirt. The bull, sighting the shirt, was filled with **wrath**. From the ire that blazed in Chester's eyes and in the bull's, it was hard to tell which one was **wrathy** and which was **wroth**. Yet one thing was certain. Both the man and the beast were mightily mean-tempered and downright angry!

wrathful See **wrath / wrathful / wrathy / wroth.**

wrathy See **wrath / wrathful / wrathy / wroth**.

wreck See **rack / wrack / wreck.**

wroth See **wrath / wrathful / wrathy / wroth**.

wright / write / right

The trouble with these three words is that they are pronounced alike: ′rīt. Yet they are different parts of speech and have separate definitions. When they are spoken, there is no problem if they sound the same. It is when they are spelled out loud or in writing that their letters have to be put straight.

Wright is a noun that is used in combination with other nouns. It means a worker, especially one in wood, such as a ship**wright** or a wheel**wright.** It generally has come to mean anyone who constructs something. Thus the word is used in play**wright** even though it is not related to write or to writing, the craft that is involved.

Write is a verb. It has many meanings, the basic ones being: to set down or express in letters or words on paper, and so on; to compose, as a song or a book; to form characters representing sounds and ideas; to be occupied in writing; to express ideas in writing.

Right is the versatile word among the trio. It is four different parts of speech. As an adjective, it means, among its many definitions, what is in accordance with what is good, proper, or just; what is correct; what is in conformity with fact, reason, or some standard or principle; what is fitting or appropriate; what is suitable; what is genuine or authentic. As a noun, **right** means a just claim or title, whether legal, moral, or prescriptive; that thing due a person by law, tradition, or nature; that which is correct; the opposite hand to the left hand; a faction, party, or other political group of a conservative or reactionary bent. As a verb, **right** means to do justice to; to correct; to redress as a wrong; to avenge; to restore to or put in upright position; to put in proper order, condition, or relationship; to resume an upright or proper position. And as an adverb, **right** means in a straight line; straight; directly; exactly; just; immediately; promptly; very; accurately; correctly; quite or completely; to a high degree.

EXAMPLES:

"**Right** the scene and **write** it **right**!" the television producer yelled at the play**wright**. "Hold it a minute, bub," Leonard Lines shouted. "I've a **right** to **write** my play as I choose. So you'd better get off my back, or it'll be the back of my **right** hand you'll be getting **right** now!"

write See **wright / write / right**.

written See **verbal / oral / written**.

Y

young / youthful

These words, as adjectives, refer to lack of age. Their shades of meanings set them apart and thus indicate they are not interchangeable modifiers. One can be young and not be youthful, yet one can be youthful and not be young.

Young is the general word for that which is undeveloped, immature, and in the process of growth. Its meanings are: being in the first or early stage of life or growth; youthful; not far advanced in growth, life, or existence; not old; having the appearance, freshness, vigor, or other qualities of youth; of or pertaining to youth; inexperienced; immature; newly begun or formed. **Young** may be applied to persons as well as to things and institutions, such as a **young** man, a **young** cow, a **young** nation. It also is a noun, meaning those who have youth; young persons collectively; offspring of animals.

Youthful has implied meanings that suggest the favorable characteristics of youth, such as vigor, enthusiasm, hopefulness, and freshness and physical grace. **Youthful** means characterized by youth; of, pertaining to, or befitting youth; vigorous; having the appearance, vitality, freshness, vigor, or other qualities of youth; still young; looking or seeming young; early in time.

EXAMPLES:

"You may think you're **young** in heart, as you're always saying you are," Lola Lingerer said to her husband, Mal, who sat slouched in front of the television set, pretending to be asleep. "Yet when it comes to your being **youthful** and useful, and helping me clean house, you're up to your usual old dog tricks!"

your / you're / yours

These words, pronounced almost the same way, are an apt example of how differently language is spoken and written. One can sound these words and, in mosts instances, use them correctly. When it comes to writing them, that is something else, for ignorance of their correct spelling, as well as their parts of speech and functions, can lead to their misuse and abuse.

Your, a form of the possessive case of the personal pronoun **you**, is used as an attributive adjective before a noun, such as in **your** book. It means of, pertaining, or belonging to you.

You're and **your** are pronounced ′yůər. That is where their similarity ends, for **you're** is a contraction of two words, **you,** a pronoun, and **are**, a verb. The distinctions that pertain to **it's**, **they're**, and **who's** apply also to **you're**. It, too, requires an apostrophe to form the contraction.

Yours is a pronoun. Like **your**, it means of, pertaining, or belonging to you. Unlike **your**, it is an independent possessive, one that can stand alone in a sentence, such as "What's mine is mine, and what's **yours** is mine." But like other pronouns, such as **hers**, **theirs**, and **its**, **yours** does not contain an apostrophe and is never so written.

EXAMPLES:

"**You're** a dear to let me wear **your** sweater on my date with the new hunk I've met," Cora Cashmere said to Lucy Lender. "Are you sure you won't need it? "No problem," her roommate replied. "It's all **yours**. Just make sure you leave a deposit on the hall table on your way out!"

you're See **your / you're / yours.**

yours See **your / you're / yours.**

youthful See **young / youthful.**

Z

zoom

This word is both a verb and an adjective. It is peculiar, the kind of word that requires one to focus on its meanings, for it hums and buzzes, and has its ups (but never its downs, some linguists contend). Yet it zips along, too.

Zoom is a true verb of motion, as its pronunciation would suggest. That is why, like zap, zing, and zag, it is an onomatopoeia, a word whose sound suggests its meaning. As a verb, **zoom** has varied meanings: to move suddenly or quickly with a loud humming or buzzing sound; to climb rapidly and steeply, as in aeronautics, or to fly an airplane suddenly and sharply upward at a great speed for short distance, or to cause it to do so; in photography, to magnify or reduce an image by adjusting a **zoom** lens; to move along at a rapid or high rate of speed. Some linguists object to the using of **zoom** with **down**, **across**, and **along**. They single out aeronautics, arguing that objects **zoom** only upward. But the use of **down**, **across**, and **along** existed long before the advent of aeronautics, and so the aeronautic sense of zoom is but one of many, all of which are recognized as standard. **Zoom**, an adjective associated with photography, describes a camera or projector lens whose focal length can be moved, allowing a rapid change in the size of an image yet keeping the image in focus at all times.

EXAMPLES:

Paulette Phocus felt the two-seat biplane **zoom** higher. Looking down, she watched the traffic, small as ants, **zoom** along the coastal highway. She steadied her camera as she adjusted the **zoom** lens. ''OK, Herman Hotshot,'' she said in the intercom to the pilot behind her. ''This is high enough. Hold her level while I **zoom** in on humanity below!''

Glossary of Grammatical Terms

A Pun My Word is a handbook on English usage and not a grammar. Even so, grammatical terms appear throughout the book that deal with the use of words, parts of speech, phrases, clauses, sentences, and other elements of syntax that constitute how we speak and write English. This glossary of grammatical terms, although not exhaustive, should be sufficient as an aid in using the book. In-depth information on and discussion of grammatical terms can be found in the grammars listed in the Bibliography.

accusative Another word for **objective**. See **case.**

active voice The form a verb takes to show that its subject is the doer of the action, as in "Emelda **likes** shoes."

adjective A part of speech used to modify (describe, limit, or qualify) a noun or pronoun, as in "Penman is a **brilliant** writer," or in "Penman is **brilliant**." See the main text for a discussion on forming the comparative and superlative of adjectives.

adverb A part of speech used to modify (describe, limit, or qualify) verbs, adjectives, and other adverbs, as in "Penman writes **rapidly**," or in "She is a **very** rapid writer," or in "She writes **very rap-**

idly.'' See the main text for a discussion on forming adverbs.

agreement The matching in form of one word with another to indicate number, person, or gender, such as in ''this car, these cars'' (number); ''a boy asks, girls reply'' (person and number); ''a girl herself'' (gender and number).

antecedent A word or group of words to which a pronoun refers.

antonymn A word of opposite meaning, as in ''prompt and late.'' The opposite of synonym. Consult a standard dictionary or a thesaurus for a listing of a particular word or words.

appositive A noun placed next or close to another to identify, explain, or supplement its meaning, as in ''Our coach, **Puntus Pigskin**, likes football,'' or ''A **conservative** at heart, Stefan Steadfast supports the Republican Party.''

article A word, **the**, **a**, or **an**, that is used adjectively before nouns, as in ''**the** book,'' ''**a** picture,'' ''**an** apple.'' **The** is a definite article. **A** and **an** are indefinite articles, **a** being used before a consonant sound, **an** before a vowel sound.

attributive adjective An adjective or modifier that is placed next to a noun, as in ''**blue** sky.''

auxiliary A form of **be**, **have**, or **do** or a **modal**, such as **will, should**, that is used with a verb, as in ''**is** talking, **has** talked, **did** talk, **will** talk, **should** talk.''

case The inflectional form of a noun or pronoun indicating its grammatical relationship to other words in a sentence. In English there are three cases: subjective (nominative), as in ''A **man**

toils, **he** toils''; possessive (genitive), as in ''**Joe's** book, **his** book''; objective (accusative), as in ''Joe hits the **ball**, the ball hits **him**.''

clause A group of words containing a subject and a predicate that acts either as an independent (main) clause, as in ''The sun rose, and her day began,'' or as a dependent (subordinate) clause, as in ''When the sun rose, her day began.'' Independent clauses can stand alone. Dependent clauses cannot stand alone but depend on some other element within a sentence. They are called noun, adjective, or adverbial clauses.

collective nouns A noun naming a collection or grouping of individuals by a singular form. Collective nouns are followed by a singular verb when the group is thought of as a unit and by a plural verb when component individuals are being referred to. See **collective nouns**, in the main text, for use and examples.

common noun See **noun.**

comparative The second of three degrees to show change in the form of adjectives and adverbs. See **adjectives** in the main text.

conjunction A part of speech used to link and relate words, phrases, clauses, or sentences. Coordinating conjunctions, such as **and**, **but**, **for**, **nor**, **or**, **yet**, join words, phrases, and clauses of equal grammatical rank, while subordinating conjunctions, such as **after**, **although**, **before**, **as if**, **because**, **since**, **unless**, **when**, join dependent clauses to independent clauses.

conjunctive adverb A word, such as **so**, **however**, **therefore**, that serves not only as an adverb but also as a connective. For use and examples, see **so / however / therefore** in the main text.

connective A word or phrase used to link and relate words, phrases, clauses, or sentences, such as **and**, **although**, **at**, **however**, **on the contrary**, **which**, **not only . . . but also**. Conjunctions, prepositions, conjunctive adverbs, relative pronouns, transitional expressions, and correlatives function as connectives.

consonants See **vowels**.

copulative verb A verb, especially a form of the verb **to be**, used to express simply the relationship between subject and predicate, such as in "The grass **is** green." Also called **linking verb**, some of which, in addition to a form of the verb **to be**, **are become**, **seem**, **feel**, **taste**, **sound**, **smell**, as in "I **seem** all right, I **feel** good, the grapes **taste** sour, the trumpets **sound** shrill, the roses **smell** sweet."

correlative conjunction Pairs of words, such as **either . . . or**, **neither . . . nor**, **not only . . . but also**, that link grammatically equal elements. For use and examples, see **either . . . or / neither . . . nor** and **not only / but also**, both in the main text.

declarative sentence A sentence that makes a statement: "Some boys like girls."

dependent clause Also called **subordinate clause**. See **clause**.

direct object A person or thing directly affected by the action of a verb, as in "The ball hit the **batter**, the batter hit the **ball**."

essential clause A clause (a group of words with a subject and a predicate), the omission of which would change the meaning of the main or principle clause in a sentence and so is not set off by commas. Also called **restricted clause.** For discussion and examples, see **that / which / who** in the main text.

exclamatory sentence A sentence that expresses strong feeling or emotion, as in "What a great day this is!"

expletive A word, such as **there** or **it**, that serves as an anticipatory subject as a means for beginning a sentence but has no grammatical function. For use and examples, see **there is / there are** in the main text.

future tense See **tense**.

gender The classification of nouns and pronouns as masculine (man, he), feminine (woman, she), and neuter (marriage, it).

genitive Another name for possessive. See **case**.

gerund A verb form ending in **ing** that functions as a noun. For use and examples, see **gerund** in the main text.

grammar A systematic description and classification of the ways and rules in which words are used, governed, or applied in a particular language; the study thereof.

homophone A word with the same sound as another, as in **to**, **too**, **two**.

imperative mood See **mood**.

imperative sentence A sentence that expresses a command, as in "Close the door!"

indefinite pronoun A pronoun that does not specify a distinct limit, such as all, any, each, everyone, one, some. See **number** in the main text.

independent clause Also called **main clause**. See **clause**.

indicative mood See **mood.**

indirect object A word (or words) that indicates to or for whom or what something is done, as in "Pass **Pappy** the biscuits." An indirect object usually can be made the object of a preposition, as in "Pass the biscuits **to Pappy**."

infinitive A verb form or verbal usually consisting of **to** followed by the present tense of the verb, as in "Almost everyone likes **to dance**." Infinitives can serve as nouns, "**To dance** means having a good time," or as adjectives, "He had no desire **to try**," or as adverbs, "But she was eager **to start**."

inflection The variation in the form of a word to show a change in its meaning. Nouns or groups of words that are used as nouns (substantives) may be inflected (declension) to show case, person, number, and gender. Verbs are inflected (conjugation) to indicate mood, tense, voice, person, and number. Adverbs and adjectives are inflected to show comparison.

interjection One of the eight parts of speech. A word that expresses a simple exclamation but has no grammatical relation with the rest of the sentence, such as "Wow! Terrific!" When an interjection stands alone, it is followed by an exclamation mark (!). When used in a sentence, it is set off by a comma, as in "Oh, let this day end!"

interrogative pronoun A word, such as **what**, **which**, **who**, used to ask a question, as in "**What** is the point? **Which** is it? **Who** has the answer?"

interrogative sentence A sentence that asks a question: "Are you ready?"

intransitive verb See **verb.**

linking verb See **copulative verb.**

main clause Also called **independent clause**. See **clause.**

modal Of, pertaining to, or expressing the mood of a verb.

mode See **mood**.

modifier A word or word group that describes, limits, or qualifies the meaning of another. See **adjective** and **adverb**, both in the main text.

mood The form of the verb, also called **mode**, that indicates the manner of the action. English has three moods: indicative, imperative, and subjunctive. The indicative is used to state a fact or to ask a question, as in "It is cold" or "Is it cold?" The imperative is used to express a command or an urgent request, as in "Leave at once!" or "Answer the phone please." The subjunctive is used to express a wish, a condition, a supposition, an exhortation, a concession, or a condition contrary to fact, as in "He talked as though he knew what he was saying." See **subjunctive mood** in the main text.

nominative Another name for **subjective**. See **case.**

nonessential clause A clause (a group of words with a subject and a predicate) whose omission would not change the meaning of the main or principle clause in a sentence. When so used, it is set off by commas: "Nat U. Rally, who has served two terms as mayor of Sky Blue, said today he would not seek reelection." Also called **nonrestricted clause**.

nonrestricted clause See **nonessential clause**.

noun A part of speech. The name of a person, place, or thing. There are these kinds of nouns: common, referring to any member or all members of a class or group, as in "boy, town, boat"; proper (written with a capital letter) naming a particular person, place, or thing, as in "Elvis Presley, Memphis, Rock 'n' Roll"; collective, the name of a group or class considered as a unit. For use and examples, see **collective nouns** in the main text. A noun functions as the subject of a verb, "The **bat** was heavy"; or as the object of a verb, "He hit the **ball**"; or as the object of a preposition, "He ran to the **base**"; or as a predicate adjective, "This place is the police **station**"; or as an appositive, "Nick Nailem, the **officer**, arrested him." See **predicate adjective** and **appositive**.

number The inflectional form of a word that indicates singular (one) or plural (more than one). See **number** in the main text.

object A noun or substitute noun that receives the action of a transitive verb. It answers the question what or whom. The object may be a word, a phrase, or a clause, as in "He saw the **firehouse**" (noun); "He likes **to fight fires**" (infinitive phrase); "Do you know **that he was made fire chief**?" (clause).

objective case See **case.**

participle A verbal used as a modifier or verbal adjective. English has three participles: present, past, and past perfect. The present ends in **ing**: rowing, hiking. The past ends in **ed**, **d**, **t**, **en**, **n**, or is formed by a vowel change: halted, said, slept, taken, worn. The past perfect adds **having** to the past participle: having halted, having said, having slept, having taken, having worn.

parts of speech The classification of words according to their particular or special function in a sentence. In English there are eight parts of speech: nouns, pronouns, verbs, adjectives, adverbs, prepositions, conjunctions, and interjections.

passive voice The form a verb takes to show that its subject is the object **voice** or the receiver of the action, as in "The tree was cut down."

past perfect tense See **tense**.

past tense See **tense**.

person The form of a pronoun and verb that is used to indicate the speaker or speakers. First person: "I am. We are." Second person: "You are." Third person: "He is. She is. They are."

personal pronoun A word, such as **I**, **you**, **he**, **she**, **it**, **we**, **they** (and inflections), that represents or substitutes for nouns.

phrase A group of words without subject and predicate that is used as a single part of speech as a substantive, verb, adjective, or adverb. Phrases are called: prepositional, "He hit the ball to him"; participial, "He saw her coming"; gerund, "Dating is fun"; infinitive, "It's simple to do"; noun, "The new tenant moved in"; appositive, "Ripoff, the landlord, knocked on the door"; and absolute, "The rent paid, Ripoff rubbed his hands."

pluperfect tense See **tense.**

plupluperfect tense See **tense.**

plural A noun, verb, or pronoun that is more than one in number. See **number** in the main text.

possessive Also called genitive. See **case**.

predicate A word or word group in a sentence that makes a statement about the subject. A simple predicate consists of only the verb and its auxiliaries, as in "Howard Hiker **has walked**." A complete predicate consists of the verb and its compliments and modifiers, as in "He **has walked in the woods**."

predicate adjective An adjective in the predicate that complements or modifies the subject. A **predicate adjective** occurs only after a form of the verb **to be** (is, are, was, were) or some other intransitive verb (become, appear, seem), as in "The sky is blue, the days seem long."

prefix One or more syllables affixed or added to the beginning of a word or root, such as **ad**, **dis**, **im**, **mis**, **re**, **sub**, **un**, **to** change or modify its meaning, as in adverb, displace, impossible, mistake, return, subdivide, untie.

preposition A part of speech. A word, such as **above**, **among**, **between**, **by**, **despite**, **down**, **during**, **for**, **from**, **in**,

inside, **into**, **like**, **near**, **of**, **over**, **to**, **toward**, **under**, **upon**, **with**, **within**, **without** (and many others), that is used to link a noun or pronoun to some other word in the sentence, as in "Take the biscuits **from** the oven, give some **to** Pappy, but save the most **for** you and me."

present tense See **tense**.

principle parts The three forms of a verb from which its various tenses are derived. See **tense**.

pronoun A part of speech. A word that is used in place of a noun. The noun a pronoun refers to is called an antecedent. The kinds of pronouns are: personal (I, you, he, she, it, we, they, and inflected forms); relative (who, whom, whose, what, which, that); indefinite (all, any, each, few, many, none, one, and the like); demonstrative (this, that, these, those); interrogative (who, whose, what, which); reflexive (myself, himself, yourself, and the like); intensive (myself, himself, yourself, and the like); reciprocal (each other, one another).

proper noun See **noun**.

relative pronoun A noun substitute, such as **who**, **whose**, **that**, **what**, which, that is used to introduce subordinate or dependent clauses. For use and examples, see **that / which / who**; **who / whom / whoever / whomever**; **who's / whose**, all in the main text.

restricted clause See **essential clause**.

sentence A group of words containing a subject and a predicate and expressing a complete thought.

singular A noun, verb, or pronoun that is one only in number. See **number**, in the main text.

solecism A nonstandard, ungrammatical combination of words, such as "between you and I."

subject A word or a group of words naming a person, place, thing, or idea about which something is stated. A simple subject is a noun or a pronoun: "The **man** ran, **he** ran." A complete subject is the simple subject with its modifiers: "The **old man** ran."

subjective See **case**.

subjunctive See **mood**.

subjunctive mood See **subjunctive mood** in the main text.

subordinate clause Also called dependent clause. See **clause**.

subordinate conjunction See **conjunction**.

suffix An ending affixed or added to a word, base, or phrase, such as, **able**, **ed**, **ful**, **less**, **ness**, **s**, that changes or modifies its meaning, as in "suitable, canceled, shameful, thoughtless, greatness, dogs."

superlative The third of three degrees to show change in the form of adjectives and adverbs. See **adjectives** in the main text.

syllable One of the parts in which a word is divided to facilitate its pronunciation and spelling, as in syl-la-ble.

synonym A word of or nearly of the same meaning as another, such as "quick and fast."

syntax The way words, phrases, and clauses are put together in a sentence; their grammatical relation; the rules that govern the relationship of words, phrases, and clauses in sentences; the study thereof.

tense The form of a verb that indicates time of action, condition, or state. English has six tenses: present, "She studies"; past, "She studied"; future, "She will study"; perfect or present perfect, "She has studied"; past perfect, "She had studied"; and future perfect, "She will have studied."

transitional expression A word or phrase that links or connects one idea to another within a sentence or between paragraphs. A transitional word or words link thoughts (and, besides, furthermore); compare like ideas (also, as well as, in the same way, likewise); contrast ideas (although, however, otherwise); show sequence and time (afterward, before, earlier, later); show cause and effect (because, hence, since, therefore); emphasize (certainly, indeed, in fact, thus); and summarize (consequently, finally, in conclusion, to sum up).

transitive verb See **verb.**

verb A part of speech that is used to assert an action, condition, or state. Verbs are transitive or intransitive. A transitive verb carries the action to the predicate of the sentence. It must answer the question what or whom, as in "Slugger hit a home run." (A home run is what Slugger hit.) An intransitive verb does not require an object to complete its meaning, as in "Slugger struck out." Most standard dictionaries indicate if a verb is transitive or intransitive, or both.

verbal A word that is derived from a verb (gerund, infinitive, and participle) and used as a modifier (adjective, adverb), as an object, as a complement, or, sometimes, as a subject. It is unable to stand alone as the main verb in a sentence. See **gerund**, **infinitive**, and **participle**.

voice The aspect of a transitive verb that shows the relationship of its subject to its expressed action: whether the subject is the doer or receiver of the action. See **active voice** and **passive voice**.

vowels Those letters of the English alphabet that form the central and most prominent sounds of syllables: a, e, i, o, u and sometimes y. The other letters, b, c, d, f, g, h, j, k, l, m, n, p, q, r, s, t, v, w, x, y, and z, are called **consonants**.

Bibliography

The American Heritage Dictionary: Second College Edition. Boston, Mass.: Houghton Mifflin, 1985.

The Associated Press Stylebook and Libel Manual. New York: Associated Press, revised 1986.

Barzun, Jacques. *Simple & Direct: A Rhetoric for Writers*. New York: Harper & Row, 1975.

Bernstein, Theordore M. *The Careful Writer: A Modern Guide to English Usage*. New York: Atheneum, 1968.

Bernstein, Theodore M. *Dos, Don'ts & Maybes of English Usage*. New York: Quadrangle/ New York Times Book Co., 1977.

———. *Miss Thistlebottom's Hobgoblins: The Careful Writer's Guide to the Taboos, Bugbears and Outmoded Rules of English Usage*. New York: Farrar, Straus and Giroux, 1971.

Callahan, E. L. *Grammar for Journalists*. Rev. ed. Radnor, Pa.: Chilton, 1975.

Chambers 20th Century Dictionary. Edited by E. M. Kirkpatrick. Cambridge: Cambridge University Press, 1983.

The Chicago Manual of Style. 13th ed., rev. and exp. Chicago: University of Chicago Press, 1982.

Ciardi, John. *A Browser's Dictionary. A Compendium of Curious Expressions & Intriguing Facts*. New York: Harper & Row, 1980.

———. *A Second Browser's Dictionary and Native's Guide to the Unknown American Language*. New York: Harper & Row, 1983.

Copperud, Roy H. *American Usage and Style: The Consensus*. New York: Van Nostrand Rheinhold, 1980.

Corbett, Edward P. J. *The Little English Handbook: Choices and Conventions*. 5th ed. Glenview, Ill.: Scott, Foresman, 1987.

Evans, Bergen. *Comfortable Words*. New York: Random House, 1962.

Evans, Bergen, and Cornelius Evans. *A Dictionary of Contemporary American Usage*. New York: Random House, 1957.

Flesch, Rudolf. *The ABC of Style: A Guide to Plain English*. New York: Harper & Row, 1964.

Foley, Stephen Merriam, and Joseph Wayne Gordon. *Conventions and Choices: A Brief Book of Style and Usage*. Lexington, Mass.: D. C. Heath, 1986.

Follett, Wilson. *Modern American Usage: A Guide*. Edited by Jacques Barzun. New York: Hill and Wang, 1966.

Fowler, H. W. *A Dictionary of Modern English Usage*. Revised by Sir Ernest Gowers. New York: Oxford University Press, 1965.

Freeman, Morton S. *The Story Behind the Word*. Philadelphia: ISI Press, 1985.

———. *A Treasury for Word Lovers*. Philadelphia: ISI Press, 1983.

Funk & Wagnalls Standard College Dictionary. New York: Funk & Wagnalls, 1973.

Grambs, David. *Words About Words*. New York: McGraw-Hill,1984.

Hayakawa, S. I. *The Use and Misuse of Language*. Greenwich, Conn.: Fawcett, 1958.

Hodges, John C., and Mary E. Whitten, with Suzanne S. Webb. *Harcourt College Handbook*. 10th ed. New York: Harcourt Brace Jovanovich, 1986.

Johnson, Edward D. *The Handbook of Good English*. New York: Facts on File, 1982.

Kessler, Lauren and Duncan McDonald. *When Words Collide*. 2nd ed. Belmont, Calif.: Wadsworth, 1988.

Kilpatrick, James A. *The Writer's Art*. Kansas City, Mo.: Andrews, McMeel & Parker, 1984.

Legget, Glenn, and C. David Mead, and Melinda G. Kramer. *Prentice Hall Handbook for Writers*. 10th ed. Englewood Cliffs, N.J.: Prentice-Hall, 1988.

Los Angles Times Stylebook: A Manual for Writers, Editors, Journalists and Students. New York: New American Library, 1981.

Morris, William, and Mary Morris. *Harper Dictionary of Contemporary Usage*. 2nd ed. New York: Harper & Row, 1985.

The New American Handy College Dictionary. New York: New American Library, 1972.

The New York Times Manual of Style and Usage. New York: Times Books, 1976.

Newman, Edwin. *A Civil Tongue*. Indianapolis: Bobbs-Merrill, 1976.

———. *Strictly Speaking: Will America Be the Death of English?* Indianapolis: Bobbs-Merrill, 1974.

Nicolson, Margaret. *A Dictionary of American-English Usage*, based on Fowler's *Modern English Usage*. New York: Oxford University, 1957.

Oxford American Dictionary. New York: Oxford University, 1980.

Partridge, Eric. *Concise Usage and Abusage*. New York: The Citadel, 1965.

Perrin, Porter G. *Writer's Guide and Index to English*. 4th ed. Revised. by Karl W. Dykema and Wilma R. Ebbitt. Glenview, Ill.: Scott, Foresman, 1968.

Quinn, Jim. *American Tongue and Cheek: A Populist Guide to Our Language*. New York: Pantheon, 1980.

Random House Dictionary of the English Language. Unabridged ed. New York: Random House, 1966.

Safire, William. *I Stand Corrected*. New York: Times Books, 1984.

———. *On Language*. New York: Times Books, 1980.

———. *Take My Word for It*. New York: Times Books, 1986.

Simon, John Ivan. *Paradigms Lost: Reflections on Literacy and Its Decline*. New York: Clarkston N. Potter, 1980.

Strunk, William Jr. *The Elements of Style*. 3rd ed., revised. by E. B. White. New York: Macmillan, 1979.

Tobin, Richard L. *Tobin's English Usage*. Indianapolis: R. J. Berg, 1985.

The Washington Post Deskbook on Style. New York: McGraw Hill, 1978.

Webster's Dictionary of English Usage. Springfield, Mass.: Merriam-Webster, 1989.

Webster's New Encyclopedia of Dictionaries. Baltimore: Ottenheimer, 1986.

Webster's New World Dictionary of American English. New York: Webster's New World, 1988.

Webster's Ninth New Collegiate Dictionary. Springfield, Mass.: Merriam-Webster, 1983.

Zinsser, William. *On Writing Well: An Informal Guide to Writing Non-Fiction*. 3rd ed. New York: Harper & Row, 1985.

Name Index

Subject Index